Advanced Praise for *A Knock at the Door*

"Ory Slonim's four decades of volunteering to save Israeli POWs and MIAs, bringing an end to their captivities—or their families' uncertainties—is one of the toughest roles in Israeli life. An amazing story that illustrates the ancient Jewish saying, 'Whoever saves one life, saves the entire world.'"

—Ehud Barak, former Israeli PM and Defence Minister,
and former IDF Chief of Staff

"Ory Slonim's gripping autobiography is a stunning blend of national and personal history.

Throughout our decades-long acquaintance, I have witnessed Ory's metamorphosis between the private, public, and third sectors—each of which he mastered—and his abilities as a successful high profile criminal attorney led to the introduction to my late father, the sixth President of the State of Israel Chaim Herzog, who mobilized him to the task of redeeming our Missing in Action. He then became the Special Advisor to the Minister of Defense, and an expert in negotiations regarding POWs and MIAs. In his work, Ory presents his life story—a moving statement by a man who intuited the import of authentic interpersonal connection, the power of eye contact, the significance of viewing every individual as an equal. It is also proof of the Ory rule: Don't complain, don't explain, let your actions do the talking. This is a fascinating piece which I wholeheartedly recommend and endorse in no uncertain terms."

—Isaac Herzog, President of the State of Israel

"Ory Slonim's life story truly deserves to be told all over the world. You have dedicated your mind to the law, your heart to children (Variety International) with special needs, and your soul to Israel's security and the fate of its missing soldiers. And you have devoted your soul and incredible sensitivity with your unique negotiating skills to securing the release of Israel's missing and captured soldiers. Truly the face of all that is good and beautiful about Israel, portraying its compassion, morality, and humanity. Your life story is an incredible tapestry of excellence, values, spirit, compassion, and leadership."

—Ambassador Dan Gillerman

A
KNOCK
AT THE
DOOR

The Story of My Secret Work
With Israeli MIAs and POWs

ORY SLONIM

WICKED SON

A WICKED SON BOOK
An Imprint of Post Hill Press
ISBN: 978-1-64293-932-3
ISBN (eBook): 978-1-64293-933-0

A Knock at the Door:
The Story of My Secret Work With Israeli MIAs and POWs
© 2021 by Ory Slonim
All Rights Reserved

Cover Design by Tiffani Shea
Translation by Tomer Ze'ev

Post Hill Press
New York • Nashville
posthillpress.com

Published in the United States of America
1 2 3 4 5 6 7 8 9 10

To Tamy, my wife, the most faithful companion of all.

To my children, my granddaughters, and grandsons, who are so dear, so important to me.

To my beloved extended family.

To the friends I've acquired at all the different stages of my life.

To all the families of the IDF soldiers who are captives or missing in action—those I've accompanied and those whose lives I didn't get a chance to be a part of—with lots of love and one single wish: that all your woes are gone forever.

And to the "special" children of Variety Israel and all those who help us in this great undertaking.

Ory Slonim, January 2021

Contents

Foreword

I have had the privilege of counting the author of this book as a friend for thirty years, ever since he became involved in the delicate area of Israel's intensive efforts to determine the status of prisoners of war (POWs) and those missing in action (MIAs). This work has been revelatory for me because it not only allots a major part of the book to these very subjects, but it also provides an essential complementary description of his origins and his multiple roles in the wide legal system in which he excelled as a highly successful trial lawyer. He was a central figure among defense teams representing senior military officers and senior public servants who were arraigned before national commissions of enquiry. His unique and deep personal empathy for his clients was one of the elements that made him an immediate choice to become special advisor to the minister of defense on MIAs and POWs. He held this position for close to thirty years, spanning the terms of several other leading figures who held this office.

His personal family background served as a powerful factor in shaping Ory's character and approach to life. His forefathers immigrated to the Holy Land about two hundred years ago under the instruction of the founders of the Habbad Hassidic sect, and they were directed to settle in Hebron—the city of the biblical fathers. Subsequent generations played major roles in the commercial and banking systems there until the year 1929, when a bloody Arab riot launched against the entire Jewish community left more than twenty dead, including several of Ory's antecedents. Events like these cannot fail to form a person's approach to life; neither can a terrorist attack in a Tel Aviv cinema in which Ory was injured, and his wife even more seriously. This must have added to his motivation to devote several decades of his life to an extremely delicate area—and for a symbolic annual salary of one solitary shekel.

Ory immediately harnessed his unique experience and capabilities to this area. As a renowned trial lawyer, he had much experience convincing clients and witnesses to share information they had originally refused to share with anyone. Secondly, he had his own knack for building mutual empathy in interrogation. He was capable of spotting lies instantly and getting the liar to confess his sin. When we first met, I was initially guarded in my approach to him. Israeli intelligence officers were prone to discourage people outside the fold from entering into Mossad's "nitty gritty." We'd had bad experiences with senior "outsiders" who entered the scene armed with impressive titles of "advisor to the minister."

Ory was an outstanding exception, and he rapidly "recruited" me and others and naturally slid into the role of a team member when necessary. He also became a key figure in maintaining the naturally tense relations with families whose absent dear ones (POWs and MIAs) were the subject of their extreme concern. They had much trust in him and felt he would state their "case" brilliantly and faithfully when discussions were held at the highest levels.

One of the most difficult cases that Israel had to contend with for over thirty years is that of missing Airforce navigator Ron Arad, who is known to have parachuted safely from his fighter aircraft in Lebanese airspace. This case challenged the entire intelligence community and successive prime ministers and ministers of defense. Over these many years it has not been possible to determine whether or not he is still alive. Considerable efforts have been made while searching for leads in Lebanon, and the possibility that the missing officer was handed over to Iran has not been discounted to this very day. This issue required a different set of approaches. Ory was privy to them through his permanent membership of the advisory group that provided both support and experience to the official running this case directly under the prime minister. It became increasingly difficult to explain to the airman's mother and wife and daughter why the Israeli intelligence community was unable to resolve this painful matter given its dramatic successes on other key issues. Ory's relations with the family, aside from his operational role as described in the book, were a model of personal empathy on the one hand and a major contribution to the anxious family.

Two of the key issues concerning any negotiation with the Hamas or Hezbollah terrorist groups holding POWs or their bodies are dealt with in detail in the book and are central to understanding some of the more complex and sensitive considerations that figure in the decision-making process. They are interrelated. These are best illustrated in the account Ory provides the reader about the role he played in the Shalit case. It relates to a soldier who was taken prisoner during a confrontation between an Israeli force and Hamas along the dividing line between Israel and the Gaza strip. Five years and four months later, he was released in return for 1,027 Palestinians, many of whom had much blood on their hands, including Yihye Sinwar, who is currently the practical leader of the Gaza Strip. Why did this deal take so much time to materialize? In the meantime, there was a regime change in Israel, and current Prime Minister Netanyahu came to power. The Hamas drove a hard bargain that the Israeli public would find difficult to digest, and there were no rules or internal regulations regarding what type of deal would be "acceptable." Ory was in the thick of this, and one of his missions was to maintain contact with Shalit's grandfather—the words in this chapter quoting the letter of the grandfather to the prime minister are surely worthy of special attention. Ory was and is a loyal voluntary servant of the Israeli government, but he does reveal some of what went on behind the scenes during the negotiations. The final touches on the agreement had been concluded a year before the exchange was implemented. It required a domestic climate that would accept such an exchange. The years before the exchange had seen an outburst of domestic demonstrations motivated by a mainly large, young, lower-middle class who felt that the State had imposed on them a very bad social deal. Only when key support for the government could be reestablished on other key issues could this deal go forward. Until such time, it was necessary to hold the fort and to invest human and gracious support for the concerned families in anticipation of a better combination of circumstances. I think it was Secretary of State Henry Kissinger who opined that Israel has no foreign policy—only a domestic one.

And one last note on the author. He became an "homme du monde"—a man of the world—at a very early stage in his legal career, and his international experience gave him the capacity to negotiate with seasoned lawyers and senior intelligence officers in many countries. Operators of this cloth are far and few around

The reader will enjoy the easy style of the author and will also learn more than appears in state-of-the-art political biographies. This a book that gives you a rare and very accurate picture of Israel from within. As you make your way, you'll get a genuine sense of Israel as revealed by an insider for the very first time.

EFRAIM HALEVY, the ninth head of the Mossad 1998–2002

1

My View on Life: Why I Wrote This Book

When my granddaughter Na'ama was ten and a half, she asked me to give a lecture to the children at her elementary school. I asked her what she wanted me to talk to the children about. "Tell them you spent time on a ship as a cadet in naval officers' course," she replied. "Tell them about interesting court cases, about your activities for the Variety children, about your involvement in the issue of captives and MIAs, about meeting important people in the world."

I was glad that my granddaughter had been listening to all my stories over the years and even managed to remember them, but I was also feeling a bit apprehensive. I'd given talks to IDF soldiers and elderly people, but I'd never given a talk to children before. I wasn't convinced that I was ready for this, or that I even knew how to do it. Anyway, Na'ama promised me that she would help me prepare the presentation.

It ended up being one of the most exciting lectures I'd ever given in my life. To my surprise, the children were completely fascinated by my stories. At the end of the talk, one of the school kids walked over and asked me how I became involved with helping captives and MIAs. "Listen," I replied, "the whole thing started completely by coincidence." He then asked me how I ended up being on the leadership team of an international nongovernmental organization dealing with children with special needs. "That was also by coincidence," I replied. When he heard

1

that it was by coincidence that I became part of the legal world and the business world—and, in fact, also by coincidence that I ended up on deck in officers' course on that ship—this ten-year-old boy asked me: "How can it be that so many meaningful things happened to you completely by coincidence?"

I was not ready for this question. It continued to haunt me for a long time after I gave that talk at the school. How can it really be?

We don't really know if "all is foreseen and permission is granted," as the Talmudic verse from *Pirkei Avot* goes—whether everything that happens is predetermined, dictated by the will of God, or if it's all pure coincidence and life just provides us with a variety of opportunities and challenges that we're completely unprepared for. It seems to me that the latter option, the coincidental one, is what happened to me in life, for the most part.

What I want to share with the reader is not just what happened to me on a personal level but also major events that occurred here in our country, including to my own family, which has lived here for so many years.

Among the large, diverse mixture of things I've done in life, there was an appearance on Israeli television: I served as a defense attorney for the historic character of Yosef Ben-Matityahu, a.k.a. Flavius Josephus—the great Jewish warlord, rebel leader, and historian from the first century CE—on the Israeli TV show *The Defendant Is Long Dead* where various historic figures were put on mock trial with testimony from professional witnesses before a panel of judges that included real historians. I delved into Josephus's account of the period when the Romans dominated this part of the world. I've met archaeologists, historians, and psychologists who had a wide array of different opinions about his writings, but all agreed on one thing: if he hadn't written this work, our knowledge of what happened during that period of history would be very scant. That was also the reason Josephus was publicly acquitted of being the "traitor" he was branded as during the course of history, a story we were all raised on and firmly believed.

The Israeli author Dr. Yuval Noah Harari wrote about human history and managed to benefit a lot of people who sat through long history classes in high school and barely managed to learn anything, and suddenly, by reading one book, learned just about everything they needed to know. After reading his first book, *Sapiens: A Brief History of Humankind*, I concluded that we live in one of the most exciting periods in the history of the human race, a time when the most important revolution happened: the digital and information technology revolution.

I'll be writing here about things that some of you experienced firsthand, in real time or were perhaps even personally involved in, and indubitably have some opinions about. It's going to be our great-grandchildren who, in all likelihood, will possess the correct perspective about this period in history, having the benefit of being able to analyze it from enough distance in the future.

It's agents of memory who write history, not historians. That is what I am: an agent of memory. I write about my own experiences and the work I've done in a completely subjective way. As someone who was involved in matters of national security, I know that there're no two people who would describe a battle they fought in the exact same way. Ultimately, the listeners and readers will internalize only the message that the storyteller or author wish to convey to them, and I do not presume to be any different. The *Oholot* tractate in the *Mishnah* states that the human body has 248 parts in it—well, this is who I am, with all 248 parts of my own being, and this is my own personal narrative. If any part of it is found later to be inaccurate or offensive, I humbly apologize in advance.

The lord God, my capacity for personal initiative, maybe some other traits that I have—and of course, a great deal of coincidence—gave me the opportunity, and indeed the privilege, to be part of some of the greatest affairs in the history of the Israeli state, and I'm going to tell you about my role in them. I won't be able to share everything about some of these affairs for reasons pertaining to national security and legal considerations. When I set out to write this book, I consulted some friends, authors, and editors who told me: "Just put down everything you want to say and let the censors do their job later." I did not heed their counsel. It is not the censors that I fear—I have complied with their directives to the letter—but rather my own personal censorship and the dictums of my own conscience.

My life also includes several decades in the business sector—a world ruled by money, power, and success. Many books have been written about this subject, and I have no desire to add my own views to the pile. I chose to focus on other parts of my life that didn't have to do with personal achievements or monetary gain but pertained to human beings and sacred values that one should uphold. Despite the hardship, the sadness, the disappointments, and the many failures involved in these dealings, I am thankful for having been on the giving and aiding side, and maybe, once in a while, I managed to make a difference for the good.

When I set out on this journey, I knew it would not be complete without enlisting the aid of people I came across along the way who had become faithful companions. I traveled the land and had exciting encounters with the children of the Variety charity organization, who grew up and turned into marvelous people; with an extraordinary bank robber I represented as legal counsel; with a long-time IDF officer in charge of casualties assistance affairs who lived to see war bring the tide of death and injury to her own family's doorstep; and with the families of Israeli MIAs—parents, siblings, and life partners—who became and remained an inseparable part of my life. Even when I thought I knew everything, I discovered new things, and so did they. The time that went by did nothing to diminish the feelings of hurt and longing for the fallen, but perhaps it managed to push aside the heavy curtain of grief, sharpen the mind, and afford us all a different perspective on things. Their moving stories, retold here among the pages of my book—in their own words and from their own perspectives—are an indelible part of the rich tapestry that chronicles my life's events. I wish to take the time to thank each and every one of the writers for their willingness to open their heart and share their stirring stories with us. Each one of them burned its image into my skin and left something in my very soul.

* * *

Many years ago, I was at a concert given by the Israeli musician Idan Raichel, which took place in the middle of the desert with thousands of people in the audience. Suddenly Idan stopped the show and to my astonishment asked to personally dedicate a song to me: "Refrain Thy Voice from Crying " It might have been the sheer surprise or maybe the atmosphere in the heart of the desert and its landscape; maybe it was all the applause that followed or just the lyrics, which describe so accurately the heart of the affairs I've dealt with all these years, but I suddenly found myself in tears.

**For in the nights your sleep is wandering
And every dream brings dread
Lend then your ear to the silence**

**The voice of grace and mercy will rise
Here it comes
For your soul is kept for him
And the time is near
When weary in your arms
He'll fall at the end of the road when to their borders
they return
Refrain your voice from crying and deny your eyes the tears
For the gate shall be opened for him
And he will enter it in a storm when to their borders
they return**

Let it be so.

—Ory Slonim

2

My Early Life: My Roots and History, Abridged

Shneurson House

Built by Chabad adherents in the 19th century
As a council house, a house of schooling, hospitality, and residence
In this house dwelled the deceased Menucha Rachel Slonim
Granddaughter of the Rabbi Shneur Zalman of Liadi
Daughter of the distinguished Chabad rabbi Duber
(Born on the Festival of Liberation—19th of Kislev, 5559)
Came to Hebron with her husband, Rabbi Ya'akov Slonim Zt'''l
And was mother to all the Chabad community in this place
Known for her righteousness and unique qualities
Admired by all residents of the town
Died in Hebron on 24th of Shvat, 5648
Buried at the Chabad Section at the old cemetery in town
Her descendants, the members of the Slonim family
Were among the heads and masters of the community
Some have been murdered in the massacres of 5689 (1929)
The house has been restored, renovated, and expanded
By the redeemers of the Jewish community in Hebron
In the years 5741–5755

In one of my secret meetings in the capital of a European nation—one of many as part of my activities to rescue IDF soldiers held captive or missing in action—I was told by the man sitting across from me (who couldn't be described as anything other than a terrorist) partly in jest: "One day, when we expel all of you from Palestine, I guess we'll keep you and your family around, because you're a native. Your family has always lived here. You're Palestinians from Hebron; you are among the sons of the Khalili."

And so, my life's trajectory was impacted by the fact that I was descended from a family that arrived in the land of Israel in the beginning of the nineteenth century and settled in the city of Hebron.

My family, originally part of the Chasidic Chabad movement, arrived in Hebron from Belarus at the behest of the movement's founder, Rabbi Zalman Shneur of Liadi—the great Jewish sage, philosopher, poet, writer, and author of the *Tanya*, one of the most important treatises in the history of Judaic thought. Like many members of our extended family, I was named after Rabbi Shneur. Many people found this name quite difficult to pronounce, and it was quickly changed to Ory, which was officially added to my Israeli ID card just before I enlisted in the IDF: Shneur Ory Slonim.

Our family became one of the most upstanding and dominant families in Hebron (alongside several families from the Jewish Sephardi denomination, including the Manni, Hasson, and Abulafia clans, among others), and its descendants were the heads of local Yeshivas and leaders of the community. The granddaughter of Rabbi Schneur, Menucha-Rachel, married one of the sons of the Slonim family and became one of the most influential public figures in Hebron, which turned us into the great rabbi's "offspring"—an affiliation that grants special status among followers of the Chabad movement worldwide: you're an "offspring"!

Through marital relations, the roots of my family tree sprouted some additional very distinguished Israeli families: Rivlin, Lipkin, and Shmerling. The family story was memorialized in the 1945 book *Chronicles of the Rabbi of Liadi's Family*, written by my beloved grandfather—one of the most meaningful figures in my life—Menachem Shmuel Slonim.

* * *

My grandfather, a native-born resident of Hebron, was a remarkable man in almost every area of life, both spiritual and mundane. He set up the first branch of Israel's National Bank (Bank Leumi) in Hebron, which was then still called the Anglo-Palestine Bank. A century later, his grandson became an attorney representing the bank.

After a few years in that management position, my grandfather, who was one of the most important and distinguished leaders of the local community, was asked to move to Jerusalem. A few years later, under grave circumstances, it turned out that this move ensured my family's continued survival; the first victim of the 1929 massacre of Hebron was the man who had replaced my grandfather in his position as bank manager—Elizier Dan Slonim, another member of the family. He was the brother of Rivka Slonim-Burg, father to former MK and future Knesset speaker, Avraham Burg.

I've encountered terrorists many times in my life, just like the ones who assaulted Hebron and killed members of my family. For instance, I crossed paths with them in 1974, when my wife Tamy and I were injured in one of the first bombings perpetrated in Tel Aviv. A terrorist walked into the Hen movie theater, killed two people and injured fifty. Years later, I would deal with them all around the world when I served for three decades as advisor to Israel's defense minister on the subject of captives and those missing in action.

My grandfather started the Bank Leumi branch in Jerusalem's Talpiot neighborhood. He was widowed at a young age and had to raise his six daughters all alone, as well as his son, Levy Yitzhak—my father.

During the 1930s the family moved to 30th Levontin Street in Tel Aviv (the house I was born in) next to the railroads connecting the city of Jaffa to Jerusalem and Tel Aviv. Today, there are only parking lots in that spot. In the future another kind of railroad would pass through the site—the newly constructed Tel Aviv Light Rail. Our childhood years were marked by the constant din of the trains passing by, and when the line was finally closed and the trains stopped running, we suddenly found ourselves surrounded by a strange quiet.

My grandfather became a businessman and, together with my father, started dealing in real estate to help people regain ownership of property that had been seized or traded due to debt. Together they founded new neighborhoods in Tel Aviv. My father, Yitzhak, owned a hotel named San Remo on the Tel Aviv waterfront, which was frequented by British officials during the time of the British Mandate. He was thirty-one (considered quite old to be a bachelor in those days) when he met my mother, Esther Lederberger. She was a refugee who'd escaped from Germany at sixteen by smuggling her way into the German delegation to the Jewish Olympics, also known as the Maccabiah Games. She stayed for a time in a Tel Aviv refugee shelter called Beit Tzeirot Mizrachi on Dov Hoz Street. She was fourteen years younger than my father. They had four children. Naomi was the eldest; I came second. The third was my brother Gili, who died of cancer at forty-six. The youngest was our sister Ricky. My brother and sisters had wonderful careers and established a huge tribe, perpetuating the tradition of large Jewish families.

During Israel's War of Independence in 1948, part of our family's home was damaged in an Egyptian air raid and we had to move to another house at the corner of Balfour and Melchett. After the house in Levontin Street was renovated, my grandfather—who'd always lived with us—went back to living there, and I moved in with him so he wouldn't have to live by himself. My sister Naomi lived with us, too, for a while. I lived with my grandfather from the second grade until he passed away, one month before my Bar Mitzvah.

A significant part of my childhood, and perhaps much more than that, was shaped by my relationship with my grandfather. No one could wish for a better grandfather. A wise man of untold accomplishments and talents, he was the one who taught me to uphold the ideals and values I've lived up to my entire life. He gave me advice that I believe young parents (at that time) were too busy to grant. He would wake me up every morning at 5:00 with a small saucer of olive oil and lemon. He told me many stories and legends; he was one of the greatest storytellers I've ever met in my life. My grandfather also taught me one of the greatest secrets of storytelling—the ability to color each story with another distinct shade each time it is retold, always preserving the essence of the tale but giving it another exciting angle.

My grandfather was a real guru and served as a mentor to all twenty of his grandchildren, who all loved him dearly. They visited him often, and he always managed to find some special way to spoil them. Whenever he bought a gift, it was always something of both sentimental and practical value. He taught me from an early age that if I wanted to receive a higher allowance, I'd have to do something to earn it. For example, he'd send me to buy him a newspaper for one Israeli pound and let me keep 10 percent as a fee.

He was an intellectual who was fluent in nine languages, an excellent cook who knew how to furnish a meal from any random group of ingredients, and a scholar who also had a great capacity for listening to others. His huge home library was a model of coexistence—it contained holy books and volumes of ancient Judaic teachings together with contemporary works by Israeli authors. After his death, part of the library was donated to Bar-Ilan University, except for a marginal number of books that now grace the relatively small library in my own study, a memento from my grandfather that I always find touching.

My grandfather hosted many of the period's great authors in his house, and he himself was a prolific reader and writer. Alongside the writers, poets, and businessmen who constantly seemed to fill the house, he was also frequently visited by the less affluent and intellectually inclined members of the local community, who told my grandfather of their lives and sought his advice on how to solve their problems. Those histories of human lives and the lessons and insights they bestowed have accompanied me in all facets of my life. They are lessons that have served me faithfully until this very day.

Grandpa Slonim never stopped learning, and most of his learning was in the context of his love for people and the way he treated each and every one of them like a page out of a book—one of the distinct traits I inherited from him. One of the most beautiful lessons of my life—the real meaning of the expression "love thy neighbor"—was taught to me by a man named Mimun, a Greek Jew from the famous Jewish community in Thessaloniki. He was a colorful character who operated a construction crane, enjoyed early Israel's nightlife, and used to go swimming with us at the Gordon Public Pool in Tel Aviv. According to Mimun, you've got to love yourself in earnest, and only then will you learn how to truly love your neighbor and your peer, something that was contrary to the values we were brought up on. But I learned the same thing from my grandfather: never treat human beings based on their titles, but try to find something special in them, something that doesn't reveal itself to the casual observer. In my view, humans are the most interesting and fascinating beings on earth, and each person I meet along the way is another incredible page in the storybook of my own life.

To this truth, I added my grandfather's life philosophy: "always be giving." But one must work hard and make great efforts in order to have something to give. And when you've reached that position, give in abundance, not just out of altruism but because it will benefit you as well. You don't go to watch a movie just to know what happens to the main character at the end; you go because first and foremost you want to enjoy yourself for a few hours.

One year before my grandfather died, he and I left the house in Levontin Street in Tel Aviv and went back to living at my parents' home, where we shared a room. I was struck with great sadness when he died of a heart attack, and I was also disappointed because the big Bar Mitzvah celebration that had been planned for me was cancelled in order to mourn him.

* * *

My childhood was concurrent with the years of World War II and the Holocaust in Europe, of which we, the children, knew next to nothing about. There was no television back then, and nobody told us what was happening over there. Every day, I would walk to Temima's kindergarten on Levontin Street. During Israel's War of Independence in 1948, when I was in elementary school, my life was marred for the first time by the experience of war. People around me were killed, injured, or simply vanished altogether. I heard one day that the son of Chaya, a woman who worked at our home, was a soldier missing in action. As a very young child, I couldn't understand the concept of someone going missing, and I would never have guessed that it would one day occupy such a tremendous part of my life—no less than thirty years of it. A concept that enfolds and envelops so much pain, helplessness, and terrible uncertainty, is almost impossible to understand and contain.

I went to the old Echad Ha'am elementary school at the corner of Echad Ha'am Street and Bezalel Yaffe Street, which (fortunately) was no longer only for boys by the time I got there. I had a science teacher named Haim Keller, who was born in the early Zionist settlement town of Rosh Pina in the Upper Galilee region. He was one of the most unique and outstanding members of the educators' community in Israel. Keller also served as the head of the local tribe of the Israeli Scouts—the Dizengoff tribe. He instilled in us an iron sense of discipline and taught me one of the most important lessons of my life: it's not "what" they teach you that matters; it's the "how." He used to take us to the local nursery for science class, in the spot where the Charles Bronfman Auditorium stands today, and 90 percent of his explanations were about the "how" of plants—how to cultivate them and what practical value they had.

When I was asked to teach criminal law procedure at Tel Aviv University, I immediately responded that I didn't want to be just a teacher, I wanted to serve as a mentor for people, to be their guide. I didn't want to teach people the "what" part of it—files filled with old court cases and rulings were widely available for the students—I wanted to teach the "how" part of being a criminal defense attorney. That was something you could only learn from other people, especially those who had real experience. How to handle the case of someone who was in a most terrible state of distress because just yesterday he or she was a senior bank manager and now they're sitting inside an interrogation room; how to talk to a police detective who's investigating your client; how to visit a person who's just been arrested for the first time in their life; how to talk to them about money when their whole life is on the line; how to talk to their family when the headlines in the press are sullying their reputation; how to speak in front of a judge; how to deal with someone who'd just been given a terrible sentence and is about to spend time behind bars; how to visit them in prison. For example, I always made sure to dress in plain clothes at the prison and never even put on an aftershave. I would never come to visit an inmate smelling of the outside world, and I would never sit and tell them about a concert or theater play I went to the other night.

At a workshop I gave to my students, I asked Ronnie Leibowitz, the infamous bank robber who was one of my past clients, to come and tell the story of his case from his own perspective. One of the wise-guy students in my course (there's one in every class) asked him if he noticed anything particular when I visited him in jail. Ronnie said that he never saw me dress luxuriously and that I never smelled of aftershave—or what could be considered "the outside world." The student couldn't believe that we hadn't prepared matching versions ahead of time. I could hardly try to explain to him that it was a lesson that I learned a long, long time ago, from a lawyer who was my mentor while I was studying law.

Someone else who later supplemented that lesson was Zvi Malchin, a Mossad operative who was directly involved in the 1960s capture of the Nazi strongman Adolf Eichmann in Argentina. Since I was never officially employed by the Mossad or Shin Bet during the long years I spent dealing with the issue of captives and MIAs—I was never really one of "their" people—I asked him to help me explore the depths of the intelligence world. Malkin didn't teach me the "what" part, either, but the "how." One example pertained to the issue of interrogations. He taught me how to talk to someone who wanted to hide the truth.

"The truth," Malkin told me, "is like a table that stands on four legs. If you strip off one of its legs, it'll start wobbling. Take off another one and it's all ready to fall down. When someone is telling a truth that stands on four legs, it's very difficult to break him. If his truth is standing on three legs, it can still stand upright somehow, but he can manage without that one leg. But if you're talking to a person who's already missing two legs from that truth, it'll be much easier for you, and if he's a big liar whose truth stands only on one leg—you'll break him easy."

His words ring true in all areas of life, but when it comes to his world, the world of espionage, he stated as an example that they'll never send an intelligence operative or spy to Germany whose outside appearance is markedly oriental, and who has no mastery of the German language. That would be a two-legged table, and if he's caught it'll be easier to break him. But if he's from German or European extraction, fluent in the German language, and with a plausible native accent, he'll have a far greater chance of completing his assignment. His words are true when it comes to the courthouse as well: the ability to break someone whose truth stands on four legs is almost impossible.

The example Malkin gave me has been following me ever since, as along with another smart piece of advice he gave me: "Say the good things about your friends. Express your appreciation for their achievements while they're still alive. Don't just speak highly of them after they've died." That was the reason that at his memorial service, I read aloud Yitzhak Shalev's poem, "Sing for the Dead Before They Die," which opens with the following stanza:

Sing for the dead before they die for what gain they
from your song when they are earless, void of understanding
let it not offend you in life to give them their recompense
in a verse. Deny your lips not the giving of a good word
in due time, for better is the word spoken when the living
hear it. Pay your due in acknowledgment for the dead 'ere they die.
For soon they pass from this land and be your eternal debtors
and that which you owe them—can never be repaid. The
words you aim to carve onto their headstone, to bear in lamenter's
locution and reminisce in seven days, in thirty days and on year
days—delay not these words! For lo
I see you exalt the names of the dead which in life not
once did you let slip a small word in favor of,
and to my heart I shall say; knew the dead your thoughts
good on them and the host of your affections—then strong
times seven, proud times seven and seven times not comfortless
they would
face each his day!

Know this: tomorrow's dead inside you all tread.
For knew you that tomorrow dies your mate, what effort
would you spare her last day merry to make? Make it so,
therefore. And merry make the lives of those who die to-morrow
for this day—'tis theirs!

I told Zvika Malkin's friends, that it's a pity people didn't tell him all their words of praise for him when he was still alive. I'm so fond of this poem, that I often use it to congratulate people on their birthdays, too, in order to emphasize the message that it's better to say a good word to someone who's still alive than sing their praises when you are delivering a eulogy.

3

Enlisting in the Israeli Defense Forces, Going to Law School, and Starting a Life

I enlisted in the IDF's Nahal brigade in 1960 and was assigned to a unit that was destined to join an agricultural community at Kibbutz Sde Boker. After a long basic training course and advanced training at Kibbutz Hatzerim, I joined the 50th Airborne Nahal Battalion, where my long romance with the paratroopers began. The commander of my unit was Ely Yadgarov, one of the legendary commanders of the IDF's paratrooper brigades—a fighter unmatched in daring—and his lieutenant was Amos Yaron. Yaron and I became close friends as the years went by, and I even served as his defense attorney when he was put on trial by the Kahan Committee, which investigated the events in the Sabra and Shatila refugee camps in Lebanon in the 1980s.

In 1961, just before we were about to go on squad leaders' course, I was sent together with other NCOs on a mission that was highly secret and revealed to the public only many years later. According to the truce between Israel and the Kingdom of Jordan, which went into effect in July 1948, the area of Mt. Scopus in Jerusalem was divided into three compounds: an Israeli enclave, a neutral zone that was no-man's-land, and a demilitarized Jordanian territory. The Israeli zone stretched from an amphitheater grove overlooking the Judean Desert up to the British Military Cemetery in Jerusalem and included the various buildings of the

Hebrew University and the Hadassah Hospital. The agreement stipulated that no more than eighty-five policemen armed only with light weaponry were allowed to be stationed in this small Israeli enclave in addition to a civilian staff consisting of thirty-five people. A convoy would drive up the mountain every two weeks through Mandelbaum Gate to bring supplies to the local staff and replace some of its members on site with fresh servicemen. Like Jordan, Israel observed the agreement only partially; the police officers were soon replaced by IDF soldiers on active duty, and weapons were smuggled into the compound, heavier in nature than the types agreed upon.

As members of the paratroopers' brigade, we were also sent to Mt. Scopus disguised as police officers, having received the required training and after making the necessary preparations. For example, we trained using police officers' standard-issue personal weapons and how to shine our shoes like they did—it turns out that policemen spend a lot more time shining their shoes than the run-of-the-mill IDF recruit. Obviously, our families had no idea where we were. During our stay on the mountain, we were constantly glued to the radio, which was broadcasting two main events: the IDF parade in Jerusalem on Israel's Independence Day and the tumultuous trial of Adolf Eichmann. It took many years for the magnitude of this event to become clear to me: we were witnessing history in the making while sitting in our positions at the IDF outpost around the Mt. Scopus amphitheater in a small "pocket" that was under Israeli control deep in enemy territory. As young IDF servicemen, we lacked the perspective that would allow us to truly comprehend the significance of this episode in Israel's history. It was made clear to us much later in life, as the long years went by and we became more mature.

Mt. Scopus was home to a branch of the Hebrew University, which was abandoned after the War of Independence. Among other things, the soldiers found a trove of fetuses carefully preserved in glass jars there, including something that resembled a "cyclops"—a creature with only one eye. I was much more intrigued to discover a pile of Israeli newspapers, among them a paper from August 30, 1929, with the headline: "The fallen—our martyrs, those who were tortured, maimed and killed sanctifying our homeland with their sacrifice." The date was according to the Jewish calendar: 17-24 Av, 5689. The third name on the list was my own family member, Eliezer Dan Slonim, who was murdered during the 1929 massacre of Hebron.

Later, I was sent to squad leaders' course and designated as the CO's radioman—the guy who carries the large radio transceiver on his back and always travels together with the unit's commander. I thought I was going to go back to the Kibbutz after the course ended, but similar to many other cases in my life, things turned out completely different than I had planned. It turned out that the IDF was providing parachute jump training for African leaders and heads of state and the senior officers in their armed forces, and there was a shortage of parachute jump instructors at the IDF Jump School. The battalion commander was therefore looking to recruit at least four guys who had finished high school and were fluent in English to teach them how to jump out of a plane. And so, I became a parachute jump instructor and did it for thirty years. I was still crazy about skydiving long after I got discharged from the IDF, and for many years, I would start my mornings with a parachute jump at the airbase in Tel-Nof and only then drive to work in Tel Aviv.

I learned one of the most important and fascinating lessons of my life at jump school—not only how to teach soldiers to do a parachute jump but also how to help people overcome their fears, another crucial life lesson for me.

They say that a coward dies a thousand deaths, whereas a brave man dies only once. The concept of fear accompanied me in everything I did in my life: a soldier's fear that his parachute won't open during a jump; the fear of a person who's been indicted and in jeopardy of losing their liberty; the fear of a mother of a soldier missing in action, wondering if she will ever find out what became of her son; and the fear of every parent of a child with special needs, wondering what will become of their child when no one is left to take care of them.

In 1963, a few months after I was discharged, Elly Yadgarov (who was later assigned to the IDF's most elite combat unit, Unit 269, a.k.a. Sayeret Matkal) was killed while constructing an improvised demolition charge that denotated prematurely in his hands, right in front of his squad members. Many years later, when I was the president of Variety Israel, I got a phone call from an elderly man who told me he'd been following my work for many years. He asked to meet with me in person and if he could purchase the Variety organization's "Gold Heart" pins, which are widely sold with the proceeds going to the organization as a donation. He wanted to share them with some of his friends at the nursing home he was living at in Tel Aviv's Afeka neighborhood.

I happened to be around that area, and I accepted his offer. I met an eighty-year-old man who appeared to be in very good physical shape. He told me, "Young man, come and sit down. I'm about to tell you a story that's been touching to me for many years, and now I'm sure you'll find it touching too. I had a son named Elly Yadgarov. My son told me about a soldier he really took a liking to, a good soldier who was maybe a tad bit undisciplined. He thought you were going to stay on and sign up for another tour of duty after you got discharged." The man's story, needless to say, was indeed very touching to me. He showed me letters where his son mentioned me. One week later, when I came back to the nursing home with fifty "Gold Heart" pins as promised, I was told that he died that very morning of our meeting. He must have known that his days were numbered and wanted to meet me before his time was up. I left the pins, which were purchased at my expense, at the nursing home so that the staff could distribute them among the local residents.

* * *

After the end of my military service, I wanted to travel somewhere abroad, but I didn't have the money for it. I went to the port in Haifa and asked a port worker how I could get on a ship and travel somewhere. He asked me what I'd done with my life so far, and I told him that I graduated from high school and served in the IDF as a paratrooper. He told me that there was hardly anything one could do on a ship with that kind of background, but he said that I seemed to be a strong man who was determined to have his way, so he suggested that I try a naval officers' course on board a ship. For that, I would have to go to the local branch of the Ministry of Transportation and ask when the next round of tests for the course were going to be held. I left the port and went to the transportation ministry office, which happened to be on Ha'Namal Street right across the road, and was told that the tests in math and English for the upcoming course were going to be held the next day and that the cadets were going to leave on a ship in one week. Without telling anyone in my family, I came back the next day and passed the tests.

One week later, I boarded a merchant fleet ship named *Eshel*. We were four cadets sailing with a crew of professional seamen, working on deck in the mornings and studying in the afternoon. During the course of a year, we sailed to Africa three times. From the Mediterranean Sea we passed through the Strait of Gibraltar and traveled to countries like Ghana, Nigeria, Congo, and the Ivory Coast. We delivered various commodities from Israel and brought back large pieces of timber that were used to manufacture products at the Kalat Afikim factory back in Israel.

It was one of the best experiences of my life. A boy who just wanted to see the world suddenly became acquainted with the life of sailors, who left their families for prolonged periods. Many of them truly had a wife in every port. I was also exposed to physical violence on board the ship—an integral part of the culture in a confined space containing people with different mentalities and traits. For the first time in my life, I got into a scuffle after getting on the wrong side of a waiter in the mess hall. The seamen didn't take a liking to the young cadets, and the waiter claimed that I treated him disrespectfully. We were both sent to the brig, each one of us held in a different part of the ship, one in the bow and the other in the stern.

At the end of the course, which lasted almost a year, I was required to pass a short seminary sailing sailboats in the Kishon River, but I gave up a naval career out of respect for my father, who wanted me to go to school before I travelled the world. I told him to enroll me in whatever classes he wanted (apart from anything to do with natural sciences) and found myself enrolled in economy, law, and accounting courses. I chose law, and in the first week of my studies at Tel Aviv University, I met Tamy. Back in those days, she was still an IDF soldier. Later, she became my wife and life partner.

* * *

Most of the lecturers in university bored me, except for Attorney Aryeh Rosenbloom. He was a defense attorney dealing with white-collar crime cases and gave amazing lectures on Israeli penal law procedure—otherwise one of the dullest subjects in the world. The way he lectured about the "how" part of it was fascinating.

I decided that this was going to be the area I would specialize in, and at the end of the fifth year of school, I was looking to intern at a law practice that dealt with white-collar crimes. I was told that the best lawyer in this field was Yitzhak Aderet, who only took three cases a year—which was one more than he wanted to take. Aderet, who employed only one intern at a time, told me there would be an opening for me in half a year.

Meanwhile, I started an internship with Zvi Lidsky, despite the fact that his practice didn't handle white-collar crime cases. It was a chance for me to become acquainted with the other side of criminal law practice—the one involving people who chose crime as a way of life. It was truly exhilarating, as I fully expected it to be. Meeting the people Lidsky regularly represented was like reading a book by the illustrious reporter and novelist Damon Runyon. I told Lidsky that I enjoyed watching what he did for a living and learning from him but that this area of law practice was not my destiny.

Around that time, in 1968, I started swimming at the Gordon Swimming Pool in Tel Aviv. I kept going for the next forty years until it was closed down for repairs. This public pool became an important part of my life's trajectory. It divided my workday into two parts—the first was devoted to work, followed by an hour and half break at the pool, and the other half was devoted to other things. Each and every day, at 1:00 p.m., I took a dive into the salt water that I enjoyed so much, since my childhood, and then sat down for a glass of beer or juice with the other regulars.

This afternoon break became a real part of my lifestyle. I met artists and actors from the local cinema and theater, military men, Holocaust survivors, criminals, and university professors. I met Nathan Zehavi there, who became one of my best friends and later a client, and the porter, Sa'adia Ben David, who became my swimming partner. Sa'adia, who immigrated to Israel from Yemen, used to travel to Poland on behalf of the Jewish Agency and get married to local Jewish girls so that they could be allowed to legally emigrate to Israel. He got five women into Israel that way, none of whom he ever saw again. It was just one of a thousand stories you could only hear with a swimsuit, the sun, and salt water.

My friends and I quickly became prominent "fixtures" of the Gordon swimming pool, and we got a chance to meet people from all walks of life who were glued together by that blissful break in the middle of the workday. Among them were Asher Havkin, who owned some gas stations in Tel Aviv and was the manager for the radio presenter Rivkah Michaeli and the famous theater actor Yossi Banay; Dov Bar, who was one of the boldest officers in the Israel naval commando, a.k.a. Shayetet 13; the Bulgarian Gang from Jaffa, who came to the pool and fed everyone *bourekas* and played Bulgarian music on a small tape recorder; Dalia Lamdani, the vice editor of *La'Isha*, Israel's first magazine for women; Heda Boshes, a famous literary critic for the *Ha'aretz* newspaper, and the aforementioned Sa'adia, of course.

I also met two of the most important people in my life at the Gordon swimming pool. The first was Nati Rotem, one of the most senior members of the Shin Bet, who dealt with airline security after he retired from state service. As acting chief of El Al's security division he turned it into one of the most secure airlines in the world. He later managed several companies for Azriel Einav and Yossi Harel, the owners of the Gordon swimming pool. Nati, who is thirteen years older than me, serves to this day as a mentor and a confidant, someone I can consult at any time and spill my guts to.

The second close friend I met at my daily repose at the Gordon pool was the actor Chaim Topol. He was playing a lawyer in the 1985 film *Again, Forever*, based on a story by the Israeli author Yitzhak Ben-Ner, which also featured his wife, Galia, and his daughter Anat. Topol asked me to take him to court with me so that he could absorb a bit of the atmosphere. I decided to take him to the court of the most flamboyant judge of the time, Shaul Aloni, whose brother was the famous playwright

Nissim Aloni. Shaul was very much surprised to see us in his courtroom. After one of the witnesses gave his testimony, Topol asked me in whispers what I thought of him. I replied that he seemed like an absolute pathological liar. At the end of the hearing, Aloni invited us to his office. At the end of our conversation, Topol asked him what he thought about that witness. The judge told him, employing a rather diplomatic tone, that it didn't appear that the witness was telling the truth. When we left Aloni's office, Topol asked me how I knew that the witness was lying. "Over the years," I replied, "you learn to observe people's behavior in certain ways, and when someone's telling a lie, you can spot it instantly."

Our paths crossed again later, doing volunteering work. Topol, who in addition to being a great actor was also a talented painter, sold portraits of celebrities he painted and donated the money to Variety, as along with the proceeds from the premieres of the show he starred in, *Fiddler on the Roof.* I helped him establish Kfar Nahar Hayarden, a small resort for children with special needs and diseases, and Tamy and I were among the donors who supported his project.

We were all hosted at the Gordon swimming pool by the owners: Yossi Harel, the legendary captain of the SS *Exodus,* the ship that brought several thousand Jewish immigrants to Israel's shores in 1947; and Azriel Einav, who worked on that same boat as the chief radio operator. Yossi's character, renamed as Ari Ben-Canaan, was portrayed by Paul Newman in the famous *Exodus* film from 1960, and Yossi was every bit as dashing and charismatic a man as Newman was. I got to meet lots of people from that generation through my friendship with Harel and Einav—the generation that built this country and did much to lay down the infrastructure in all matters related to state security. Most of them were ten to twenty years older than me. I've always had a tendency to have older friends; their wisdom charmed me, and I loved hearing the fascinating stories about the people who were involved in the founding of the state of Israel, many of whom had the ear of our heads of state.

Beyond the fact that they were history in the flesh, Harel and Einav were also shrewd businessmen. They were partners in a host of different ventures worldwide, the largest of which involved importing meat into

Israel from various nations in South America. Azriel Einav was a man with a first-rate sense of humor and was a veritable master when it came to the art of negotiation. In one of the many lessons he imparted to me, he told me about the time he was conducting a very strained negotiation with an Iranian businessman, which had reached a deadlock. He felt the Iranian didn't have much respect for his business acumen and asked him to halt the negotiations for the span of one week. "I'm about to have surgery anyway," he said. "We'll see each other again after I'm fully recovered."

"My dear friend," responded the Iranian with great concern, "what kind of surgery are you going to have?"

"Plastic surgery for my face," replied Einav. "I'm going to trade it in and get a different one. It looks like I have the face of a complete idiot, judging by the way you're been treating me." The Iranian burst into laughter, and the deal between them was successfully concluded later that day.

During the decades I spent going to Harel and Einav's pool, I also had some business ties with them, and I served as their legal counsel on matters of international civil law. I did not normally deal with civil law, but it gave me the benefit of learning from both of them many secrets about the international world of trading, business, and banking.

And that's not all: thanks to Harel I even got involved in show business. He had invested in the production of a film whose script was written by his daughter, Sharon Harel, and the famous Israeli filmmaker Avi Nesher. Yossi Harel asked me to supervise the work on his behalf. I told him that I knew nothing about filmmaking, and Harel said I only needed to oversee the production and make sure everything was going smoothly. And so, I found myself acting as a representative for the investors in a film about the IDF Nahal Brigade's army band, featuring some of the biggest pop hits and biggest stars of the era, including Tuvia Tzafir, Gidi Gov, Gilat Ankori, Sasi Keshet, Dafna Armoni, Meir Swisa, and Gali Atari. I didn't have much work to do from a legal perspective, but I had an incredible experience supervising the work on this highly successful film, which was seen by over half a million people in Israel and ended up becoming a cult classic—*The Band*. I was later also partially involved in the production of *Dizengoff 99* on Harel's behalf, which featured Anat Atzmon, Gali Atari, and Gidi Gov. It also ended up having a real cult following in Israel.

Like a horse that longs to go back to its stable, I was drawn every single day back to the Gordon public pool, where I met people who lived in neighborhoods that I'd never been to, who didn't go to school with me, didn't serve in my unit in the IDF, and didn't sit in the chair next to me at university. It's a very healthy experience for a man to break out of his social and cultural shell once in a while. The Gordon public pool was like the stage for life's drama—a library without books.

* * *

After half a year at Zvi Lidksy's law firm, I had a 1.5-year internship with Yitzhak Aderet, which played a huge role in my professional life. He was like a religious authority figure for me, much like a rabbi. I wanted to be just like him.

I worked with Aderet on big legal cases that often made it to the courtroom. The first thing he taught me was a phrase that he learned during his studies in England—"Never complain and never explain."

"I want this phrase to guide you both in work and in life," he told me. "If you're complaining, you only expose the fact that you're in trouble, and nobody can help you anyway. Instead of complaining, think about the exact thing that made you want to complain. And don't try to explain things either. Just fix whatever needs fixing." Several days later he sent me to handle something at the courthouse. I wanted to explain what happened when I came back, and he told me: "Don't explain anything. You'll fix it tomorrow." That was a monumental lesson for me. Ever since, I've always tried to do less explaining and spend more time fixing and improving upon things, though I do not always succeed in that.

I learned something else from Yitzhak Aderet that I attempted to implement during most of my life, something that became my personal philosophy in the business realm: instead of dealing with a million different legal matters, it's better to deal only with several large, interesting cases that would allow me to make a decent living and work only until the afternoon. Yitzhak Aderet would refuse to take a case that required him to work into the night; he preferred reading books during those hours. When you make a conscious choice to minimize the amount of time you spend working, you become much more productive and focused. When I was working, I did nothing else. I was completely absorbed in doing my job for those hours. I devoted the rest of my time, beginning with the afternoon, to things that nourished the soul. This meant that the hour and a half that I spent at the Gordon pool was no less important than other things I did that day.

I believe that there's a paradox about life's experience: by the time you gain all the necessary experience and knowledge, you no longer have the strength to apply them. It's like getting a comb when you've grown bald. I've tried to live up to that single principle throughout my whole career: don't wait for retirement to do the things you want to do; try to do them here and now.

In my view, work and career are not goals. They can only serve as a means toward a goal. Despite that, you have to make sure that they're fascinating, a good fit for your preferences, and they allow you to get compensated financially at a reasonable rate that will allow you to do the things you love doing—as much as life's circumstances allow for that. Just like we shouldn't wait for someone's death to sing their praises, we shouldn't wait to live only when we have the time or the money to live well.

I was operating in accordance with this philosophy even when I didn't have the means. I became a freelancer on the day I first received my license to practice law in Israel, before I ever had a single client. Tamy and I made sure to celebrate even when we were flat broke. We took two mortgages for our first apartment in Tel Aviv's Neve Avivim neighborhood.

I didn't want to spend my life waiting for better days. "Life is short and death is unimaginably long." So goes the saying attributed to King Solomon. I fell in love with the character of Zorba the Greek, who consumed life like a delicacy. I love people who treat life as a feast. I didn't want to get to a point where I looked back and felt regret about something I didn't do.

* * *

After consulting Yitzhak Aderet, I decided to open my own law practice. He told me I was better off starting my own firm and not working for a paycheck at someone else's. All I knew, after several years spent thinking about this decision, was that I wanted to deal with white-collar criminal cases.

Among the many books I read, I was fascinated by *Courtroom: The Story of Samuel S. Leibowitz* by Quentin Reynolds. It helped me begin to understand the philosophy behind why there are lawyers who serve as legal defenders for criminals.

Years later, when I was teaching law at the Interdisciplinary Center in Herzeliya, a student asked a question that may sound a bit stupid at first but is, in fact, a very deep question: "If someone is accused of having committed an offense while being completely innocent, why would they even need a lawyer?" In response, I came up with an imaginary story that explains why I think every human being has the right to receive legal aid in circumstances they don't understand and have no idea how to deal with and that sometimes involve the whims and arbitrary judgments of the local authorities. The story is as follows:

A man is standing on the balcony of his house and watering the plants in his windows, same as he does every day. Suddenly, the watering pot hits the planter, which falls on the neighbor's head, resulting in his death. So, an innocent man who had nothing but good intentions is suddenly faced with the predicament of having taken another man's life. He is then investigated by police officers who, wanting to get more pieces of the puzzle, start questioning the other residents in the building. One of the neighbors recalls that a few years back, there was a very serious dispute between the person who was watering his plants and the man who was killed. Now the officers have a motive, and who knows what the man's true intentions were. He's now faced with a murder trial. Who could possibly come to his aid now and save him from this calamity? The man is unfamiliar with the legal system and how to defend himself against the accusation.

I had a client once, a manager of the digital division in the Union Bank of Israel, who had a terrible gambling addiction. Every night, he told his wife that he was involved in a secret affair tied to the security of the state of Israel and promptly proceeded to go to a local gambling den, where he lost most of the money he made. To cover his losses, he embezzled the bank's money and was eventually convicted and sent to jail. That was the only place where he could successfully complete a rehabilitation program because there was no possibility of gambling in prison. That was the kind of client I chose to defend.

When I left Yitzhak Aderet's firm, I trailed my way around different properties looking for a small office I could rent for myself. As I searched, I kept running into a lawyer named Binyamin Levinbok, who had been my lecturer in university for civil law procedure. He was also looking for a room to rent. We decided that this was no chance meeting and rented a two-room office space together. In 1970, we rented an office at the basement level of Echad Ha'am Street in Tel Aviv. That was where I took my first steps as a criminal lawyer. Success came almost immediately, when I chanced to become involved with one of the biggest trials in the country at the time.

Several years later, Benny Levinbok went back to working for the firm he was a partner in previously, which became one of the main firms representing Israel's banks in court. We remained good friends until his death.

* * *

In 1973, the Yom Kippur war broke out. I was drafted for seven months. I served as a parachute jump instructor, and our unit was also involved in making supply drops for IDF combat units fighting in the field. At some stage during the conflict, we were flown to the Fayid Airfield in the Sinai Peninsula, which we took from the Egyptians. A field hospital was established there, and wounded men and bodies of those killed in action (KIAs) were brought in from the entire region. We helped to land helicopters at the airfield and were also unofficially tasked with unloading the bodies and wounded from the aircraft. Many were soldiers that I had trained as a jump instructor. It was one of the most traumatic experiences of my entire life...perhaps the most traumatic of all.

The war caught me at a time when we were about to move from the office we had to another office on Balfour Street. By this time, I was a father of two children, Erez and Anat. I was paying rent for two office spaces at the same time and found myself without any source of income. I had to take a loan from a fund that was set up by the Israeli Bar Association in order to help lawyers who were drafted during the war.

Before the war broke out, I took Uri Yaffe, a friend from the Gordon pool and an El Al pilot, to buy furniture for the new office at a place owned by Marcel, a merchant who bought and sold at the local flea market. I left the furniture in his store so that it could be treated to a new coat of polish. I went back to Marcel's at the end of April 1974 to let him know that I didn't have any way to pay him for the furniture that I bought. As soon as Marcel laid his eyes on me, he fainted straight away. When he came to, he told me that because I had been gone for so long, he was sure that I got killed in the war and he'd made a vow to never sell those pieces of furniture to anyone else.

Marcel refused to cancel the order and said that I could pay him in installments, as much as I could spare. I left a bundle of checks at his place, and I still have the furniture I bought from him to this day in my office. Several years ago, a collector of antique furniture came to my office and told me that apparently neither Marcel nor I knew what we were literally sitting on. The table and closet were one hundred years old, brought to Israel by German missionaries from an order associated with the Templars.

Life slowly returned to normal. The clients came back. Tamy was pregnant with our third child. And then, fate struck again. I came back alive from a war that had claimed the lives of thousands of Israeli people and almost died in a cinema in the city I was living in.

It was a particularly rainy winter day, one of those days when everyone preferred to stay home under a thick blanket. On that day, I had the mind, for some inexplicable reason, to go to a comedy show by the "HaGashash HaHiver" group, whose members were also among my friends form the Gordon pool. I drove to the "Hadran" offices at Ibn Gvirol Street to get tickets, where I was told that there was not going to be a show that night. I insisted on going out on that stormy day and bought tickets for the movie *A Man Named Flatfoot*, which must have been the worst film in the history of modern cinema. I bought four tickets with the notion of trying to seduce some other maniacs to come out of the house that night, and my efforts bore fruit: I managed to get Asher and Rina Havkin to go out with my wife and me.

We went to the Hen Cinema on Dizengoff square in the pouring rain. We were two minutes late. Our seats were in the gallery. Ten minutes after the beginning of the movie, there was a terrible explosion right behind us. A terrorist was throwing improvised explosives that he'd fashioned out of empty tin cans full of iron nails into the hall. The couple sitting right next to us was killed instantly. Tamy looked back and was hit in the eye by a piece of shrapnel. I covered her with my arm and was hit by a piece of shrapnel that got under my hand and lodged itself at the edge of my diaphragm. My good friend Asher was lightly wounded in the temple, while Rina remained unharmed. The terrorist himself was killed due to a malfunction in the improvised munitions he was carrying, which were strapped to his body with a belt.

Terrible panic erupted in the movie theater. People ran and trampled one another, desperately attempting to escape the hall. Dozens of taxi-cabs evacuated the wounded to the Ichilov Hospital, where Tamy and I got separated. They initially thought that my injuries were far worse than hers, because the piece of shrapnel hit me in the chest and it had become terribly bloated. The intern who received us was Dr. Nachum Verbin, a doctor from the Mezakh IDF outpost on the banks of the Suez Canal, who had just returned from captivity in Egypt. I had an X-ray done, which showed that the injury was minor—a piece of shrapnel and nothing more. Tamy suffered an injury to the lens in her eye and had to go through surgeries that lasted all night. Professor Moshe Lazar, a renowned Israeli eye specialist, later went on a seminary abroad to learn a new methodology of eye operation specifically for Tamy's specific injury, so that he could continue treating her.

The names of the people who were injured in the bombing were soon published, and lots of people who knew us streamed into the hospital, including friends from the Gordon swimming pool, who came with a bag full of cash in case we had to pay the surgeons. Another friend from the pool went over to our house and took the kids to his place to watch over them.

It took a long time for us to recover physically, especially Tamy, who was hospitalized for a month and still has a disability in one of her eyes. I wouldn't leave her hospital bed. Due to the large number of X-ray images that had to be taken, Tamy's pregnancy had to be terminated. The piece of shrapnel that entered my body got very close to my heart, where it remains to this day. Despite everything we went through, we didn't have any lasting trauma from this event—no anxiety, no anguish of any kind, and also no desire for revenge. We decided that we were going to go on with our lives normally.

Tamy got pregnant again very soon. All our friends were waiting for her to give birth with great excitement. We had a baby girl, who was born with a very serious congenital heart defect. The doctor said her chances of survival were very slim. Sadly, she died no more than twenty-four hours later.

Several years later we had our next child, Yonathan, whose birth not only brought us great happiness but also marked a victory over the injuries we suffered in the terrorist attack and the unsuccessful pregnancy that followed.

My wife, Tamy, hasn't been sitting by idly, either, and has had many successes through the years. At the beginning of our relationship, she allowed me to do my internship before she did hers and, while I completely dedicated myself to this task, she made sure we made ends meet by working at the legal department of Bank Leumi. She ended up becoming one of the bank's most valued senior attorneys. One day, she told me that someone at work spoke to her in a highly offensive and denigrating manner, and I immediately suggested she quit and start her own law firm dealing with civil lawsuits and banking. Naturally, she responded by asking me if I'd completely lost my mind. Asking someone like Tamy, who had spent her entire life working as a salaried employee, to open her own law practice was like telling her to jump out of an airplane without a parachute on her back. I found her an office together with a lawyer friend of ours and told her not to worry, the clients would assuredly come. Tamy opened her law practice in a small room in Ra'anana and quickly moved to her own office in Kfar Sava. She recruited some good people and set up an excellent firm, which today has twenty-five professionals on its roster. Tamy made an outstanding career for herself, and I'm so proud of her for making the decision to challenge herself—a choice that was in stark contrast to everything she believed.

As I noted above, Tamy and I started our life together in Tel Aviv with two mortgages, both of which were paid off ten years later. Because we wanted our children to have a good education, we bought a house in Ra'anana and lived there for the next thirty-four years. Several years ago, our daughter Anat suggested that we all live next to each other. We were in Australia when she called us on the phone and told us that she'd found a piece of real estate in the countryside, in the Israeli Moshav community of Haniel. And so, we moved to the beautiful district of Emek Hefer.

4

My Appointment as Special Advisor on Captured Israeli Soldiers and Those Missing in Action

The subject of IDF captives and MIAs started appearing in headlines in the press as far back as 1948. But up until the 1980s only IDF command was authorized to officially handle this issue, and the authority to do so rested with the head of IDF Manpower Directorate. When tangled dealings with foreign elements began to complicate the issue, such as the Jibril Agreement of 1985, and public opinion was loudly being heard and began to play a role in such considerations, civilians were asked to assist Israel's defense ministry. The first to do so was Attorney Shmuel Tamir, followed by Attorney Aryeh Merinsky and later me, starting on a voluntary basis and continuing in the same way for the next thirty years.

The person who enlisted me was Israel's president at the time, Haim Herzog. In 1986, he asked that I handle the subject of captives and MIAs for a short stint alongside officials from the IDF Manpower Directorate. I accepted his offer. At that preliminary stage, there was no title for someone acting in this capacity. The first two years were very hard, because the various public bodies making up the elaborate system entrusted with maintaining Israel's defense—including, first and foremost the IDF brass—didn't like working with civilians who didn't rise from the ranks. I told Brig. Gen. Elkana Har-Nof, the military advisor to Israel's defense minister at the time, Yitzhak Rabin, that I was constantly feeling like the odd man out, an outsider. He suggested that I be given the official role of special advisor to the minister of defense for matters of captives and MIAs. I would receive a higher security clearance, which would upgrade my role and make the system treat me more seriously. And so it was. On September 8, 1988, I was officially appointed to this role in return for a salary of one Israeli shekel per year. Our list of MIAs from the ranks of the IDF at the time included Zachary Baumel, Yehuda Katz, and Zvika Feldman who were captured in the Battle of Sultan Yaqoub in 1982, in addition to Yossi Fink, Rahamim Alsheikh, Samir As'ad, and Ron Arad.

In one of my meetings with Defense Minister Rabin, I told him that it was impossible for only IDF command to handle this subject and that other elements must be involved in the process. Rabin agreed and suggested that I voice my opinion to Nahum Admoni, director of the Israeli Institute of Intelligence, a.k.a. the Mossad. Following my meeting with Admoni, the Mossad also became a part of the picture, and Admoni appointed a special team to handle IDF captives and MIAs led by Shabtai Shavit, who later became chief of the Mossad himself.

My appointment was extended by defense ministers in all successive administrations. Since I didn't answer directly to any part of the system, I was involved in everything. I handled the negotiations, intelligence gathering, and also relations with family members of the captives and MIAs. Combining all three proved to be problematic at times. Some people thought it improper, claiming that someone who was directly affiliated with the families couldn't handle the professional side of it, too, because it could serve as a source of conflicting interests in the process. I told those critics, "You can't let the families sit around waiting for a meeting with the defense minister. They can come and have a meeting with me anytime they want."

In the course of my work, I've met the kinds of people that a normal person rarely gets to, and I still managed to maintain a crucial division between all my different roles. Thus, for instance, I could come back from a secret meeting and sit down with the family members of a missing person without telling them a word about the meeting that just took place.

I became a part of those families' world. Relations between us were always open and honest, even though we certainly had some disagreements, and there was even anger involved sometimes. Each one of these families, whose lives had been completely thrown into chaos overnight and who suddenly found themselves thrust into the spotlight and the public eye, is an amazing story in itself. Some of them continue to be faithful companions, confidants who supported me during some of the hard times we've had dealing with these issues. You never truly become immunized to it. One of the seventy-three IDF soldiers who were killed in action in the helicopter disaster of February 1997 was Avi Efner from the northern city of Kiryat Tivon. His father worked at a company that I was a board member of, and naturally I planned to attend the funeral. On the morning of the funeral, as usual, I was talking on the phone to Batya Arad, mother to the missing IAF navigator Ron Arad, and she asked me where I was going to go that day. I tried to evade her question, but she pressured me and I finally told her where I was headed. Batya, who was a very unique and strong woman, insisted that I let her talk to Raya, the bereaved mother, before the funeral. When I met Raya later that day, I found it extremely hard to relay Batya's request, but she saw in my face that I was deeply troubled by something, and as soon as she heard what it was about, she asked that I connect her to Batya immediately. I stood by Raya as she talked to Batya on the phone, one moment before she was going to say goodbye to her son forever, and I saw an expression on her face that I simply couldn't fathom.

Many years later, Raya told me about the content of that phone call with Batya. "The night of the helicopter disaster, at 2:00 a.m., IDF officers from the local city's liaison unit arrived at our house and informed us that Avi was missing in action. The feelings of uncertainty were absolutely unbearable. What if he was lying somewhere wounded? What if he was unconscious and couldn't call for help? Where was he? The hours went by, and the house was full of family relatives and friends—everyone was worried and filled with a feeling of incredible tension and complete helplessness. In the small hours of the morning, the IDF liaison officer's mobile phone suddenly started ringing. I heard him say, 'Are you sure?

Is it official?' and for a moment I was filled with great happiness. 'They must have found him.' He was alive. Obviously, the information that was just relayed to him was the exact opposite. Avi was one of the first to have his body identified. Together with the horrific pain, a strange calm descended upon the entire house.

"That's what I was telling Batya in our phone call just before the funeral. Batya shared my grief with very touching words and told me about the first official message she received from the IDF after Ron ejected from his aircraft on October 16, 1986, and about the uncertainty regarding Ron's fate which has been with her ever since. I told Batya that it was terribly hard when we received word that Avi's body was identified, but it was preferable to the awful feeling of uncertainty. From the several hours that I had to endure, I know that there's nothing worse than the feeling, of simply not knowing. Batya responded, "'I envy you.'"

This story emphasizes how unbearably hard the uncertainty is for the families of a missing person, and it is a feeling that becomes an inseparable part of their lives thereafter.

During the Gilad Shalit affair, I was teamed up with Hagai Hadas and later with David Meidan. When the prisoner exchange deal was about to be finalized, I was on an organized tour of Tibet. The head of the team, David Meidan, promised that he would send me a secret signal agreed upon in advance at the moment of truth. When I received this signal from him, Tamy and I left the group, and after twenty-six hours on the way we landed back in Israel at 3:00 a.m. Several hours later, we were engaged in a fascinating conversation with Gilad's mother, Aviva Shalit, at their home in Mitzpe Hila.

Until the mid-1980s, Israel had to deal with the return of captives and MIAs with state actors on the other side of the negotiating table. But from that time, the other parties were terrorist organizations, and working with those was a completely different endeavor. It wasn't an organized state entity, but a band of violent civilian people who had completely different decision-making processes and considerations.

When I was a child, my grandfather asked me a question that, unbeknownst to me, would have awesome significance for me later in life: "If the world's boxing champion stepped into the ring and had to face a young man from the slums holding a broken glass bottle, who would win?"

"The champion," I replied.

"No, my child," said my grandfather, "the winner would be that boy from the slums, and he would win quickly, because the champion learned that it's illegal to hit below the belt, whereas the boy wouldn't be constrained by any of the rules."

The state of Israel—a democracy with all of its advantages and flaws—is that world champion forced to abide by the rules of the game when facing that boy from the slums with a smashed bottle in his hand. A terrorist organization doesn't follow any rules. A state has a highly organized process of decision-making. That was the backbone of every part of my activities. It is the duty of the state, which sends soldiers to the field of battle with the risk of being taken captive or killed, to bring them back home. This duty is one of the most fundamental moral values that we uphold.

* * *

In 1992, while I was deeply involved in the recovery of captives and MIAs (and in addition to my career as an attorney) I met with Danny Angel, owner of "Angel Bakeries," and Kenny Greidinger, one of the owners of Israel's "Rav-Hen" movie theater chain, in the lobby of the Dan hotel in Tel Aviv. They asked me to join the management team of Variety, a global nongovernmental organization engaged in aiding children with special needs and their families. They hinted that later I might also be appointed to head the organization. Mira Avrech was then acting president, and the CEO was Yonah Klimovzky, who was once director general of Israel's Prime Minister's office under Menachem Begin. She was later replaced by Irit Admoni Perlman, daughter of former Mossad chief Nahum Admoni. When I told them that I was far too busy to be involved, Angel and Greidinger convinced me to come in "only for a year or two" and then resign.

I agreed and in 1994 was appointed president of Variety Israel. I really thought I would only be in this role for a year or two, but from that moment on, there was no turning back, and I never wanted to. We managed to turn Variety into a wonderful organization. In 1996, the global Variety group inquired if I was interested in becoming a member of the organization's board of directors. I was appointed to the position of global vice president the following year and started my work in the international arena. We aided millions of children in fifty different countries. It was exhilarating to see how the world opened its heart and started giving on a truly global scale.

In 2002, I was elected to be president of the global organization—the first Israeli citizen to hold this position. The inauguration ceremony was held in Chicago and was attended by 1,200 members of the organization from all around the world. Israeli flags flew in the hall, and "Hava Nagila" played in the background. It was one of the most exciting and emotional events in my life. The guest of honor was Buzz Aldrin, the second astronaut to walk on the moon. I served as president for two years, until 2005, and as chairman of the board until 2007.

My position as Variety Israel president was taken by Udi Angel, who informed me at our first meeting, when I offered this position to him, that he was a very busy man. I told him the same thing they told me—come in for one or two years only. I managed to convince him the same way they managed to convince me. When my term as global president was finished, Udi wanted to give me back the reins, but I declined. I wanted him to stick around and remain on the board of Variety. We decided that the "elders of the tribe" would weigh in on this question. They ruled that I would be appointed chairman for life and that Udi would remain president and be eligible for reelection every two years. It's been fifteen years since we started working together manning the helm at this NGO, and we both enjoy doing it with a great deal of love and friendship.

I never thought I would spend so many years at the head of the organization. Over the years I kept asking myself how and why I persisted in this particular endeavor of helping children and not, for example, elderly people or battered women. I concluded that children's cases were touching for me because, unlike others, they hadn't had time to experience the good in life; they were struck by the hand of fate right at the beginning of the road. Also, there's nothing that makes people happy more than children. First, it's our own childhood, then it's the children we bring into the world and the joy and pride of raising them to adulthood, and finally when they end up having their own children—our grandchildren—who provide us with pure bliss. Not that I dismiss the needs of other people who need help, but we live a relatively short life on this earth, and one has to decide how to spend that time to better humanity.

My involvement with Variety allows me to practice what I find myself preaching to anyone who's willing to listen: find a cause to volunteer for and do it for your local community. The world we live in is becoming an increasingly alienating place. We eat faster, make love faster, walk faster, talk faster. I suggest slowing down. Let yourself stop. Marvel at the road you're taking, get a look at the scenery, enjoy that which the world has given us, and do good. If you do nothing in this life but work, earn a living, and accumulate material wealth, it is inevitable that sooner or later a significant part of your life will become all but tasteless.

I've met children from all over the world. I found that it's much easier to send a message of coexistence and promote peaceful international relations when you're talking to children. They have not yet formed a coherent set of opinions and views about the world around them. They don't have any prejudices yet, and they're not "political animals." And all children in the world have at least one thing in common: they need to be loved.

They say that "he who saves one man's life, it's as if he had saved the entire world." And I want to paraphrase that idiom: he who raises a smile on the face of one individual, unique child, it's as if he kept the entire world alive for a day. It's a terrible thing to see a sad child. I'd been given the awesome privilege of not only raising a smile on hundreds of thousands of children's faces all over the world but also to promote the state of Israel's good reputation. It's true that I can't give a blind child back their eyesight, but I can provide them with the means of seeing without seeing—with a computer that speaks to them using a Braille keyboard. I can give him back his smile.

43

* * *

One day during the year 2001, when I was acting as the vice president of the global Variety NGO, I received a surprising phone call. "Is this Ory Slonim?" A representative of some government office was on the other side of line, and after I confirmed my identity, he said solemnly to me, "I wish to inform you that you've just been selected to light a beacon on Independence Day."

For several years I had been out of the country on Independence Day and did not watch the annual beacon-lighting ceremony because the international conference of the Variety organization was held at the same time. I already knew that I was going to be a very likely candidate for president of global Variety, and was supposed to be at the conference abroad. I couldn't skip it. When I said this to the man on the other side of the line, he was confounded. "Sorry, is this Ory Slonim?" I confirmed again that it was. "Are you listening to what you're saying?" he asked. "You must be confused. I'm talking to you about the most important ceremony for any Jew in the whole world."

It took me about thirty seconds to admit my mistake. My heart and mind were so devoted to Variety—as they are to this day, in fact—that I did not understand the magnitude of the honor that had been bestowed upon me.

During the rehearsals for the ceremony, I received the text that I was supposed to read. I asked that several changes be made. Among other things, I asked to change the wording related to the return of the captives and MIAs. These were sensitive words, all the more for the families whose loved ones we had not managed to bring back yet. In the end, my recommendations were accepted, and I read the following official statement on the night of the ceremony:

> I, Ory Slonim, Resident of Ra'anana, Son of Yitzhak, may his memory be a blessing, and Esther, may she be distinguished for a long life, seventh generation to the Jewish settlers in Hebron in the 19th Century, special volunteer advisor to all defense ministers since 1988 on IDF POWs and MIAs, I dedicate most of my

44

time to my role as President of the Israeli Variety organization, a branch of the world's largest international aid organization for children, and I am honored to light this beacon on the 53rd Independence Day for the State of Israel.

In honor of those who are constantly engaged, a little openly and mostly secretly, without any consideration for the expense of time, effort, and disappointment, in the sacred task of bringing back soldiers who were captured, went missing in action, or were abducted by the enemy and maintain close contact with their families.

In honor of those who willingly take it upon themselves with great love and generosity, the awesome human responsibility for caring for the destitute children of the world, improving their condition, and promoting a better future for them.

In honor of the faith that we have in our duty and our power to fulfil the Prophet Jeremiah's promises: "I will comfort them, and make them rejoice from their sorrow… thy children shall come again to their own border."

And to the glory of the State of Israel.

On the day of the beacon-lighting ceremony, we were all hosted by the chairman of the Knesset at the time, Avraham Burg. He said that among the lighters of the beacons was "uncle Ory"—a term we'd never used before when talking to each other as family members—and told everyone present that his uncle Eliezer Dan, his mother's brother, replaced my own grandfather Menachem Shmuel as manager of the bank in Hebron and was later murdered. "If his grandfather had kept his position," he said, "Ory wouldn't be here to light a beacon today." It made me realize that the fact I was descended from a family from Hebron was going to follow me wherever I went, like it or not.

The beacon-lighting ceremony that year was dedicated to promoting the value of volunteering. I stood on the podium alongside eleven other people, most of whom I wasn't personally acquainted with, but who had dedicated their lives to doing good deeds. It was, without doubt, one of the most inspiring and uplifting moments of my entire life. I was chosen to light a beacon thanks to, and in honor of, the two passions that go with me everywhere—the Variety organization's children and the soldiers taken captive or missing in action. I am their faithful envoy, and I served as their envoy on that memorable evening on Mount Herzl as well. I did not at any point feel the bitter cold, nor did I hear any of the applause. I felt lightheaded due to the excitement. I have no other way of describing my feelings that evening.

I have received many awards in life. Among others, I received the President's Award for Volunteering from President Haim Herzog and the Presidential Award of Distinction from president Shimon Peres, an honor also bestowed on Henry Kissinger, as well as former US presidents Bill Clinton and Barack Obama. Despite that, I've never deliberately done anything to win the honor that has fallen to me, but I was glad that I could use it to further the issues dear to my heart. And, yes, admittedly after years of doing all this hard work, it's nice to know that there are those who acknowledge your efforts.

5

Public Inquiry Committees

The utter chaos in Lebanon played a crucial role in the narrative. Israel made a strategic alliance with the local Christians—they helped us and we helped them, with the understanding that our goal was safeguarding Israel's northern frontier. It was my first acquaintance with the situation in Lebanon, and despite having delved into this theater of war during the period when I was dealing with captives and MIAs, I still barely knew anything about it. The questions that stood at the center of the subsequent investigation were many, but the major ones were why we allowed the Christian militias into the refugee camps in the first place, whether we had any knowledge in advance about the massacres that were about to be perpetrated, and whether we'd done enough to prevent them.

During the committee's investigation, I met a well-known arch-terrorist from Lebanon in Jerusalem who told me, "Listen, you're considered to be a nation of some very smart people, but you're actually being pretty thick-skulled with all your values and principles. There's one thing you don't know how to run—your investigative committees. You put all your generals and high-ranking officers on trial and then publish some conclusions. We do the same, but in reverse order: first we decide what conclusions we want to publish and then we build the case around them. You're playing on an unfamiliar playing field which has a very particular set of rules, but you live by completely different rules."

We both burst out laughing, but today I realize that it wasn't funny at all. The state of Israel is a democracy with a democratic process of decision-making, balances, and safeguards. That's the basis. There are political parties, opinions, a free press. But we're located in a region that operates in a completely different manner; there are no coalitions, and if there's any political opposition, it is swiftly dealt with. There's no free press to speak of; there's no process of decision-making. It's that same old boy from the slums holding on to a broken bottle, which my grandfather told me about.

The claims brought against Amos Yaron were that he failed to properly assess intelligence regarding military action by Christian forces in refugee camps that violated the laws of war, that he failed to take the necessary steps to stop their actions and protect local civilian populations, and that he failed to alert the IDF chief of staff of the immediate threat to those populations.

After the preliminary stages of the committee's discussions were finished, I claimed, on his behalf, that at the time when the Phalange (Christian Lebanese forces) entered the area, he took measures above and beyond what was normally expected in such circumstances, that the reports that reached him were irregular and uncorroborated, and that he had no knowledge of any unprovoked, unjust killings. I further stated that on Friday, September 17, Amos Yaron relayed his concerns to the IDF chief of Northern Command and that, following his report, the Phalange's actions were immediately halted, and they were ordered to remain at their base. Additionally, in a meeting with the commanders of the Phalange forces, Yaron did not receive from them any early indication that would raise any concern.

In the beginning of the legal summary that I submitted to the committee, I wrote that "it would be proper and just that the committee consider the full scope of the evidence and testimonies collected in accordance with the events' actual time of occurrence. The degree of caution that must be exercised by any judicial tribunal demands that it remains impartial and evenhanded in its inquiry into the reasonable discretion of a competent, experienced professional whose decisions and actions are subject to review by the tribunal." To this I added, "As a senior commander with extensive professional experience, who has not passed the responsibility to other levels in the chain of command, neither above nor below in rank, Amos Yaron took all the necessary actions, having exercised reasonable discretion and far above that, in accordance with the available data, the intelligence, and the reality on the ground prevailing at the time when he was in command of his division. During that time, and after carefully weighing the circumstances and the full consequences of his decisions, it was not possible for him to act except as he acted."

Amos acted nobly. I've represented many people, and I've seen with my own eyes how they behave during times of distress. Amos acted with great courage and composure. He didn't do what so many others do—look for someone else to shift the responsibility to.

There was not one time when he tried to lay even a milligram of the responsibility on someone else. While others invited witnesses and questioned them, he did not ask to investigate anyone. Although he was among those warned by the committee that their standing as public officials might be tarnished or that they might be held liable in the investigation, Amos chose not to use his right to testify a second time, to examine witnesses, or to present new evidence to the committee. In fact, at that very same time, he was on a public diplomacy mission to promote Israel's reputation in the United States.

On one occasion, a low-ranking soldier testified before the committee. I told Amos that I knew the soldier's words weren't true and that I wanted to question him. Amos firmly objected. "I am a senior IDF officer," he said. "I will not have my lawyer investigate a sergeant in a cross-examination to protect me." As an attorney, I thought he was wrong from a purely professional perspective, but it really was a noble thing to do on his part.

* * *

Dealing with public investigative committees is like putting a pot of cholent in the oven: even if you put all the correct ingredients in it, you have no idea what's going to come out at the end. When you're sawing a piece of wood, chips fly off. When you examine all the different variables and environmental conditions in a laboratory setting, it's possible to say things should have been done differently, but life is not a laboratory and war much less so—especially the war in Lebanon, which we weren't fighting on our own. Sadly, war is a place where people are injured, killed, or captured.

I've come to realize over the years that one's chance of coming out of an investigative committee unblemished with a supposed "Certificate of Merit" to hang on the wall is close to zero. Even if their conduct was truly spotless, they'll be smeared somehow; you just don't know how deep they'll be wading in it.

The committee slapped Yaron with a harsh sanction: he would be barred from any command post for three years. I felt that he was terribly, terribly wronged. In my view, reprimanding him should have been enough. In any case, the punishment was completely exaggerated.

I was not alone in this conviction. The legal expert Claude Klein, one of the greatest jurists in Europe, said to the press that there's no comparable instance in the history of investigative committees where such harsh conclusions have been drawn like those in the case of the Kahan Committee. He described the committee's regard for Yaron as "completely dumbfounding. The assertion that he should not be entrusted with a commanding role for three years is the kind of thing one would never expect from an investigative committee, only from a court of law."

Amos was disappointed and expressed great anger at the committee's decision. Rightfully so. His conduct did not result in anyone getting injured or killed. He acted precisely as a commander in the field should have acted under such circumstances, and he ought not have been punished, certainly not to this extent. But he gritted his teeth and pressed on. None of his friends turned their backs on him, and he kept moving forward in the new path that had been marked for him—off the field of battle. Amos Yaron remained in his position as the IDF Chief Infantry and Paratrooper Officer, later served as a great head of IDF Manpower Directorate, and as a civilian, he became the director-general of the Israeli Defense Ministry.

The Kahan Committee was a traumatic national moment for all of us. The Israeli state is constantly at war in a hostile, foreign arena with no clear rules of engagement, and he who is unfamiliar with the cruel law of the jungle on this kind of playing field can get terribly burned—and sometimes die.

The IDF's top brass, possessing untold experience in the theater of war, didn't know how to stand in front of the committee. The result was that, today, IDF officers prepare for a committee in advance, long before one is ever established, or as the Israeli journalist Eitan Haber put it: "A soldier goes to war, and comes back home trailed by an attorney."

And that is why you have to think a thousand times before setting up an investigative committee. Not every public dispute needs to turn instantly into a commission of inquiry that passes judgment and sometimes publicly seals people's fate. This measure should only be reserved for the most pivotal and critical of historic events.

My generation was raised on the verse from the book of Ecclesiastes, "A good name is better than fine perfume." It's a simple thing to destroy someone's reputation, and by the time you manage to prove what's been alleged never really occurred, the damage has already been done, sometimes irrevocably. In the twenty-four years I served as chairman of the Israeli Press Council's court of ethics, I've learned in the most visceral manner that words can kill.

I'm not opposed to the establishment of investigative committees as a general rule. I'm merely pointing out the need to put an emphasis on the extreme judiciousness and caution that we must all exercise when we judge people on what happened in hindsight. That's the meaning of the phrase "experience is the best teacher." The first to act fails, and the one who comes after is bound to learn the lesson. We must therefore be extremely prudent and mild when we judge people for their supposed failings.

* * *

During my career, I hardly ever ran into someone who acted as bravely and decently as Amos Yaron. I choose to end this chapter with the words he said to the government after the committee's conclusions were published:

> I did not come here to ask for mercy. This is not a personal problem of mine. I accept anything you in this administration decide. That is democracy, that's what I was brought up on, and that's just what I'll teach those who come after me.

> It's true that one should not testify as to the nature of his own conduct, but in the last war I had the privilege of commanding thousands of soldiers and hundreds of officers. The war began when we landed at the northern part of Sidon on June 6, and, as far as we were concerned, ended four months later in Beirut. It wasn't my war. It was the division's war, a war in which it was continuously engaged. There were two distinct goals to this war: the first—performing operations with a minimum of casualties. The second—observing every last moral principle that was part of our moral and operational upbringing in the corps. That was hard to accomplish. It was clear to us in what kind of arena we were fighting. It was a densely populated urban area, full of civilians. Day by day, hour after hour, one moment after another, it was necessary to issue orders to the troops about adherence to high moral standards and rules of engagement in combat.

> I remember the first problem I encountered. I received a report immediately after the landing that we were being fired upon from a church. There was great confusion. The enemy's firing at us from a church? It went on and on just the same way all through the fighting. Should we return fire or not? For us, as warfighters, every house with laundry hanging out the windows posed a moral problem. All because of the fact that we adopted a rule that said that any house that has laundry hanging outside—was a house that you weren't meant to shoot at, even though we were constantly under fire from those locations.

My personal predicament plays no role here. But it is an issue for IDF soldiers, whom I wish would never have to go on any future wars. We learn lessons from previous wars, and if the soldiers of the IDF go on future operations, people may be harmed. It's important that there be no element that challenges the things we were brought up on, like the willingness to take responsibility. It's important to think about what kind of officers we want to recruit in the IDF in the future. Field commanders are the fundamental foundations of the military, not the staff officers, whose important role I do not for one moment dismiss.

I have no claim or critique against even one word in the committee's report. There's only one thing on my mind at the moment, our legacy, what we should leave behind for those who come after us and the values upon which we need to raise them.

With such admirable words, I cannot but thank my good fortune for having been tasked with defending the man and the officer who is Yaron, despite the tremendous challenges and dire conditions. The insights I gained from this affair serve me to this day.

6

The Egged Bus 300 Affair: The Price of Truth—and the Lies

It was the evening of April 12, 1984. Four Palestinian terrorists armed with knives took over the Egged bus on line 300, which was making its way from Tel Aviv to Ashkelon. They forced the driver to divert from his normal route and drive to the Gaza Strip. The passengers were held hostage inside the bus by the hijackers, who, in exchange for them, demanded the release of 500 Palestinian terrorists—members of the Fatah organization who were imprisoned in Israel. They had in their possession a suitcase which they claimed was full of explosives and said that they would not hesitate to detonate it and kill all the passengers. It turned out the suitcase was completely empty.

The IDF and Israeli police stopped the bus on the outskirts of the city of Deir al-Balah, in the central Gaza Strip, and circled it there. The IDF chief of staff, Moshe Levy, instructed the Chief Infantry and Paratrooper Officer, Brig. Gen. Yitzhak "Itzik" Mordechai, to plan a tactical operation and perform a takeover of the bus. The elite Sayeret Matkal unit, commanded by Lt. Gen. Shay Avital, broke into the bus the next day at dawn, rescuing the passengers and killing two of the terrorists. Irit Portuguez, a young female IDF soldier in regular mandatory service, was killed in the short battle that ensued. The two remaining terrorists, Majdi Abu Jamea and Subhi Abu Jamea, were tied and moved to a nearby field, where they were interrogated by forces on the ground.

Among the many IDF fighters in the field alongside Itzik Mordechai at that time, there were also some friends of mine from the service in the paratroopers' brigade back in the 1960s—people from the School for Parachuting Training and Commando Warfare.

I was a parachute jump instructor in the school's class 15. In my decades of service in the corps, both regular and in reserve, I sent hundreds of soldiers and officers into the air in parachute courses and drill exercises—from the first Douglas C-47 Dakota jets, where you would emerge from the aircraft door and almost fly into the tail of the plane when you made the jump, to the American Lockheed C-130 Hercules, which still serves to launch IDF paratroopers into the sky today. Many of the people I met during those years became friends for life, including those who continued to serve and reached the top command echelons of the unit, which was then involved in both parachuting and counterterrorism. Some of them are also related to this incident—the Line 300 affair—and their part in this story is disclosed here publicly for the first time.

Although I remember everything related to the affair very vividly even today, I reconstructed it again before writing the book with my good friend from the service, a special friend to this day, Col. (res.) Amir Sheleg, commonly known by his nickname, "Habash." When I met Habash to discuss these events, he was gravely ill, suffering from a serious disease that he was battling, brave as a lion, the same way he fought as an IDF soldier all his life. I asked him to write for me the special story of his life, the story of the baby who was abandoned on the day he was born and became a colonel in the IDF, because that man deserves to have his story told. Habash complied with my wishes, and his life's story is included at the end of this chapter.

Habash, who was a parachute jump instructor in one of the classes after mine, is one of those who chose to continue serving in the corps, and during his illustrious career, he became the commander of the School for Parachuting Training and Commando Warfare. The other friend associated with the affair is Lt. Col. Avraham Tzedaka, who was also a parachute jump instructor and served as the commander of the IDF's counterterrorism unit (LOTAR). Lt. Col. Tzedaka and Col. Sheleg are the ones who shared with me and my other paratrooper friends, in real time, the suspicion that there was an attempted cover-up, although we had no evidence of this at that stage.

Lt. Col. Tzedaka, who was then the commander of LOTAR, was on site together with Brig. Gen. Itzik Mordechai. Col. Sheleg and his team were also on the ground, but they did not at any point come into direct contact with the terrorists. After taking over the bus, eliminating two of the terrorists, and detaining the two other terrorists, the commanders wanted to get information as quickly as possible about any chance of a boobytrap or explosive charges that may have been left on the bus. The surviving terrorists were taken by the fighters, including Itzik Mordechai and Tzedaka, for an initial interrogation. The interrogation included the use of force, and at its conclusion, the terrorists, still alive and walking on their own two feet, were handed over to a team of field operatives from Israel's General Security Services, commonly known as the Shin Bet, for further questioning.

What happened between the field interrogation and the terrorists' transfer to the Shin Bet would later be at the center of this affair and rapidly morph into an unprecedented defamation campaign. The arrows of blame were about to be pointed directly at Brig. Gen. Mordechai and his team, alleging that he was the one responsible for the deaths of the terrorists in custody, while the defense would insist that the terrorists were alive when handed over to the Shin Bet investigators. But none of this was anticipated in the first days after the incident.

* * *

My involvement as an attorney and a paratrooper who served for several decades with most of the people caught up in the affair began shortly after the incident, which initially led me to the gut feeling that something terrible was going on and that there was definitely a plot. Even the paratroopers who were on the ground realized this, as Col. Habash told me at the time of writing this book:

As soon as the incident was over, when the rumors started to spread about the killing of the terrorists and finger-pointing started in the direction of Itzik Mordechai, an officer from among Tzedaka's "gang" called me and said that Tzedaka wanted to meet with me urgently. We arranged to meet at a restaurant in Gedera.

It was the morning after the incident, and I waited about an hour for them to arrive. At the meeting, I first heard from Tzedaka (who was very agitated) all the details about the incident and how it unfolded and about the interrogation that took place in the field, including the physical beating of the terrorists. He emphasized that the two terrorists were indeed beaten very harshly, but at the end of the interrogation they were transferred to the hands of the Shin Bet while still being very much alive and standing on their own feet. We said goodbye to each other at the end of the meeting, but none of us could predict how the event would soon escalate.

Ultimately, none of the terrorists came out alive from this incident. In an official IDF spokesman's report on the results of the operation, it was stated that all the terrorists were killed, but photos taken by Israeli press photographers—as well as reports in the world media—indicated that two of them were taken off the bus while still alive. The affair started to spiral from this point with increasing velocity. All hell broke loose, a pandemonium of press publications, investigations, and a series of different events, all with the purpose of attempting to determine who caused the deaths of the terrorists.

Habash went on to say: "Tzedaka was in great distress. He was there and witnessed everything with his own eyes, and now he was watching how the truth, which he also saw with his own eyes, was subjected to opposing and completely outrageous interpretations. At this point, I decided to introduce him to you—a fellow member of the unit, a personal friend, and an attorney who chanced to have quite a bit of experience in such affairs."

With Habash's mediation, I met with Lt. Col. Tzedaka and heard his full version of it, the one he'd already told Habash the day after the incident. I still did not know at this point that in the span of a very short time I would be asked to be involved in the representation of Brig. Gen. Itzik Mordechai as a defense attorney, together with other faithful friends from the paratroopers' brigade: Attorney Dror Hoter-Yishai and Attorney Yehuda Tuniq (who were also friends of mine) in conjunction with his representation by Attorney Amnon Goldenberg.

The Israeli defense minister, Moshe Arens, appointed the Zorea Committee, staffed by Maj. Gen. (res.) Meir Zorea and, in compliance with the request of the Shin Bet, member Yossi Ginossar. The legal counsel for the committee was Ilan Schiff. The accusing finger was unambiguously—and inexplicably, at least to the paratroopers who were at the scene of the incident—pointed in the direction of Brig. Gen. Itzik Mordechai on the grounds that he caused the terrorists' deaths from blows inflicted with the butt of his handgun.

Mordechai insisted that while it was true he had beaten the terrorists, he used reasonable force to take control of them, with three purposes: to determine within the shortest possible time frame whether there was any further danger to the lives of civilians and IDF servicemen, whether there were any explosive charges on the bus, and whether there were any other terrorists in the vicinity. Quite spontaneously, a team of friends and several jurists had been assembled to assist Mordechai in his legal battle. I was among them, as I stated. In addition, dozens of IDF paratroopers and infantrymen contacted us and expressed their desire to help. The feeling was that we were on the verge of a serious campaign, large parts of which were unknown to those who were involved, and the parts that *were* known raised significant doubts about their very existence.

Mordechai hired the services of Attorney Dr. Amnon Goldenberg and his team, who immediately went into action and held discussions in preparation for the Zorea Committee. During my legal career, I worked together with Attorney Goldenberg on dozens of cases, trials, and investigative committees, and we were close personal friends. He also taught me at university and was one of my favorite teachers there. Amnon Goldenberg was a truly gifted legal practitioner, a wise man, well-educated, and possessed the manners and grace of a British gentleman. Highly qualified and accomplished in almost every area of life, he had but one "weakness": he hadn't served in the IDF paratroopers' brigade. I point this out because, around that time as things began to start escalating and while I was slowly starting to get an increasing sense that a "scheme" that we didn't have the details about was definitely brewing, I began to act more like a paratrooper and less like a lawyer. I had a strong instinct something was afoot that was distorting what would otherwise be a purely legal matter.

I knew the work that Amnon was doing in regard to evidence and the legal aspects of the case would be handled with the greatest degree of care and expertise. But the thing that began to dawn on me—and I'm not saying this in retrospect; I'm talking about things that happened in real time—was that we were faced with something that raised suspicion and consternation at a level that cannot be described in words. And so, while Amnon's office dealt with the practical side, I, along with some others, started to address a part of the story that had never been publicly told before—a conspiracy against Itzik Mordechai. We did not fully know the details at the time, but we knew for sure that it was absolutely real.

I began to receive phone calls from members of the paratroopers' brigade who told me what was going on at the Zorea Committee. "The Shin Bet is way more powerful than you are," I was told by one of them. "They know how to investigate everything they think needs to be investigated, and they use methods that leave you in the dust, without the slightest idea how to tackle them."

The people who contacted me suggested that I look into what happened in the Tyre disaster in Lebanon, which had happened two years earlier, in November 1982, when the military government building in the city of Tyre collapsed and ninety-one people were killed. Seventy-six of them were IDF soldiers, policemen, and Shin Bet personnel. The rest were Lebanese detainees.

At the head of the committee investigating the killings of the two Lebanese terrorists was Col. (res.) Meir Zorea, who was known as a straight and honest man. The previous Zorea Committee, the one that had investigated the Tyre disaster, concluded that leaks from gas balloons likely resulted in the explosion and collapse of the building as opposed to hostile terrorist activity.

My contacts told me that there was very intense influence in the activities of the Zorea Committee from the head of the Shin Bet, Avraham Shalom, and the commander of the Shin Bet's northern regional division, Yossi Ginossar. "What the Shin Bet did with regard to that committee is exactly what they're doing now, in the Zorea Committee of bus line 300."

Years later, the Israeli journalist Ronen Bergman wrote in his book *The Point of No Return* that a military police investigation into the Tyre disaster found evidence that the explosion at the complex was caused by a car bomb, but it was decided not to publish the conclusions and stick to the official version, which proved more palatable.

Recently, the Tyre disaster, which had troubled me so much in the past, returned to the headlines again. According to new evidence published in an article by Itai Ilanai in "Yedioth Ahronoth," a study conducted by former Shin Bet man Nachman Tal found that the disaster in Tyre was the result of a car bomb attack and that the man behind it was Imad Mughniyeh, who was destined to become the leader of the Hezbollah's military wing in Lebanon and who, according to foreign press sources, was later assassinated by Israel. Even then, it was alleged, Avraham Shalom and Yossi Ginossar were involved in attempts to prevent a genuine open investigation into the incident. The determination that the explosion resulted from a gas leak made it easier for Israeli political leaders and generals to continue with the military campaign in Lebanon and absolved from any responsibility the members of the intelligence apparatus whose job was to prevent precisely this kind of terrorist attack.

I got to know Nachman Tal, the Shin Bet operative, very well during the years that I dealt with the issue of captives and MIAs. Years after the Line 300 affair, the overreach of Shin Bet members in the context of investigative committees was a major concern in the numerous conversations we had. Nachman tried to explain to me how unfamiliar I was with the capabilities and methods that were in use then—and I emphasize the word *then*—by the Shin Bet. In his praise, I would say that he never slandered any of the Shin Bet members or tried to sully their reputation or make accusations against them. He also never divulged any specific information about the director of the service and his subordinates regarding the Line 300 affair. Being a Shin Bet officer, he strictly obeyed the principles he had been relying on throughout his life: what happens inside the organization is kept inside the organization and is not shared with "outsiders." Despite his adherence to these rules, I could sense from him that "something very bad" was happening there.

* * *

I admit that during that time, in the midst of the Line 300 affair, I didn't have the leisure or ability to address these allegations and warnings. I was completely occupied with providing legal aid to Itzik Mordechai, and it did not occur to me to delve into the subject deeper and explore how one could orchestrate a cover-up in a country where the rule of law prevails—all the more when this cover-up targets not the nation's enemies but a senior IDF officer. I then spent the next few years learning, like all the rest of us, that even in countries like the United States, incidents such as the Watergate affair and others occurred. They were completely incomprehensible to many people who had to deal with them in real time, but those who understood just a little more than the others and perhaps even suspected a little more than others also conducted themselves and acted differently in the end.

After hearing the stories about Lt. Col. Tzedaka and Col. Habash regarding what happened in the field and what was happening in the Zorea Committee of Line 300, the stories from many other people about the Shin Bet's conduct, and the unequivocal version of Itzik Mordechai himself, and after I learned—as much as I could back then—about the Tyre disaster, I came to realize that someone was playing us for fools. Someone was trying to hatch a plot of some kind, and in order to uncover it, it was time to adopt a radically different approach. We needed to do so without abandoning all the legitimate efforts being made by the excellent team of jurists led by Amnon Goldenberg. And so, on the one hand, I received regular reports on all the purely professional legal aspects and, at the same time, was contacted by more and more IDF officers who'd been summoned to testify at the committee. From their accounts, it was increasingly clear to the Itzik Mordechai crew and me that there was definitely a plot. Itzik Mordechai was the victim of an elaborate, sinister conspiracy, but we didn't know to what extent it involved the head of the Shin Bet and his senior representative on the committee, Yossi Ginossar.

Habash remembers those days well. "The smear campaign was inhumane and downright scary," he reminded me recently. "Tzedaka was terribly anxious. He told of his summons to appear and testify before the committee and about the inhuman pressures exerted on him there, especially by Yossi Ginossar. They told him if he adhered to the narrative which they defined as the 'truth,' it would go a long way toward improving the outcome for him, and that if he didn't, the consequences would be dire. That's when I took him to see you again."

In my second meeting with Tzedaka, I told him that he must steel himself and stick to the truth. After Tzedaka gave his testimony to the committee, I approached Yonah Blatman, the state attorney. "There's something wrong here," I told him. "I'm getting visits from friends summoned to testify at the Zorea Committee who say they've received threats."

Yonah Blatman did not accept my claim that something was improper with the committee, and he made kind of a veiled "threat" of his own. "Listen my dear friend, Attorney Ory Slonim," he told me, "you are an excellent lawyer, but if you continue in this vein, you're going to get yourself disbarred. Your relationship with officers involved in the affair could prove to have a detrimental effect on you." I responded that I was doing my work faithfully, in a decent and upright manner, and that my relationships were with officers who were fighting on only one front and had one truth. I added that what we were feeling was simply unacceptable for me. We said goodbye to each other as friends, as I knew he had been cheated by the cover story of the head of Shin Bet.

I'm sure that Blatman—an honest and professional person—wasn't aware of everything about the committee either, at least not at the time. He was a reliable and trustworthy member of the judicial system, and I believe he simply could not conceive that there might be a plot and a conspiracy planned and orchestrated in such an elaborate way.

We tried to handle the matter using our own ways and our meager means. We got smart. To some extent, our actions did indeed entail some intervention into the proceedings. For example, when Tzedaka was invited to attend a meeting in connection with his testimony, we instructed him to go but with a clear warning about the excessive involvement of Yossi Ginossar in the affair. We handled terrified IDF officers facing the risk of dishonorable discharge from the military, and we were there to bolster their confidence. We told them that there was probably someone sitting there trying to guide the witnesses and give them directions, even though we had no tangible evidence of this at that point. We thought it impossible that the truth we knew for certain—one hundred percent, no guesses, no conjecture—could be distorted by anyone.

* * *

In a report published by the committee on May 20, 1984, it was determined that the two hijackers were killed by blows to their heads, yet no one was being held responsible for their deaths. It was decided to bring Itzik Mordechai to disciplinary proceedings before Maj. Gen. (res.) Haim Nadal, formerly the President of the Military Court of Appeals, for conduct unbecoming an IDF officer.

I accompanied Itzik Mordechai to the disciplinary hearings. For him, even the decision to do nothing more than discipline him was simply out of the question. He knew with absolutely certainty that he was innocent and that his conduct was unassailable. On the night before the trial, a memorial conference was held in Ramat Gan to commemorate the establishment of the Paratroopers' Brigade. The IDF Chief of Staff, Moshe Levy, stood for a picture there alongside Mordechai in a clear demonstration of support.

The trial opened on Friday, August 16, 1985. In his testimony before Maj. Gen. Nadal, Itzik argued for two hours about the operational needs that forced him to act as he did, and he claimed, in the most unambiguous terms, that the blows the terrorists suffered had not resulted in their deaths. Two days later, at a meeting I attended with Itzik Mordechai (and which lasted only a few minutes), Maj. Gen. Nadal announced that he was acquitting Mordechai of all charges. He accepted the rationale behind Mordechai's actions, and even acknowledged that, when there are risk factors in the field, reasonable force can be lawfully used to obtain information.

"My heart explodes when I think what might have happened had general Yitzhak Mordechai not been such a strong man," I was quoted saying in the papers. "A less resilient person might have gone to extremes. Itzik's silence, from the time of his indictment and until the present, is an expression of the strength of his faith in his own righteousness. At such moments, no legal counsel, no monetary compensation, or encouragement can alleviate the hardship. One can only be sustained by an inner belief in one's own rectitude and purity of action and intention."

During that time—when we still didn't know the horrible truth in its entirety—I was calling what happened in the trial a "blood libel." "An entire system stood against him," I said. "The Attorney General, the State Attorney, the investigative committee, the Criminal Investigation Division in the IDF's Military Police Corps, and the media—everyone. He repeatedly said, 'I'm innocent,' and was flatly given one, single answer: 'We don't believe you.' Faced with this system was a lone man who could not cry out because he was wearing a uniform. Now, shouldn't all those who have smeared him step forward and apologize to him? Although Mordechai is not at all interested in an apology, it is puzzling that no one bothered to say 'we were wrong.'"

Itzik celebrated his acquittal in an evening of group singing at his house, surrounded by the many friends who supported him. "I always believed in the rightness of my path," he said. "This is the way I was educated and the way in which I educate my subordinates: to love the land and its people, to adhere to the highest of values and to the sanctity of human life, to be steadfast and accomplish your mission to the fullest in every condition and in every circumstance."

It took another two years until it was publicly revealed, following the testimony of three Shin Bet operatives, not only that our suspicions were very much grounded in reality, but that the truth was even more hideous and frightening than we ever imagined. The trio—Reuven Hazak, Rafi Malka, and Peleg Radai—testified that while they were in the field, when the interrogation of the terrorists took place, Shin Bet chief Avraham Shalom instructed the head of the Shin Bet's operations unit, Ehud Yatom, to eliminate the terrorists because he said, "Terrorists who try to instigate a hostage crisis don't come out of this alive." Yatom and his team proceeded to beat the two terrorists with rocks and an iron rod until they had both gone to meet their maker.

All hell broke loose. There was a massive police investigation, a state attorney was forced to resign before the probe was concluded, Shalom and his Shin Bet operatives were granted amnesty from the Israeli president with no subsequent challenge from the Supreme Court (but according to the article I read, there was a challenge and the SC upheld the pardons). The affair finally came to a close, but it continues to bleed to this day.

* * *

Years later, my friend, Attorney Amnon Zichroni, contacted me and asked me if I was willing to meet with Yossi Ginossar. Other people who knew Yossi Ginossar and me, including senior members of the IDF and Shin Bet, thought we ought to see each other. They maintained that Yossi acted the way he did, not because he had any personal motive, but because as a Shin Bet man, he believed—perhaps due to the highly reprehensible standards prevalent then in the service—that he was doing the right thing. Our mutual friends thought we should get to know each other, clear the bad blood between us, and maybe (so they said) a common language could be found.

I refused to meet Ginossar at first, but in the end, I relented and accepted Zichroni's request. I met an impressive, charismatic, smart, and intelligent man. We spoke for about two hours. Yossi explained to me that as a Shin Bet man, he was merely doing what he was instructed to do, same as the others. I found it very hard to accept his claim that one of Israel's secret service arms, whose mission is to battle our enemies, would act in this manner against a senior IDF officer. Yossi tried to convince me that Itzik Mordechai was promised that no harm would come to him. I couldn't bear to hear that sentence. "How can you assure someone that they will not be harmed after you made your claims and acted in front of the whole world as if he was the one who killed the terrorists?" I rebuked him. "If Itzik Mordechai hadn't been such a strong man in his personality and character, he would never have lasted out there."

Since that meeting, I met with Yossi Ginossar several other times in private. But I just couldn't let go of my feelings of bitterness toward him due to the past.

Ginossar had an impressive ability to communicate with people. If he hadn't passed away at such an early age, he would in all likelihood have gone a long way in the business he was engaged in. Ronen Bergman, in his book *By Any Means Necessary*, wrote that thanks to my influence and also thanks to Zichroni's warm recommendation, Ginossar was appointed by Yitzhak Rabin to be the government coordinator for captives and MIAs. He added that while Ginossar was in office, he also "secured his own interests in dark dealings with PLO chairman Yasser Arafat and other Palestinian officials."

Indeed, I was the one who recommended Ginossar to Rabin. I was also the one who pressured all defense ministers to appoint one person to coordinate all the operations regarding prisoners of war and missing persons vis-à-vis all the powerful bodies handling the issue: the IDF, the Shin Bet, the Mossad, the intelligence agencies, and the government. A committee was appointed to review the proposal, and the pressure I exerted finally bore fruit and led to the appointment of the coordinator. When Rabin mentioned Yossi Ginossar as a likely candidate for the job, I said it was a great idea. However, I never learned what kind of dealings Ginossar had with the Palestinians, and I didn't care about it. I have always tended not to believe what I read or hear about people. I prefer to distill things and judge each person by myself, according to my own impressions.

Yossi Ginossar was appointed to the position that I never wanted to fill. My role had no official designation. I did everything that I saw fit to promote the issue of captives and MIAs. I would refer to my position as "The Knocker on Doors." I knocked on the door of anyone that I thought could be of help. When you knock on the door, sometimes it opens, and then you go inside and make connections. If they don't open the door for you, then you try to open it using other means. You knock on any possible door to find the POW and MIA's whereabouts and links to those who may be able to assist you in this goal. You use any negotiating tool to bring them home.

That's what I did with Yossi Ginossar. We knocked on each other's door, and when we discovered that we had a common language and that we could help each other, we gradually expanded the opening. After three decades of dealing with the issue of captives and MIAs, I can say today with a great deal of satisfaction that I did not get into conflicts with anyone. I sometimes said the harshest things to people and had the harshest things said to me, but I was always guided by my sacred purpose. That was the most important thing. I am not a man of strife and quarrel, and I know how to set aside things that might hinder the promotion of the sacred goal. That is precisely what I did in this case as well.

Despite that, and although I did not have any personal resentment toward Yossi Ginossar, after everything I personally experienced in the Line 300 case—and especially when examining all the hard facts in retrospect—I cannot accept all his explanations. I remain steadfast in my belief that it was lucky for the conspirators behind this terrible plot that they were faced with such a strong man who had such great faith in his own truth and such good friends who believed him and believed in him. If it weren't for that, the affair could have ended in a completely different and terribly tragic way.

As someone who witnessed the events closely, the Line 300 affair is one of the biggest traumas in the history of the state of Israel. It wasn't just a conspiracy against a senior commander in the IDF, but a grievous injury inflicted on Israeli democracy itself. Fortunately, there were those who sought to right the terrible wrong that had been committed, even if their work was late in coming.

7

The Knocker on Doors: Soldiers Captured by Terrorists and MIAs

I was still in the midst of my long reserve service during the Yom Kippur War in 1973, when I traveled with Col. (res.) Amir "Habash" Sheleg to visit one of his relatives who had just returned from captivity in the hands of the enemy. At that time, prisoners of war who were brought back to Israel following the armistice agreements, first with Egypt and then with Syria, were gathered by IDF command in a special facility located in a recreational resort at Zichron Ya'akov, which was closed to the public and converted for that purpose. The goal of this was to have all the released captives investigated in one place—away from their families and the pressures of the outside world—about the circumstances of their captivity and their conduct during the time they spent in enemy hands.

Habash's relative and other released POWs told us that they had to sit through interrogations several times a day and they weren't allowed to go back to their homes or meet with their families. We saw people returning from captivity and experiencing a second trauma. It was a traumatic experience for us, too, but back then we still didn't realize—like many other people in our country—what a grievous mistake it was to welcome the returning captives home like this. It took many long years before anyone dared to criticize what had happened at the facility in Zichron Ya'akov, until they realized that it was possible to make different choices.

The experience of visiting the facility and the strong impression it left on me continued to haunt me for a long time.

Those were precisely the things that were on my mind when Israel's president, Haim Herzog, contacted me in 1986 and offered me an opportunity to join the efforts to return captives and MIAs to Israel. At the time, I didn't have the same conviction as I do now, that there is nothing more important in the world than securing the return of the men and women who were ordered to go to war on behalf of our country and our people. Those killed in action are obviously beyond help; you can only provide support for their families. But the wounded need to be rehabilitated. Those who have suffered emotional traumas, including those who have been held in captivity, must receive all possible assistance; they must be supported tirelessly. And regarding those still missing in action—every effort must be made, and any price can and should be paid, to try to bring them home.

When Herzog approached me, the only parties handling captives and MIAs were the IDF (specifically the IDF's Manpower Directorate) and the unit for detecting missing soldiers (EITAN), which I later became an officer in. In the 1980s it was decided to appoint, alongside the Manpower Directorate, a public civilian figure who would handle the issue from the outside, probably due to mounting pressure from the families of MIAs. The first to serve in this capacity was Shmuel Tamir, a government minister, Knesset member, and attorney. Tamir opposed the Jibril deal of 1985 in which 1,150 terrorists were released in exchange for just three IDF soldiers—Hezi Shai, Nissim Salem, and Yosef Groff. Tamir sought to resign after the deal was approved by the government, but Defense Minister Yitzhak Rabin, fearing his resignation would cause Jibril to be tougher, refused to accept it and persuaded Tamir to postpone it until the deal was finalized. Attorney Aryeh Merinsky replaced Tamir and served briefly in this role. I met Tamir and Merinsky—both lawyers involved with white-collar crimes like me—as friends of my great mentor, Attorney Yitzhak Aderet.

I was forty-four, a father of three, and already a pretty successful lawyer when Herzog—whom I had met years earlier when we were both on opposing sides in an arbitration proceeding—offered me a chance to get involved in a profession that I knew next to nothing about. I didn't think twice about it, because I honestly thought even back then that this was a sacred cause. However, even after I consulted with a few friends, some of whom were veterans of the defense establishment, I still did not understand exactly what I was getting into. I couldn't imagine that I would be swallowed up in this endless activity, in which there's never a dull moment, while continuing to work as a lawyer handling some of the biggest legal cases in the country. It's not an easy thing to appear in court in the morning when your head is troubled by what you're going to say later that afternoon to the mothers of MIAs like Batya Arad, Miriam Baumel, or Pnina Feldman.

The reference to the redemption of prisoners originates in ancient times. In the *Gitin* tractate of the Talmud, Chapter 4, *Mishnah* 6, it is stated: "One must not redeem the captives for more than their price is worth, for the risk of amending the world." That is, one must not pay an exorbitant price in return for captives for fear that the act will encourage further abductions. Rabbi Meir of Rothenburg, one of the greatest medieval masters on Jewish law, followed this Talmudic tenet when he was captured and imprisoned in 1286 while trying to unlawfully emigrate to the Holy Land. The king of Germany, Rudolf I, demanded a huge sum of money in ransom. The Jewish community collected the required sum and planned to pay and secure his release, but the Rabbi of Rothenburg was adamant that he should not be released in exchange for the money and ended up dying in prison.

Rabbi Shlomo Goren addresses this subject in his book *Theory of the State* (*Torat Ha'Medina*). His remarks were written following the controversial Jibril deal. He wrote: "It is possible that in the case of prisoners of war who have been captured while fulfilling a mission of the country that sent them to the missions of war, there is a sacred duty to do everything for the purpose of their release and one must not observe any of the restrictions of the tractate 'One must not redeem the captives for more than their price is worth,' because our soldiers were captured in the service of the state. It may be that the state has the undisputable duty of redeeming them and preventing them from being in harm's way, even to the slightest degree, and there are no restrictions on them in respect to redemption of captives.... The state must redeem them with any funds it can possibly allocate to it and for any price in the world, because the responsibility for their lives rests with the state, which sent them to the battle they never returned from.... Due to the responsibility of the state and the military to keep soldiers safe at all costs, we may also have had to release them in exchange for the release of hundreds of murderers. Although the release of the terrorists could have put the country and its people in greater jeopardy, there is no cost to the lives of our soldiers who were captured in a mission on our behalf, while performing their national duty and military roles."

The great Jewish philosopher and physician Maimonides ruled: "The redemption of captives takes greater priority than the livelihood of the poor and cover for their bodies, and you have no greater deed than the redemption of captives, because the captive is among all the hungry, thirsty and unclothed, and is in danger of losing his life too. Ignoring the need to redeem captives goes against the laws: 'Do not harden your heart or shut your hand against your needy fellow' (Deuteronomy 15:7); 'Do not stand idly by while your neighbor's blood is shed' (Leviticus 19:16); and 'Do not rule over them ruthlessly' (Leviticus 25:53), and cancels out the following good deeds: 'You must surely open your hand to him' (Deuteronomy 15:8); 'Your brother shall live with you' (Leviticus 25:36); '...Love your neighbor as yourself' (Leviticus 19:18); 'Rescue those who are drawn to death' (Proverbs 24:11); and more. And there is no greater deed than the redeeming of captives."

But it wasn't Maimonides or Rabbi Goren that made me accept this role and, in a very short time, understand the complexity of this subject. It is a world of its own: the captive and the captor's sides of the equation—with all the intricate psychology of the relationship between the parties—the family that was left behind, the state, and the circumstances of the captive's release. My life has revolved around this complexity for more than thirty years.

* * *

During the time when I was just starting to get involved in these matters, the IDF was handling all MIAs, including people who were still missing from as far back as Israel's War of Independence in 1948, but I was initially sent to deal with the "fresh" cases. This included Zachary Baumel, Yehuda Katz, and Zvika Feldman, who had been missing (and still are) since the bloody battle between Israeli and Syrian armor units in Sultan Yacoub, in the Beqaa Valley of Lebanon on June 11, 1982; the Druze soldier Samir As'ad, who disappeared in 1983; and Yossi Fink and Rahamim Alsheikh, who were captured during an ambush in Lebanon in 1986.

The case of Ron Arad, an Israeli Air Force navigator who parachuted and was captured alive by the enemy in Lebanon on October 16, 1986, was not in my personal care at that time. There were several teams investigating his case, both in the army and in a captives and MIAs task force set up in the Ministry of Defense under Uri Lubrani's management. I wasn't an active member of the team yet at that point, as I did not have an official role with the required security clearance; I received this clearance only in 1988, at which point I was entrusted with confidential details of the Ron Arad case and met with his family. I had a strong conviction that the Ron Arad case was being handled with such great care and determination that it would be resolved in a very short span of time, which, sadly, was never to happen. Only in retrospect, and only after many years, did I realize that secret and highly classified parts of the case were not shared with me in full, including very significant negotiations conducted with the enemy.

I began to study the subject of captives and MIAs in depth and met with people who were involved in the field and close to it: military personnel, intelligence community members, prisoners of war returning from captivity, families of MIAs, and religious figures involved in the process. I wanted to know everything. A big part of my job, at least as I understood it, was the connection with the families. I'm not a psychologist, but I served as a sturdy figure to lean on for most of the families of the captives and MIAs for a long time. For some of them, I inevitably sometimes served as a source of great disappointment, and rightly so. I learned to understand the anger that was directed at me. I might have been angry, too, as a family member of a missing person. I was a civilian, not an IDF officer and not a minister in the government. I volunteered to be in this capacity. I didn't receive one shekel in return for my work and did not ask for it. I didn't even take the one shekel that was later symbolically put into the books as my yearly salary. Brig. Gen. Shimon Hefetz, who was the military adjutant for Defense Ministers Moshe Arens and Yitzhak Rabin, and later for Israeli Presidents Ezer Weizman, Moshe Katsav, and Shimon Peres, once told me that he wanted to give me a modest gift and presented me with an IDF commendation badge that had one Israeli shekel glued to the back. "I know that you never received a salary," he wrote to me, "so at least be kind enough to accept this one shekel from me."

Despite the fact that I was a volunteer—and maybe precisely because of it—I often turned into the families' punching bag. I was the target for all their arrows of anguish because I just happened to be there. I was the messenger, and the messenger is always the one to receive the punishment for bad news. As far as the families were concerned, I was the one who represented the kingdom, even though that was not exactly the case formally. I completely understood their position and their terrible pain, but I've often had difficulty dealing with it. I suffered a lot of grief and had a lot of horrible moments. I heard things that are hard to hear, but I certainly toughened up in the process, during which I realized that the anger and discontent were not because of me, but due to this frustrating situation and because of those whose job was to solve the problems. Families were angry and desperate and hoped that somebody from the outside world of the public service could assist with the issue a bit better or in a different way. This was the situation, and I understood that my role was to build more trusted relationships in these delicate situations. Despite the disappointment I have often caused them, I still maintain close relationships with most of the families.

I used to be asked every now and then how exactly I referred to my position. I have come to the conclusion that the most appropriate definition is "The Knocker on Doors." As discussed earlier, my job was to knock on the doors of the whole world and their cousins, in Israel and abroad, from the most junior military officer up to the level of heads of states, to never allow the issue to be struck from the agenda, and to do everything in my power to bring the captives and MIAs home. Sometimes, when someone like the defense minister or prime minster is busy with his many different tasks and has a huge, monumental burden on his shoulders, they need a reminder about the captives and the MIAs. So, there I was, knocking on every possible door that is unworthy of me stepping up to and knocking on. As the saying goes, when you enter the vineyard you have to ask yourself if you really want to eat the grapes or simply kill the guard. For my part, I really wanted to eat the grapes.

I realized pretty quickly that there was a strong need to upgrade the way that the issue of captives and MIAs was being handled. I wanted to take it to the next level. It wasn't enough for the IDF and its Manpower Directorate to manage it. Dealing with this subject requires covering many broad areas, and therefore more elements had to be involved, such as the Mossad. For example, the ultra-Orthodox child Yossele Shumacher was abducted in the 1960s and smuggled from Israel into the United States by his grandfather and uncle, who feared his parents would return with him to Russia and raise him to be an atheist. In one of my many meetings with Defense Minister Yitzhak Rabin, I asked him how it was possible that Schumacher was brought back to Israel using intelligence gathered by the Mossad and many other bodies, but when it came to our soldiers, only the IDF and the Manpower Directorate were authorized to deal with it. Rabin agreed with me and sent me to meet with Nahum Admoni, the head of the Mossad.

I went to the Hadar Daphna house, an office building in Tel Aviv, and met with a man who looked like a Hollywood movie actor and really fit the bill as an intelligence community man. I told Admoni that I was there on behalf of Defense Minister Rabin, who, like me, now thought that the Mossad should be involved in the investigations into the IDF's missing soldiers. After all, the Mossad was derived, in part, from the Institute for Immigration B—the clandestine operation to retrieve Jewish immigrants and refugees from World War II and ship them to Israel in the late 1940s. Its primary historic role was to help getting people to

Israel. Admoni told me without a moment's hesitation: "You're absolutely correct." He formed a senior team called the "Shon" (the Hebrew abbreviation for "captives and missing persons") and put one of his best people in charge of it, Shabtai Shavit, who was himself already one of the leading candidates for the position of director of the Mossad. This team, made up of senior officers in the organization, continues in its work to this day. Its mission is to locate any intel that can possibly be of use in regards to the MIAs in the IDF—what happened to them and where they were located—without holding any negotiations.

I was, in fact, the catalyst for the Mossad's involvement, which led to a significant upgrade in terms of the measures and resources allocated for these endeavors. The amount of human and financial energy that has been invested since then in trying to learn what happened to Israeli captives and MIAs and returning them home is unprecedented and unparalleled in the world, and I say that with the highest degree of certainty. I've developed a personal connection over the years with all the teams that worked on this issue at the Mossad. I was sometimes directly involved in what they did, as I will later reveal. Quite a few times, I created the connection with a particular source somewhere in the world, and the Mossad took it from there.

I met with the deputy director of the Shin Bet at the time, Ya'akov Peri, who would later become the Shin Bet chief, and got his organization to join our efforts as well. The Shin Bet handled everything related to interrogation and espionage, as well as anything to do with the MIAs in Israel's sovereignty. At the time, there were two people who fell under this category—the soldiers Avi Sasportas and Ilan Sa'adon, who had been kidnapped and murdered on Israeli soil. The two were kidnapped within Israel and this was the only case that the Shin Bet dealt. All others were caught or captured out of Israel and dealt by the Mossad and IDF intelligence.

* * *

Needless to say, there was a tremendous benefit to having a large, professional, and multi-armed team involved in the operation. The disadvantage, which I increasingly became aware of over the years, was the difficulty in getting all of the different bodies to maneuver together and act in concert. I am proud that I managed to do so for so many years without starting unnecessary internal conflicts. I had an excellent relationship with almost every one of the people who worked with me, not least because of the sanctity of the mission, and also because they appreciated the fact that I was a civilian volunteer dealing with this painful endeavor from morning to night.

Many people had trouble understanding why I was doing this. There were even those who were constantly looking for hidden motives, trying to figure out what I was getting in return for it. Well, the only thing I gained from it was a lot of heartache. Yonah Baumel, Zachary's father, who, along with his wife, Miriam, mother of Zachary, was moving heaven and earth trying to find out what happened to his son and bring him home, asked me many times why I was dealing with the issue, why I was leaving my family behind on long trips, spending money, and experiencing grief over and over again. I tried to be humorous in my reply: "Because if I didn't, I'd never get the chance to meet a wonderful guy like you." And that was the truth.

* * *

The person who was then in charge of this matter in the Ministry of Defense was Uri Lubrani, and he had a team of intelligence officers at his beck and call. The most prominent of these were Col. Reuven "Rubke" Ehrlich and Col. Yitzhak Tidhar, who were sitting in Lubrani's chamber on the second floor of the Ministry of Defense building in the Rabin Military Camp in Tel Aviv, also known as Ha'Kirya ("The District"). Uri was a highly experienced diplomat who served as Israel's ambassador to Uganda, Rwanda, Ethiopia, and Iran, and was coordinator of government operations in Lebanon. He had a wide array of global connections, including excellent relationships with elements in Lebanon and Iran, owing to his unique personality. He was a very well-educated man, with lots of knowledge and emotional intelligence; he knew how to speak to anyone in their own language. "Rubke" Ehrlich, who is today the head of the Intelligence and Terrorism Information Center at Israel's Intelligence

Heritage Center in Ramat Gan, was a case officer and one of the biggest experts in the service on anything related to Lebanon. Yitzhak Tidhar was also a brilliant man with vast knowledge of Lebanon. They've all done much to help me understand a great many things about Lebanon and the people who live there, with whom I was often in close contact.

At the same time, I was constantly in contact with the casualties department in the IDF Manpower Directorate—the people caring for the MIAs' families at an individual level—as they were the main avenue through which I made contact with all the families. Naturally, these are people who have to be smart, sensitive, and highly empathetic.

I had a particularly special connection with the chief of Casualties Assistance, Col. (res.) Varda Pomerantz, who returned to military service at the end of a period of higher education studies shortly after I took up my post. I was told that she was a uniquely capable woman who could break down steel doors. "But you better be aware," my contacts added, "that if you can't get on her good side, there'll be hell to pay." The warning was unnecessary. I met a very smart and special woman whose level of openness and sincerity (and to some extent the craziness of her positive attitude) were extraordinary. There was a difference of opinion between me and Varda almost every day, but that's only because we both knew that our shared mission was bigger and more important than anything else. As far as I'm concerned, Varda was my entry ticket to the more sensitive part of the issue of captives and MIAs, which is the connection with the families. We both sojourned in this world for several years. We were in almost daily contact. Varda is one of my favorite people, because of who she is and because of all the hard work she's done.

Varda's story is the story of our quintessential national tragedy. During Operation Protective Edge in 2014, Varda—who for years lived daily in the world of bereavement, pain, and uncertainty—suddenly lost her son Daniel when IDF ground forces entered the Gaza Strip. On the morning of the funeral I arrived at the house where Varda and her husband, Avi, were living. "I told you" were the first words she said to me as I hugged her. She didn't have to explain what she meant. After all, having worked so closely with her, I had often heard those words come from her mouth. She knew that one day the bearer of bad news would come knocking on her door too.

Varda's replacement in this post was Brig. Gen. (res.) Itamar Barnea, a clinical psychologist and former jet fighter pilot who, during the Yom Kippur War, was severely wounded and taken captive by the Syrians. I'd never gone to a psychological therapy session prior to that. Itamar Barnea, who later became the chief psychologist of the Israeli Trauma and Resiliency Center (NATAL, an Israeli association that deals with trauma victims on a services background), was also my personal psychologist in those days. With his track record—as a pilot, an injured serviceman, a prisoner of war, and a psychologist and therapist who helped families— who could be better suited to be my own therapist? To this day, whenever I have to face some dilemma, he's my shoulder to lean on and my listening ear. He serves as my psychologist, filling in for all the ones I never found the time to go to.

I could consult with Itamar on any dilemmas I had with the family of an MIA. He was the one who helped me deal with the dual nature of my role—my attempts to gain information on MIAs on the one hand and to maintain the connection with the families on the other. I often came back from a trip to some godforsaken rural place in Lebanon after negotiating with one of many villains who may have held the end of a thread that could lead to actionable intel, and I would suddenly get a phone call from Batya Arad asking: "Can you drop in for a cup of coffee?" Well, of course I *could*, but what was I going to tell her? After all, I wasn't authorized to make reports on anything, and I wasn't at liberty to divulge even a shred of what I knew. I was meeting with Batya almost every day at some point, passing through the nursery she worked at when on my way to the office. I was always careful, as I was with other families, never to allow her to harbor any illusions. My greatest fear was to transmit the optimism I sometimes returned with after a meeting in a European capital to the families because it wasn't always based on firm foundations. And woe to me if I let the grief of these families, and the terrible frustration of a life of constant uncertainty, be compounded with false hope. That's exactly the time when I needed Itamar Barnea to tell me that it wasn't a good day to meet with a particular family, because they were mad at the whole world.

Another person who became a kind of confessional priest for me, albeit from a different angle, was the military secretary for Defense Minister Rabin, Brig. Gen. Elkana Har-Nof, a senior military man with invaluable experience. There was unique chemistry between us right from the first few meetings. He was the one I voiced my frustrations to when I felt like valuable information was being withheld from me, and that I was being treated like nothing but a stranger or a guest who's dropped by for a few brief moments. My attempts to fit in and "belong" to the defense establishment and government bureaucracy were going from swimming in an Olympic pool to towering waves in a roiling sea. I wasn't on anybody's team; my designated area of work was this one single issue.

Elkana provided me with a very broad shoulder to lean on. He was the one who allowed me to go into the defense minister's office whenever I wanted to try some new strategy, and he was also the one to tell me when Rabin was sitting with Air Force pilots working on a military operation and it wasn't the right time to go in. He also taught me how to write using military style and jargon—concise and to the point. Until then, I was filling the page with voluminous paragraphs…like a lawyer.

There were other people in the defense minister's office who helped me understand how to function within public service, a system which I was not part of: Shimon Sheves, who was close to Rabin personally and politically and later served as director-general of his office as prime minister; Oded Ben-Ami, who served as Rabin's media consultant; and more than anyone else, Haim Israeli, Defense Ministry member since 1950. Mr. Israeli served under fourteen defense ministers, the first of them being David Ben-Gurion himself, and on the fiftieth anniversary of Israel's independence received the Israel Prize for his special contribution to the state and to society. To my joy, he agreed to be one of my sponsors. Without these people, it's likely that I would have had a heart attack over the years—or just got discouraged and quit.

The almost two-year period in which I dealt with the POW and MIA issue without any designation for my role and without being officially appointed by the defense minister was almost completely unbearable. Without an official appointment, the issue of my security clearance was also not addressed, so I had no access to information regarding some of the secret moves that were being made. This kind of compartmental-ization was extremely difficult for me. I was not personally offended by this because I understood that these were the rules of the game, but the fact that I was not involved in many of the important things that were happening and that I did not even know about some of them, made it very difficult for me to do my job. It was an intolerable feeling on the practical-operational level, and above all else it proved a hindrance to me when I had to deal with this important issue with regard to navigator Ron Arad. His capture was an area in which information and operational considerations were highly compartmentalized, and I was consistently left out of the picture.

One of the events that I did not participate in due to the lack of security clearance was the connection that the Lubrani team created with the so-called "Ranger" described in Ronen Bergman's book, *By Any Means Necessary*.

Jamil Sahid, also known as "The Ranger" (Ha'Sayar was the nick-name attached to him in the Israeli intelligence community), was a Shi'ite Lebanese businessman who operated in Africa. He was also affiliated with Nabih Berri, head of the Shi'ite Amal movement in Lebanon, and frequently donated funds to him and his organization. With the help of Attorney Amnon Zichroni and his client Shabtai Kalmanovich, Uri Lubrani met with the "Ranger" and got the immediate impression that he was a serious guy who could provide real actionable information about the fate of Ron Arad. The "Ranger" did indeed succeed in bringing us an authentic letter written by Ron Arad—who at the time was being held in Lebanon by Mustafa Dirani—and two pictures of him. The state of Israel found ways to repay Sahid for his help, including obtaining licenses to transfer goods to Lebanon, and even managed to rescue his sister's son, who had been sentenced to death by the courts in Sierra Leone for having been involved in a failed attempt at a military coup.

With the mediation of the "Ranger" and additional contacts, the conditions for the release and repatriation of Arad were clarified: money and the release of Palestinian terrorists. Unfortunately, at precisely that point in time, in 1988, the vicious Palestinian terrorist campaign known as the First Intifada broke out and was mistakenly attributed to the terrorists released in the Jibril prisoner exchange deal just a few short years earlier. Defense Minister Rabin, beleaguered by the harsh public criticism about his role in the Jibril deal, refused to approve the deal to bring Arad home. One year later, the Sahid reported to us that Dirani had kidnapped Ron Arad from the Amal organization, and he was no longer in their hands.

Years later, when I read the interviews with Uri Lubrani, in which he said he regretted not putting a lot more pressure on the policy makers (Shamir and Rabin), it was even more frustrating for me. That pressure might have changed Ron Arad's fate. Lubrani's remarks, which I have no doubt were said in all frankness and with a pained heart, made me realize that if I had been part of the business and if I could have gotten close enough to the defense minister and prime minister, then maybe—just maybe—I could have increased the pressure and ensured the continued negotiations with the "Ranger."

Incidentally, for purposes of this case, Amnon Zichroni received an ad-hoc security clearance from Meir Shamgar, the Supreme Court president at the time, while I, as I said, was not given this privilege. I only learned about this many months later.

I had known Attorney Amnon Zichroni for many years as a colleague who'd spent far longer than me in our profession. We sometimes met at the old Café Tamar on Sheinkin Street in Tel Aviv, which was close to both our offices. Zichroni was already a veteran lawyer by then, and among other things, he served as an attorney for the aforementioned left-leaning *Ha'Olam Ha'Ze* magazine. We became friends, despite the difficult conversations we had sometimes about his pacifist worldview and his decision not to enlist in the IDF for that reason. Amnon tried to explain to me the reasons behind his views and his decision. It was obviously hard for me back then to understand the decision not to serve in the military for ideological reasons. I still respected the fact that he chose to share his perspective with me, and over the years our friendship deepened. Attorney Zichroni greatly assisted our efforts to obtain information about captives and MIAs, and there were many endeavors in this area he initiated that I wasn't involved in at all. The biggest issue on which we collaborated fully was in connection with the German lawyer Wolfgang Vogel. I was deeply involved with the enquiry, and I will reveal the details in a later chapter.

* * *

Ultimately, it was Elkana Har-Nof who helped me solve the compartmentalization problem, which led to me being appointed a special adviser to the defense minister in exchange for a salary of one Israeli shekel per year. On September 7, 1988, the IDF chief of staff, the Shin Bet director, the head of the Mossad, the head of the IDF Manpower Directorate, the head of Military Intelligence (AMAN), and Uri Lubrani all received a letter that reads as follows: "Attorney Ory Slonim has been appointed by the minister of defense to be his special adviser on the subject of soldiers who became missing in action, prisoners of war, or abducted by the enemy. Attorney Slonim will handle two areas: A. Advising the Defense Minister on soldiers missing, taken captive, and kidnapped; B. Maintaining regular connection with families. Attorney Slonim will facilitate cooperation, mutual briefings, and advisement on the abovementioned subjects with all relevant elements and bodies engaged in these endeavors while focusing on continuous full-time working relations with the head of AKA (IDF Manpower Directorate) as the designated person in charge of the issue in IDF command. Signed: Elkana Har-Nof, military secretary at the defense minister's office."

This move by Har-Nof enabled me to perform my duties in a practical and highly efficient manner. I was now included in the discussions at the highest levels. But it also came with a price: I made the decision that, in my personal life, I wouldn't touch anything related to state security matters—and definitely not something that would provide me with an income.

Har-Nof's letter changed my life. The moment it was signed, I was suddenly blessed with the ability to pick up the phone and call the chief of AMAN, the Shin Bet director, or the Mossad director and ask to meet with them, and they wouldn't be able to tell me to call back in two weeks. I was now operating on behalf of the defense minister, and that was of great significance. Additionally, the defense ministers for whom I was working now had far more appreciation for me for having given up many of my business endeavors and private affairs to devote time to this mission.

Since entering the legal world in the 1970s, I'd managed to find time to serve as an attorney for large entities, including some of Israel's banks, and appear on investigative committees dealing with major events in Israel's history. The people I met—even if we didn't play backgammon together on Friday afternoons—knew who I was and where I was coming from. Whenever I called on someone whose help I needed—Finance Minister Yitzhak Moda'i, for example, whom I was working with on a case I will discuss in a later chapter—he knew who it was and what it was about. Some of Israel's defense ministers were people I "grew up" with during my army service, such as Ehud Barak and Shaul Mofaz, which meant that I had no problem explaining why I needed to meet with him. Those connections were very important to survival in a system that didn't take kindly to strangers.

To the people operating in this system, I've always been nothing but a guest, and it didn't matter if this guest has been in the system for thirty years. I've never been "one of their own." By nature of their activities, each one of the secret agencies had to retain and fiercely guard its own territory. They did not want to send a person who wasn't a fully trained company man, someone who rose from the ranks, on a life-threatening operation—something that actually happened in my case (and will be told in the chapter "Operation Dirani Brothers"). As I mentioned, many of the heads of the intelligence and security bodies had a hard time accepting my presence, stemming from their apprehension in welcoming anyone from the outside, including people who came from other agencies. For example, AMAN had a difficult time working with a person who also reported to the head of the Mossad, and the head of the Mossad had a hard time talking to a person who also reported to the defense minister. I can definitely understand their misgivings—who would want their organization to be "infiltrated" by a person who answers to the defense minister and tells him exactly what file they had open on their desks? I got that, and I never made reports to the defense minister while going over someone else's head. A copy of every report I sent to the defense minister was also sent to the specific body I was working with. I didn't just do it for the sake of courtesy; I did it because I didn't want to be "neutralized" at work and left out of the discussion.

One of the biggest challenges I faced was getting people to not be afraid of me. I think I succeeded in this task, even if sometimes there were those who thought twice about sharing things with me, and I can understand that too. To survive the way I did, for several years in an almost impossible role, whose definition might be the broadest in existence, you have to be sensitive from morning to night when working with your partners in this sacred mission. Each had his own agenda and personal issues, and if one does not take into account all the different components—failure is a very likely outcome, and then it's time to go home.

"It's not easy for a civilian, someone who is not an integral part of the security apparatus, who was not born and raised in it, to deal with such sensitive and delicate issues, like the ones you had to deal with," I was told by Defense Minister Moshe Arens, with whom I worked for part of that period, when he heard that I was writing a book. He died, sadly, right before the book was set for printing in Israel. "I know this feeling very well; I was neither a soldier in the IDF nor part of the defense establishment. I served in the US military and had experience in the military and in state service in Washington, D.C., and still I served as Israel's defense minister for two full terms. To me, each one of us civilians is actually a reservist in the service of the country, and that's exactly what you were. You handled the issue of IDF captives and MIAs like you were born to do it."

Since receiving this appointment, I have become well acquainted with the Arad family. The family dimension, which I was already very familiar with, was compounded by another facet, because there were also a wife and a daughter involved, which made the picture a bit more complicated. Each member of the family carried their pain and frustration and found a different way to deal with it. My mother, a smart woman who didn't know anything about state security and knew very little about my actual work, once said to me: "You men cannot understand a mother's love to the living being that comes out of her womb." I'm afraid I cannot but agree with this statement.

Following my work on the case of the Arad family, I've often faced claims that this case of the missing navigator received a greater priority when compared to the treatment of other missing persons. Similar allegations of discrimination in treatment came to my ears during the campaign to negotiate for the release of Gilad Shalit, the soldier held captive by the Hamas in the Gaza strip. I learned to ignore these claims. After all, I knew perfectly well that no effort was spared to bring back any of the MIAs, and it didn't matter in what unit they served, as they were sent by the state. For me, they were truly all my sons.

* * *

From the day that my world became intermingled with the IDF captives and MIAs until I decided to concentrate more on the world of aiding children with special needs within the Israeli and global Variety organizations, I was often asked by friends and partners about my exact place there.

Was it serving as a companion for families who wanted my involvement and helping the good people—the officers of the IDF Manpower Directorate and other departments in the IDF—who were engaged in this difficult and sacred work? Was it aiding those bodies involved in the intelligence and operational effort to obtain information on the captives and MIAs and to try to bring them back to Israel through negotiation or operational means? Or was it initiating my own moves and creating channels of communication with different elements, both friendly and hostile, that might be able to help? Even after a few good years of dealing with the subject, and after thousands of conversations, meetings, and initiatives; lots of heartache and disappointment; and even some exciting and uplifting moments, I do not really have one definitive answer. It was probably a little of everything.

While working on this book, I met with my friend Haggai Hadas, a Mossad operative, who was at the head of the team involved in securing the release of Gilad Shalit. I told him that I had a hard time describing my own role. After the meeting, Haggai wrote me a moving letter. In his own special words, he described what I couldn't—and still can't—say today about myself.

This is what he wrote to me:

Ory, you were trusted by all the members of a family, which a huge "mountain" suddenly fell on, one bright day. Such a family to me is like a blind man standing in a busy city street, with completely unrecognizable sounds and noises blaring from all sides, and the poor man is completely unequipped with the ability to distinguish a friend from a foe, tell between good and evil, between what's permitted and what's forbidden, tell right from wrong, he does not know when to bend and when to raise his head. You succeeded, thanks to who you are, in containing the family and safely leading it through the busy streets. To build the family's ability to have the right proportions for each article in the newspaper, for each minister's statement, for another Hamas propaganda video, for a report from the negotiating team or for any other kind of noise and to enable it to maintain its sanity. If I had to try to define what skills you possess, I would say that these are basically three skills that are in the same person: an ear for filtering noise, judicial thinking and expressiveness using body language, verbal language and choosing the right timing to speak to the family. In the same way, you also applied these skills in your contact with other parties: the negotiating team, international mediators, and members of the supporting military unit.

As an expert in negotiation, your angle of thinking is layered with knowledge, based on practical, rich, diverse, lifelong experience. We spent a lot of time analyzing people, statements, moves, and opportunities while trying to assess what's right and what's possible in the face of what could be potentially harmful. Negotiation is a battle of the minds. A sophisticated negotiating team must utilize many different kinds of stratagems. Over the years, you have equipped yourself with the tools and skills, which are well-integrated into the activity that has been carried out in practice.

And, in addition to all these, you are also the master of organizational memory. Unfortunately, there is no complete and organized record of all the actions taken by the various bodies and teams that have been active in the field over the years. Moreover, there is no code of operational conduct which has been definitively outlined and approved by the political echelons. Each event is handled at the discretion of the elected leadership and command. You, in addition to having been in the field for many years, have another advantage: your memory and your ability to transmit the knowledge without appearing to be overbearing or patronizing when addressing your collaborators.

Indeed, during the early years of my work on the subject, I felt that, despite it being so important and even sacred to many in the system, the bodies involved in it were not sufficiently coordinated, and their modes of cooperation and exchange of information were severely lacking. Many good people explained to me that this is simply the way of the world, where each one of the agencies involved keeps information and activity confidential and inside its corridors, and the compartmentalization—especially in the intelligence and operational areas—is their absolute prerogative. It's true that at the end of the day, the minister or prime minister in charge of the subject is the one who is supposed to know everything there is to know, but naturally, he or she is concerned with many different state, defense, and policy issues that involve the administration and security of the state. The subject of the IDF captives and MIAs, with all the many factors involved, must therefore be organized by only one person. It should be someone with experience and the widest possible backing from the prime minister or the minister of defense, someone who will be afforded all the possibilities, full and completely transparent, for the fulfillment of this special task.

From the very first days when I studied the subject, and after conversations with many different parties, I saw myself as an envoy—a messenger that publicly proclaims the need for such an appointment. Already in my first work meetings and personal meetings with Defense Minister Yitzhak Rabin, this was the first topic on the agenda.

Rabin appointed Uri Lubrani to be the head of the captives and MIAs team at the time. Lubrani and with his staff were indeed the most suitable people for the mission, but the feeling, which was shared by me and others I spoke with, was that the cooperation and openness with the more secretive of the intelligence agencies were incomplete. Indeed, over the years, Rabin had appointed a number of teams and committees to examine the issue. They all came to the same conclusion: the mission should be handled by one person who "knows everything." I saw these decisions as a good outcome and even, I daresay, a modest achievement I could crown myself with for all the efforts I made.

Another important issue that I raised during each meeting with the defense minister was the integration of the captives and MIAs subject into every conversation—whether on political or state security background—with leaders and senior executives in foreign nations. This combination, in the right dosage and in the right places, was meant to convey a message that the issue was a high priority for Israeli administrations.

Since, naturally, prisoners of war and missing persons, as well as the information about them, are held by hostile elements, it is always advisable to also include bodies that have already established contact with our enemies and rivals. At the time, I believed that alongside my involvement in other areas, I could help (thanks to my personal and business relationships with my clients as a lawyer)—with efforts to reach elements in Iran with whom we had no direct and visible connection, or to communicate with other hostile entities, including those in Syria and

Lebanon. I believed that it was also necessary to combine economic and political interests, through which we might be able to obtain information and even possibly bring back our captives and MIAs, regardless of the work of the Mossad and the Shin Bet, which were already tirelessly dealing with this subject.

Indeed, over the years I have personally assisted in such moves, always in full and open cooperation with members of the secret agencies engaged in it. Despite being an outsider, I managed to gain the trust of members of the intelligence community and secret bodies that compose it. Eventually, they learned to accept my presence and respected my work alongside them. All the initiatives I have led over the years have been coordinated and reported in real time to state agencies.

I made personal connections—always using my full name and never undercover—with Syrian, Iranian, and Lebanese elements, as well as with antiques dealers and arms traders, and in one case, even with an organized crime boss. I reached out to elements in the USSR, Germany, Austria, the United Kingdom, and African countries, including several terrorist organizations. Their members agreed to meet me only after using their own connections to make sure that I was not an "agent." The background checks confirmed that I was, indeed, a lawyer, who did not deal with security matters except for this single humanitarian issue, and were usually conducted after receiving a series of organized newspaper clippings, from Israel and the rest of the world media, on the trials and legal affairs I dealt with as a lawyer, as well as my extensive activities in Israel and the global arena as part of the Variety organization. This vetting had a great impact on the level of confidence created and my subsequent ability to reach elements that had been apprehensive about meeting with official or covert Israeli elements.

Some of the stories about my meetings around the world will be told here, in the following chapters. These include a series of encounters in Denmark with Mustafa Dirani's brother, which are revealed here for the first time; an informal meeting with Austrian President Kurt Waldheim, due to the severing of the official ties between the state of Israel and his administration at the time; a meeting with then-president of Kenya, Jomo

Kenyatta, who was friends with Iran's leaders; a somewhat amusing meeting in Moscow; and a surprising encounter in New York. I will also reveal details about some meetings with Iranian agents, who were in working relationships with some of my clients in Europe and with terrorist-related elements in Lebanon.

I still can't tell you about some of my meetings. They will have to remain confidential, possibly forever.

8

A Mother Cries Out for Her Son, Killed in Action: The Haunting Words of Col. Varda Pomerantz

"Worse than the worst of all…"
Col. (res.) Varda Pomerantz, formerly chief of casualties, mother to Daniel Pomerantz, killed in action in Operation Protective Edge, 2014

I could say that a missing son is worse than the worst of all. Absence is the worst calamity. Death is terrible. Believe me, I know what a terrible blow this is, to experience the death of a child. But bereavement is definitive, it is absolute. You don't find yourself drifting from life to death and tormenting yourself with your own thoughts. Is he suffering or not? Is he being fed or being starved? Will he ever come back? You know that he's dead.

Although I have dealt with death and bereavement almost all of my life, I have always been the happiest person in the world, because I knew how to appreciate life and not deal with nonsense. I knew how to enjoy every blooming flower and always find a sunbeam, emerging somewhere from among the dark clouds. When my son Lior was injured in combat, I was strutting like a peacock in the Tel Hashomer hospital. What's an injury compared to what might have happened?

But at the same time, I always knew that one day I would lose a son. After all, I saw it with my own eyes: tens of thousands of people were killed while defending the state, so why should my house be passed over? By what right? I was very close to the writer Naomi Unger, whose son Nitzan was killed in 1984 by accidental discharge of one of his teammates' guns during a Nahal brigade's paradrop exercise. Naomi started fighting for prevention of accidents in IDF drills and operations and wrote a book titled *Stopping the Bullet*. I recently read the book again and was amazed to discover that I already told her as early as 1985 that I knew it would happen to me too, that I would lose my son. I didn't know which one of them and I didn't know how, and I only had two sons at the time.

Knowing it didn't make me an anxious mother. I was perfectly happy to send Daniel, the youngest of my sons, to the Golani brigade because that's the unit he wanted to serve in, but when operation Protective Edge began, I said: "As soon as the ground forces go into Gaza, I'm dead." On June 1, I was at a relative's wedding. I met there an IDF mental health specialist, an officer whom I knew from my time in the service and who helped us handle the cases of returning prisoners of war. I told her that I was going through a very difficult time, that I was dreaming at night about an IDF civilian liaison officer from the city of Rehovoth, him of all people, who came to inform me about my son's death. I even considered, for the first time in my life, to go myself and seek emotional support from the IDF's NATAL unit.

About ten days before Daniel was killed, Ory and I were invited to celebrate the fifty-year marriage anniversary of Mordechai and Hadassah Fink, the parents of the late IDF soldier Yossi Fink, which was organized by their daughters. We were the only ones invited who weren't family members, and it was a great honor. While we were sitting at the reception, feeling elated, an alarm started and everyone ran for the shelter. A few days later, I also joined the family of bereaved mothers.

I spoke to Daniel on Friday morning. I recorded the call, knowing full well that this was going to be our last conversation. He knew it, too, but each of us was protecting the other. Daniel told me that they were told to write something in case…. It was very important for him to tell us all where he left his letter for us. I thought that the army was going crazy if those were the instructions they gave to the troops, but when I checked it later, it turned out to be wrong. Not only did they not tell the soldiers to write such a letter, but the soldiers under Daniel's command, who saw someone sitting and writing this kind of letter, called on him and said to him: "Pomeranz, don't let him write this stuff." Daniel invented this story to protect me, so that I wouldn't know that he himself knew that he was going to be killed. When Daniel talked to me, at 9:31 a.m., the letter was not yet written. He wrote it only an hour later.

On Sunday morning I told my husband, Avi: "Today is not a good day for us." Many years after I was discharged from the army service, I decided to completely disconnect from the past and changed my phone number. But I also saved the old phone with the previous number. The old phone wouldn't stop ringing that day. I waited for the officers from the IDF liaison unit, for hours on end. And all this time I pleaded within my heart: "Just don't put me in the position of a son who's missing in action, anything but that. Just come already and let me know, don't leave me hanging between heaven and earth, between life and death. Don't let me fall into this pit of despair, that place that I simply don't understand, to this day, how I could possibly endure."

* * *

How symbolic this conversation is, taking place on the thirty-sixth anniversary of the Battle of Sultan Yacoub. You can't escape this historic event. It's an integral part of my shared life story with Ory.

The IDF Casualties Department was established as a lesson from the Yom Kippur War, which was a terrible national trauma in terms of the amount of casualties and the way they were treated, as well as their families. The whole country was in disarray. We still have people missing from that war, all of them officially classified as soldiers Killed In Action whose place of burial is unknown. But did all their mothers and fathers, most of whom must have already passed away since then, really believe it?

In fact, under the circumstances, I was serving at the time in the Golani brigade, as an officer in the now disbanded IDF Women's Corps (CHEN), stationed at the Golan Heights, in charge of casualties. At the time, the military had absolutely no framework for dealing with the families of KIAs, and every division commander or adjutant turned the (usually) two female officers in their division into Casualties Officers. And so, Ruth Frank, the division's social care and relief officer, and I, CHEN officer Varda Nimtsovitz, began treating the cases of the families and the wounded soldiers. We did the best we could, but what can a twenty-one-year-old girl possibly be able to do without any prior preparation or training? My own mind did its best to repress the traumatic events of that war to this day.

In late 1975, as a lesson from the Yom Kippur War, the army decided to set up an array to handle the families' cases. I was fortunate to have been offered a role in the field. I must admit, to my great regret, that everything we know today has been learned through the sacrifice made in the flesh and blood of soldiers killed and missing in action and standing upon the shoulders of their families. Those who laid the foundations for the conception of treatment for the families of captives and MIAs are Col. Dvora Tomer, former IDF Chief CHEN Officer, and Col. Rabbi Ephraim Tsemel, who worked in this field in the Israeli Air Force. The two were thrown straight into the cold water, during the chaotic situation left over from the Yom Kippur War.

In 1981, when I was head of the Family Liaison Branch, there was already a whole written doctrine in the "Shon" unit, dealing with prisoners of war and soldiers missing in action, through two established centers: Center for Detection of Missing Soldiers (EITAN) and the Family Liaison Center. The job of the Center for Detection of Missing Soldiers was, as its name implies, to locate them and find information about them, and the role of the Family Liaison Center was to provide support, based in part on knowledge which came from the detection center. Ory, who came into the field a few years later, had a supervising role: he used his particular capabilities to link the proximity to information with the proximity to the families. Before he appeared on the scene, the field was plagued with "horse thieves," people who preyed on the families, took advantage of them, failed to disclose the correct and accurate information about their loved ones, and in my opinion also used them as pawns for political and personal gain, as it happened, for example, in the treatment of MIAs from the Battle of Sultan Yacoub.

To my astonishment, less than a year after formulating the doctrine of care for the soldiers and their families under the Shon's supervision, it had its first trial of fire following the Battle in Sultan Yacoub, on June 11, 1982, where we experienced at once a mass of soldiers missing in action. During the incident, a direction for a particular course of action was being examined, which could bring about a solution to the mystery. I knew who was going to be traveling and what they were going to do, and in a preliminary hearing I said that nothing should be disclosed to the families in the meantime. It's important for me to explain that our approach was to tell families the truth, and nothing but the truth, but not always the whole truth. Why should these families, who are so devastated as it is, wait nervously for days on end? And what's more, it was nearly time for the Jewish New Year celebration. I myself could hardly breathe due to the mounting stress and pressure waiting for the results, and I could hardly imagine how difficult they would find it to cope with it, and in any case, there'd be nothing for them to do about it.

It was clear to me that I was ready to "lie" to them, because that was the right thing to do, but there was someone else on the team who thought otherwise and chose to leak the test results to a young girl in one of the families. That was not part of my work method or ethics, nor Ory's. None of us ever "meddled." This mission was sacred to us. These families were sacred and so was their care, and I say this as someone who has had to bury her own son and is willing to be a footstool for the families of the MIAs even today.

As a result of that test, Cpt. Zohar "Zorko" Lifshitz was brought back to Israel and received a military funeral and burial in the military cemetery in Holon. At least his family had the comfort of a relatively quick way to have a tombstone over their loved one's body, in contrast to the families of Zachary Baumel, Yehuda Katz, and Zvika Feldman, who are still classified as Missing in Action to this day. Zorko's mother, the late Dvora, like many other bereaved parents, visited me when I observed the seven days of mourning over the death of my own son. Zorko was freshly married to a lovely young girl, Ronit. A few months after Daniel was killed, we received a message that a joint march would take place along the Israel National Trail, in memory of Zorko and Daniel, at the request of the families of both Zohar and Ronit. The march, which we attended, occurred on March 13, 2015, and was held as part of a commemorative project on the Israel National Trail initiated by Raya Efner, mother to one of the IDF soldiers killed in the 1997 Helicopter Disaster. Another circle strangely came to a close.

The contact with the families was always continuous and close, and the senior officials were attentive and genuinely interested in their situation. I remember the late Yonah Baumel, Zachary's father, who was very ill and got hospitalized for a long period of time, part of which he spent completely unconsciousness. I made sure to visit him daily, no matter what time of day or night. Professor Avi Rivkind, who treated him, asked to meet the officer who comes to see him every day. He told me that after every time I visited, the values on Yonah's chart changed for the better. At some point, Professor Rivkind announced that Yonah was in critical condition and was now on his deathbed, that those were his last hours, and that if the defense minister wants to say goodbye to him, now would be the time. Yitzhak Rabin changed his entire schedule so that he would have time to come over and say goodbye to Yonah Baumel, and like an incredible miracle, this special man suddenly came out of it and recovered. I think this story teaches us the importance that our leaders attach to the issue of captives and MIAs and their sincere concern for them and their families.

The call for Ory Slonim to serve as the defense minister's advisor on captives and MIA issues is further proof to me of that. After getting back the soldiers who were taken captive at the Battle of Sultan Yacoub, in two different rounds, we had three remaining soldiers who were missing in action—Zachary Baumel, Yehuda Katz, and Zvi Feldman—and I left the unit to pursue higher education for a while. Even during my time in school, I was assigned tasks on this sensitive and important subject, and for that purpose I always had an IDF uniform in a bag kept in my car in case I needed to change. In the end, my studies were cut short and I returned to work in my position as Chief of the Casualties Department. During my studies, Ron Arad was taken captive in Lebanon. There was a feeling, in the beginning, that he was going to come back home very shortly.

When I returned to the army, I fell straight into Ory's arms, who was already in his role. In retrospect, I know that they warned him about me, that highly opinionated woman with her big, dirty mouth. Ory was the one sticking up for me before he even got to know me. He was scheduled to give a lecture up in the north, at an event that was set up long before I returned to my position. When it was time for him to do the lecture and I was already on duty, the organizers of the event asked Ory not to bring me with him. Without thinking twice, Ory said: "Then I'm not coming either." We were both free of these foolish games of respect and ego.

I was glad for his presence right from the first moment. I have always had good relationships with the families of the MIAs; my door was always open with them, but Ory, who was a civilian trusted by the topmost echelons, had his own abilities. Peacefully, with an impressive and dignified presence that inspired the highest degree of confidence, with modesty, eloquence, and sensitivity given to every individual, his ability to forge personal relationships with people. This is probably something you're born with. There are very few people who could be given the status of a family member among the bereaved, the way Ory was received. It's a very fine line, and most people don't have the ability to walk it. Ory had that kind of integrity, the soul, and the ability to tell the truth and nothing but the truth—and when necessary, not the whole truth. I'm not sure that Ory knew, like me, what he was getting into, but I know that, whether by pure chance or otherwise, they brought the best man for the job.

Ory was an anchor for me. When he joined the team, it helped to alleviate my feelings of loneliness. I suddenly had someone to talk to, share the hardship involved with my connection with the families, a bond that would never break until the day you died. Who else could I talk to about everything, the way I talked with him? We spent many hours together on long distance trips and had conversations into the night. Ory has become a real shoulder to lean on. His knowledge, personality, intimate and professional connection to the job. We worked as a team in full cooperation, mostly because he was the one who made it happen, perhaps. It's a priceless gift.

We were soul mates. We went through so much together. Every family and its unique story. In the case of Samir As'ad's family, I had a little trouble. Maybe because it was a combination of modernity and tradition, maybe because I didn't feel that I knew the Druze community's customs well enough and didn't feel strong and safe enough there. The support I got from Ory, who was more naturally accepted there, was a huge relief for me.

We went together through the abduction events of the soldiers Ilan Sa'adon of Ashkelon and Avi Sasportas of Ashdod, who in my opinion were a national trauma—soldiers who were kidnapped here, on Israeli soil, and we had not a single clue that would lead to them. We went to sleep with Sa'adon and Sasportas, we got up in the morning with Sa'adon and Sasportas, and in between, we talked about them all the time. We bonded with the two families, who were so different from each other and shared the same fate. The Sa'adons were a family with many children. A widowed mother whose missing son was the youngest of her ten children and was her whole world, and now she didn't know what to do with herself. The Sasportas family were an amazing couple who coped with this complex and difficult situation very nobly. I really loved both families. When Rachel Sasportas came to see me when I was mourning my son, I almost broke down completely.

I was at a meeting with the assistant for the head of the rehabilitation department when they rang and told me that the defense minister was looking for me. On the other side of the line, Yitzhak Rabin told me in his uniquely deep voice: "Varda, a bereaved mother is standing right outside my office with a gasoline can and threatening to set herself on fire." I told him, "I'll be right there." Within minutes, I managed to convince her not to do it and held her in a warm, loving embrace. I put her on a taxi home. I learned only later that Ory was in the office at a meeting with the defense minister exactly at the same time, in which he told him about the mother's threat and said to him: "Varda is the only person who would be able to handle this."

* * *

The families of Yossi Fink and Rahamim Alsheikh, who were then classified as soldiers killed in action whose burial place was unknown, were an inseparable part of our lives. I vividly remember the day Ory and I came to visit them with a rabbi, and told them: "Although their bodies have not been recovered, they're not with us and we only have pictures of them, we know for sure that they are dead and we know who's who."

When the Fink family was finally assured by all the people entrusted with their care that Yossi was dead, they enlisted to become our soldiers. They showed incredibly strong character and nobility in spirit when they decided not to publicly demand that the IDF engage the enemy in combat for the restoration of the bodies. The Alsheikh family, wonderful and gentle people, if my memory serves me correctly, decided to adopt this approach as well. I remember it like it was yesterday, when I said to Hadassah and Mordechai Fink: "There's nothing that's going to bring back Rahamim and Yossi, but if others were to take the risk in the fight to recover their bodies from the hands of the enemy, or if the price was paid for it with living people from Israel's jails, the terrorist organizations will conclude that there is no need to keep captives alive, because we're also willing to pay this price in exchange for dead bodies. If we're willing to pay so dearly just to give Yossi a funeral, why would they keep the next Yossi alive?"

I truly don't have enough words to describe these noble and powerful people. They allowed us to accept the deaths of Yossi and Rahamim and didn't drive the entire country crazy in a public battle to have their bodies returned while endangering the lives of other people.

Their noble choice allowed the system to devote most of the resources at its disposal to obtaining information on the fate of Ron Arad and the soldiers who went missing in action at the battle of Sultan Yacoub—Zachary Baumel, Yehuda Katz, and Zvi Feldman. Unfortunately, to this day, they have not been returned home.

9

Legal Defense for One Party

"In Jewish lore, captivity is regarded as the worst fate of all. This percept is founded upon a verse from the book of Jeremiah: 'Thus said the lord: those destined for death, to death; those for the sword, to the sword; those for starvation, to starvation; those for captivity, to captivity' (Jeremiah 15:2). The Babylon Talmud cites Rabbi Yochanan's interpretation for this verse: 'Each subsequent challenge in this verse is harsher than the one preceding it: the sword is worse than death, hunger is worse than the sword, captivity is worst of all, for it encompasses all of those' (Bava Batra 8b). The torments of the sword and the agony of the body which is injured are worse than death; starvation and the pains of the body and the soul who devour themselves are worse than the torments of the sword; and captivity is worse than death, the sword and starvation, because it incorporates all of those evils.

"What does that mean? Why does captivity encompass death, the sword, and hunger? What could possibly be worse than death, from the torments of the sword and from starvation? The twelfth century sage Rabbi Shlomo Yitzhaki (Rashi) explains thus: 'The captive is at the mercy of the idolators (pagan worshippers of astrology and the Zodiac) who can do with him as they please, whether his fate may be his own death, torment with the sword, or hunger.' That is, captivity is worse than death, worse than the torments of the sword, and worse than the agony of famine, and encompasses all three of them, since in captivity the captive is subjected to the wiles and whims of strangers. That does not necessarily mean that captivity entails certain death, torture with the sword or starvation, or any other treatment—on the contrary, the essence of captivity is nothing beyond the fact that the captive is held by an outside element, that is, the very fact that he is being held in captivity."[1]

The concept of captives and MIAs enfolds a rich and varied microcosmos of human thought and emotion which has been part of human history for thousands of years. Thousands of research papers and books have been written about this subject, including academic works, personal memoirs, and theses. The last thing I want to do is write another one of these works.

After years of deliberation, during which I began to write the book several times—beginnings that were shortly nipped in the bud because it was very difficult for me personally—I finally decided not to write another book on captives and MIAs. I wished instead to give the readers a small glimpse of what it's like for someone to be thrust into this kind of work without any prior planning and to remain engaged with it for nearly three decades. The practical side of this issue is a world of its own. The topic of captivity has been addressed since the writing of the Jewish scripture and the Qur'an. It can be found in a large body of other historic and religious edicts, at religious, national, military, legal, and political levels, and in international art. I shall not deal with all of these, though they are fascinating. All I want is to share, from the perspective of my very own personal and limited experience, is the moral side of the field.

Before taking up my position and over the years ever since, I read a lot about this subject—books written by people who spent time in captivity,

---

[1]   Elad Lapidot and Merav Mack, eds., "Prisoners of War—Law, State, and International Judgment," *Captives*, Jerusalem: Van Leer Institute.

interviews with liberated prisoners of war, many books by negotiators who worked on prisoner exchange deals, articles by statesmen who had to make decisions in this area, and works by high school and higher education students who chose the area of captives and MIAs as the subject of their academic research. (I was also interviewed for such works over the years.) I wanted to gain the greatest degree of understanding about the issue as possible, and I wanted to minimize the number of mistakes I and my partners might be making.

Among other works, I read Professor Amia Lieblich's book *Except for the Birds*, about ten IDF soldiers who fell into captivity in Egypt and spent three and a half years there during the War of Attrition between 1968–1970. I read Dr. Ronen Bergman's book *By Any Means Necessary*, which covers the secret battles of members of the Israeli intelligence community in their attempts to obtain information about the fate of MIAs and bring them back home. I read the book *Captives*, edited by Merav Mack, which discusses various aspects of the issue of captivity. I also read *Hanging by a Thread*, the personal accounts of Tammy Arad; Karnit Goldwasser's *The Way to You*; and the memoir written by Sarah and Yossef Katz, *Where Art Thou*. I met hundreds of people who dealt with the subject from a variety of different angles: people who returned to Israel from captivity in enemy hands; the family members of people who did not return, or those who were indeed brought back, but were unfortunately no longer among the living; members of the intelligence community, including field agents and members in special operations units; and soldiers for whom captivity or the possibility of being captured was an inseparable part of their lives in the service.

I learned that when it comes to captives and MIAs and the efforts to bring them home—whether alive or in a coffin—this is nothing but an infinite void, a truly bottomless pit. There is not one case that resembles another, and even when you think you have some insight, often something completely contradicts it. I realized that no matter what I learned, there were things that I could never understand.

This book is just what I chose to share without any pretense and with the clear knowledge that some things would be unacceptable to some of readers. Perhaps some might have done things differently had they been in my shoes, but this was my way, and I always followed my own convictions.

* * *

For the past forty years, it's been a world of terrorist organizations and factions squabbling for power and attempting to dictate other people's fate while operating in a completely different manner than state actors. I have to go back once again to the imagery of that neighborhood bully clutching a broken glass bottle, or, if you wish, a flaming kite like the ones launched by Hamas terrorist agents in Gaza and flown into Israel's territory. Those kites could set fire to thousands of acres of agricultural fields and sometimes cause far greater damage than the sophisticated weapons used in the modern theater of war.

That is what fate had in store for me. During the years I spent dealing with the issue of captives and MIAs, I faced only nongovernmental organizations and not countries. Dealing with a terrorist organization is nothing like dealing with a country, not even in the case of a nondemocratic regime.

During Israel's first few wars, our servicemen fell captive to Egypt, Syria, Jordan, and Lebanon. Getting them back home was completely different than dealing with a terror group; they operate differently, utilize different decision-making processes and different methodologies, have different interests, and the amount of influence that nation states have over them is markedly low. Dealing with them is therefore far more difficult and, in my bitter experience, a lot more frustrating.

When Gilad Shalit was held in captivity by Hamas, I appeared on television alongside Amos Levitov, an Israeli Air Force navigator who had spent time in captivity in Egypt. (Levitov is one of the POWs mentioned in the book *Except for the Birds* by Professor Amia Libelich.) Amos dealt frequently with the subject of captivity in wartime and was writing and giving lectures on it. During the conversation between us on the subject of Shalit, he told me, "We were sitting in captivity and waiting to be released, without anyone struggling on our behalf among the Israeli public or in the press."

I replied, "You're right and I understand what you're trying to say, but there's a difference between these cases. You were held captive by a state and not a terrorist organization. It was a long and terrible time you spent in captivity, but it was also a completely different kind of predicament, and they (Egypt) dealt with it in a completely different way. And in all honesty—and I hope you'll agree with me on this—sitting in captivity with other members of the armed forces you were serving with, even in the harshest conditions, is entirely different from sitting in captivity alone in a dank cell for five years with no one to keep you company."

The concepts of "success" and "failure" are highly problematic in this field. You can hardly ever say with absolute certainty that you've "succeeded." In my view, the title for the book *By Any Means Necessary* by Dr. Ronen Bergman, one of the foremost experts in the field, truly demonstrates this grave problem. Saying that "the state of Israel would use any means necessary" is both true and untrue. It can be soothing but can also cause terrible outrage. This statement has been made far too many times, including by me, I must begrudgingly admit, until I finally learned that you just can't say these words. While it's often clear what *needs* to be done, in all likelihood, it cannot possibly *be* done. I experienced the utmost satisfaction being one of the people in the field, but I also experienced the most horrendous frustrations and disappointments. Sometimes, in spite of employing any means necessary, we still couldn't do it.

While it's a great idea in principle, there's no such thing as "by any means" in practice. A country can't really do anything it wants to do. When a head of state says, "I will do *anything* in my power to bring back those held captive," they might send troops to extract the captives, even if it means that some of these troops would come back in a casket, whether the operation succeeds or not. But is it truly a legitimate choice? Do you have the liberty to risk the lives of so many people? There's no such thing as doing "anything" in life. *Anything* is a purely theoretical concept.

The great difficulty in operating in this field and the many uncertainties and reservations it entails has stirred up heated debates over the years.

What is the right price to pay in exchange for the return of captives? Is it appropriate to raise a great public outcry in order to try to bring them back, or does the commotion just get in the way and cause the price to be raised? Should, then, the people entrusted with the issue quietly be allowed to act and fly under the radar?

I've always tried to avoid taking part in this public debate. After all, both sides are right and both make strong, reasonable arguments, so what's the point? One side says a killer with blood on his hands should not be released, and the other argues that even despicable murderers should be freed in exchange for someone's son who's been taken captive, and in my view they're both absolutely correct.

When I appear as an attorney in court, I serve as legal defense for one party only, one side in the dispute, which presents its version of the events and wishes to avoid a conviction or a penalty. I do not represent the opposite side, which seeks to place the defendant behind bars. The same is true of the captives and MIAs. My mission was to be an advocate for only one of the parties. My job was to return the captives and MIAs to Israel and to be there for the families who longed for their return or, in the more difficult cases, to try to find out what had happened to them.

I always repeat to everyone's ears, again and again, this mantra that I stick with: a country that sends its soldiers to fight in its service must also bring them home, dead or alive. When I lectured once on the never-ending and uncompromising duty of the state of Israel to bring its captive soldiers back home, I was approached at the end of the lecture by one of the most wonderful people I ever met: Professor Robert (Israel) Aumann, the Nobel laureate in the field of economics in 2005, whose main area of expertise is game theory. His eldest son, Shlomo, was killed in the first Lebanon war in 1982. Professor Aumann told me that according to game theory, I am in error—and so is the state—in agreeing to the release of more than one terrorist in exchange for one Israeli captive. It will only lead to a new formula, according to which the next deal will require the release of a hundred and the one after that a thousand—a well-known argument in the country ever since the 1985 Jibril deal.

I replied, "Professor Aumann, I truly admire you. You're right about that, but I'm probably right too. Both of us will remain right, yet I will try to convince you that if there's any possibility to return someone home, we will pay a price—even if it's not according to game theory—and fulfill our duty to those that we sent to fight in a war on our behalf. We don't pay such a high price for the captives just because they're worth a lot, but because we are the ones who sent them to the battlefield."

I said the same thing to dozens of rabbis I met. They all reminded me of the *Gitin* tractate in Jewish law: "One must not redeem the captives for more than their price is worth," reminiscent of the sage Meir of Rothenburg, who'd refused to be released and wasted away until he died in his cell. My response to this has always been the same: "This religious edict is correct, but it was published at the time when there was no sovereign Jewish state and no requirement by state law for mandatory service in the armed forces. All you had was the duty to redeem a person who had been captured when his captors demanded ransom for their release. However, today we live in a country where the law requires serving in the military. Regardless of the humanitarian aspect and the pleading of the compassionate Jewish heart, we have an obligation to free those who were sent to battle on our behalf and in the name of the law. If it were up to these young people, they may well have preferred to go to university or lie on the beach in Thailand instead of serving in the army. But they were sent to war, and they should go with the knowledge that we will do everything it takes to bring them back home. If Israel operated an army of mercenaries who knew that being held captive is one of the professional hazards they may face, I might think otherwise."

I learned to live in peace with criticism leveled at me for my worldview. Whenever anyone told me that there's a great chance that among the people liberated from Israel's jails in exchange for captives there were some who would resume their murderous terrorist careers, my response was: "We will continue to pursue them and fight them even after their release and they will meet their deaths before they have the chance to commit any wrongdoing ever again."

I am well aware of the fact that other approaches to this issue exist and that some of them have merit. In the prisoner exchange deal with Hezbollah in 2008, Israel decided to release Samir Kuntar, a Lebanese terrorist who viciously murdered members of the Haran family from the northern city of Nahariya. He killed the father, Danny Haran, by shooting him in the back, and his four-year-old daughter, Einat, by smashing her head against a rock on the Mediterranean beach while attempting to make his escape back to Lebanon by sea. Meanwhile, in the Haran family home, Danny's other daughter, two-year-old Yael, suffocated to death when the mother, Smadar, placed her hand on the infant's mouth to keep her from crying and alerting Kuntar and the other terrorists to their hiding place. Smadar was the only survivor. In addition, Kuntar shot two Israeli police officers to death during his flight. He was apprehended while still alive. When I was asked why the Israeli government agreed to release him, even though we knew with almost complete certainty that, in exchange, we were going to receive the IDF soldiers Udi Goldwasser and Eldad Regev in coffins, I replied, "For me, 99 percent certainty is not enough."

There's a part of our lives that entails making decisions, knowing that the validity and degree of justification inherent in them can and will be questioned. Is it right that a head of state decides to send soldiers into battle, knowing full well that some of them will not return? Is it proper, and can it be allowed, to risk the life of one person because of the mere possibility, no matter how remote and uncertain, that another human life could be saved?

I am not a missionary who follows a single dogma. I maintain my position while showing respect for any dissenting opinions. And I concede, I am not objective, and I have no desire to be. There are roles that require one to be completely impartial—a judge in the court or a referee on a football field who must put aside what he believes in and adhere to the facts in front of him, or an Israeli medical doctor forced to perform surgery to save the life of a terrorist who was injured during an attack in which he killed others. The doctor must ignore his personal feelings, which might be that the person under his care should be sentenced to death for his crimes, and act in accordance with his professional commitment to save the terrorist's life. But not everything in life is objective.

Professor Aumann's argument, which is founded upon game theory, is logical and very much correct, but it does not stand the test of reality. If you have two soldiers who are in captivity and there are 10,000 terrorists sitting in your prisons, then you can certainly expect a problem in advance. The starting point is different and, accordingly, so are the expectations on each of the sides in the conflict. In the negotiations to retrieve the body of IDF soldier Samir As'ad in the 1990s, we returned to the Palestinian Territories only one deported person because in this specific case, that was in the interests of the other side.

Abductions have become an effective weapon, one of the most brutal in our modern world. When your enemies are digging a tunnel that reaches a civilian settlement, it is obvious that they intend to take prisoners in order to have a powerful bargaining chip for future negotiations. Abductions are sometimes more effective than killing. The killing, cruel and horrible as it is, ends with that person's funeral, albeit with all the deep sorrow and grief it entails. But when you're dealing with a kidnapping, it's all just the beginning: for the captive, who may have to endure the physical and mental scars of captivity until his last dying day, for the organizations who conduct the negotiations, for the families, for the public, and the psychological warfare that will be employed. This issue engages our lives at every level, not to mention the terrible uncertainty, especially for the families who have no idea what happened to their loved ones.

The chilling phone call—about which I wrote in the beginning of the book—between the bereaved mother Raya Efner, whose son Avi died in the 1997 Helicopter Disaster, and Batya Arad, who to this day does not know what became of her son Ron, is the essence of this whole story: there is bereavement, which is the most terrible thing in the world, and then there's uncertainty, and that's also the most terrible thing in the world. The fact that Varda Pomerantz, as a bereaved mother says in the chapter she wrote for this book, that uncertainty is worse than the worst of all, makes it easier for me to say the things I've been saying to myself and to others all these years.

Another point that has been the subject of much debate and controversy is the extent to which public outcry keeps the issue of the captives and MIAs on the public agenda to actively promote their release. On this subject, I also believe there is no right and wrong answer, and what is true in one case is not necessarily true in another. The families and the general public in the country do what they feel is right. However, they serve no practical role in the matter. The duty of returning the captives and MIAs rests solely with those who bear the burden of state leadership.

There's no doubt in my mind that the circumstances of Gilad Shalit's case made the campaign for his release more meaningful and perhaps more understandable. In this case, we had very reliable information about a captive soldier who was still alive and well only twelve kilometers away from the country's borders, and you couldn't help but ask: If we have such a large army with some of the best intelligence in the world, why can they not bring him back? In the case of Gilad Shalit, I also have no doubt that the support and involvement of the public had a great impact. Leaders in a democratic state are political people, and even if the good of the state should always be their first priority, public opinion and the public eye weigh greatly upon them, and a leader cannot help but be influenced by these considerations.

It looks like this is just one more issue that everybody's right about. Those Israeli citizens who marched in the streets in June 2010 to promote the return of Gilad Shalit—and who wholeheartedly believed any price should be paid to get him back—were absolutely right. And those who claimed that the terrorists released in return for Shalit would go right back to killing again (a claim that has, unfortunately, proven true) were also right. Each party had its job to do. Trying to get him home was the least I could do.

* * *

One shouldn't enter a role like this while harboring any illusions. I believed—and I still firmly believe it even today—that working on these cases was a true "Mitzvah," a sacred task and a great good deed, even if much of the task was almost certain to end in failure. There are other people who take on roles with similar responsibilities, in which there's never an absolute victory: a physician who helps terminally ill patients or a physiotherapist who helps people with disabilities, for example. It's true that their patients will probably never recover, and a paraplegic will never be able to stand on his own two feet, but they may be able to spend the remainder of their lives with better conditions and be afforded a higher quality of life. That was also the role I took on: trying to help people, if ever so slightly, to deal with the awful predicament they were facing.

This was completely in contrast with the legal world I was part of at the same time. In this new world, I wanted to do everything in my power to keep the case from ending in failure. And between these two opposing worlds, there was also a third world in my life—the Variety charity— which is a combination of all worlds: I can't cure people with disabilities but I can help them to enjoy a more comfortable life and provide them with a slightly higher standard of living.

The truth is, in this field of captives and MIAs, the words "success" and "failure" have a different meaning. If I managed to provide even the slightest bit of help to families forced to live with such terrible uncertainty, then let that be my reward. I've always done whatever I could for them. There's only one thing I never did: I never lied and I never deceived. At most, I didn't disclose everything that I knew at the time, but I always told the truth. It also wasn't my job to be the bearer of news. There were many others whose job it was to perform that task.

Absolute success—return of the captives—was not the only yardstick by which you measured success, even if it was the ultimate goal. On the way to attaining this supreme goal, many other positive things can also be achieved. I've read in Ronen Bergman's book that "Uri Lubrani said he didn't want to meet with families; that was Ory Slonim's job." Uri Lubrani also made this statement in public interviews.

Although I've been criticized quite a bit due to the fact that I maintained my personal connections with the families and continued to hold meetings with them despite my other endeavors in the area of negotiations, intelligence, and operations, I don't regret it for a moment. Only a fraction of state officials in charge of this matter (including Shin Bet and

Mossad officials) ever met with the families over the years. Many told me later that these meetings were harder for them than highly dangerous, covert missions in the field. On the other hand, it provided them with things they'd never experienced before. For example, a friend and colleague, a Mossad official, once told me that he understood me the moment that he met Tammy Arad, the wife of the missing navigator Ron Arad, after years of refusing to do so. "It gave my mission tremendous significance," he admitted, "and at the same time, didn't jeopardize it from an operational standpoint in any way."

For each of the families, I fulfilled a different need. When Udi Goldwasser was abducted in Lebanon in 2005, his wife, Karnit Goldwasser, asked me to come and see her quickly. I paid her a visit under a barrage of rockets being fired on her hometown of Nahariya that very day, even before Udi's parents managed to come back to Israel from their trip abroad. I would meet with the families of the captives very frequently, at their request. It's difficult to look into a father's pained eyes and not tell him that someone called saying he had a tape of his son who was held in captivity. After all, scammers were calling the family endlessly with such stories, so I said nothing. Occasionally, the family of a missing soldier called my house, heard from my wife, Tammy, that I was abroad, and asked that I come to see them as soon as I returned home. I went, but I wouldn't tell them whom I'd met with or what they'd told me, even if it made the family angry at me. I was simply not at liberty to tell them what was going on.

There's no single formula for encouraging and mentally supporting a family that's living in an agonizing and continuous state of uncertainty. Sometimes we just talked about life in general. We even indulged in gossiping at times. As far as they were concerned, the encouragement came from the knowledge that there was someone devoting most of his time to bringing their loved ones home and that it was someone they could call on at any time of day and talk about anything.

I had an open-door policy for almost all the people involved. If I thought that a good word from a certain IDF commander who knew the family's son might help, I called that commander and asked him to drop in and wish the family a happy New Year. If a meeting with the defense minister was scheduled but the family would have to wait for another three weeks, I would ask to have the meeting earlier.

I could even get involved in relationships within the family—disputes and altercations that arose due to the terrible tension. Sometimes I even had to deal with very prosaic issues. One family complained about a leak in a water pipe at their home. I asked the local mayor to repair the leak within an hour. In the midst of the sea of pain the family was stranded in, knowing there was someone who could make sure the water pipes were fixed quickly—strange as it might sound—that, too, provided them with a measure of comfort.

10

The Spy Trader

When Steven Spielberg's movie *Bridge of Spies* was screened in Israel, I was invited to the premiere. The film tells the true story of the trade that was made between the United States and the Soviet Union, in which the Russian spy Rudolf Abel, who was imprisoned in America, was released in exchange for the American Air Force pilot Francis Gary Powers, who was captured by the Soviets, and a young American student falsely accused of espionage and imprisoned in East Germany. The negotiations were led by US Attorney James Donovan, played by Tom Hanks, who negotiated with the representatives from East Germany.

I was absolutely glued to the screen. It immediately brought me back to the days when I had been involved in similar contacts and deals. I recognized similar and exciting lines running parallel to my own endeavors as an attorney enlisted by Israel's government for such missions. Of course, I actually knew that German mediator very well, whose character was given a very similar name to the one collaborating with us in reality. I have no doubt that the people who wrote the script and built his character read a lot about the German lawyer and "spy trader," Wolfgang Vogel, and probably even met people who knew him.

Dealing with captives and MIAs has provided me with some extraordinary experiences that few people go through. I encountered a completely different world and entered it quite naturally, which sometimes surprised me no less than it did others. Soon, the sacred goal that I struggled to achieve turned me into a man who led a kind of double life.

On the one hand, a lawyer who manages public trials that receive extensive media coverage in my home country. In that world, I never had to worry about security and never met secretly with a person whose name is not even listed in the hotel register where he's staying. On the other hand, in my involvement with captives and MIAs, I led a life where there were many secret meetings in European capitals—meetings with people I never dreamed of meeting—in restaurants where you had to enter through the back entrance and with different rules of the game that required discipline and absolute secrecy. In my case, confidentiality wasn't required just because of the nature of the subjects and contacts I dealt with but also because I did not want to sow false hopes among the families of Israeli captives and MIAs, with whom I'd been in constant contact for years.

On this issue, only the outcome was important, and, sadly, in most cases we did not succeed in meeting our objectives. I had to keep the faith and hope in the hearts of the families but without allowing them to live in an illusion. I was afraid sometimes that even my body language, which is generally known to be no less significant and clear as the words you use, would inadvertently convey to the family something that I didn't want to tell them...or that I shouldn't.

In this secret world, I met different and absolutely fascinating people, but a person like the Wolfgang Vogel, who was engaged in the trading of spies, I had never met before or after. He was a smart and sophisticated man, a handsome, dapper gentleman who took pleasure in dressing sharply and was particularly fond of neckties, and a high-profile public figure whose favor was highly sought-after by heads of state and secret agencies. Diplomats are representatives of states who must report all their actions to their superiors. Wolfgang Vogel answered to only one authority—his own bank account.

* * *

One of the ways to obtain information about the fate of our captives and MIAs was to get help from people who did this kind of work for a living.

There are scarce few individuals who fall under this category in the world. People who helped to secure the release of political prisoners, mainly from Soviet and Eastern Bloc countries, for example. These are professionals who specialize in managing complicated negotiations. Usually, they were engaged in exchanges of spies and secret agents, especially between sovereign countries.

The German lawyer Wolfgang Vogel, who lived in East Germany at the time, was one of the most famous people in the history of the "trade" in spies, kidnapping victims, and political prisoners. He began to deal with the issue in the 1960s and 1970s and was instrumental in the most famous prisoner exchange deal that Israel was involved in, in which Nathan Sharansky, Russian Zionist activist and later Israeli parliamentarian, was released after years of imprisonment in the Soviet Union.

During the period we'll be examining here, in the 1970s and 1980s, Vogel also began to make regular contact with Russian spies, including those who spied against the state of Israel. In January 1983, Marcus Klingberg, a professor of epidemiology and a researcher at the Israel Institute for Biological Research (IIBR) in Ness Ziona, was arrested by local police. He was charged with espionage for the Soviet Union and sentenced to twenty years in prison, which he served in the Shikma Prison in Ashkelon in solitary confinement under a false identity. Except for the people involved in this affair, no Israeli citizen knew of his existence. Klingberg's daughter, Sylvia, and his French attorney, Antoine Comte, then contacted Attorney Wolfgang Vogel in Berlin and asked for his help. Vogel was amazed to learn that he—the world's greatest trader in spies— did not even know about the existence of the Soviet spy being detained in Israel. Klingberg was considered back then, and perhaps even today, to be one of the highest-ranking Soviet agents captured in Israel, and it was important for the people who sent him to Israel to provide him with assistance and negotiate for his release.

At the time, Vogel was in contact with Attorney Amnon Zichroni, who'd asked him to assist in the case of another spy whom Zichrony represented: Shabtai Kalmanovich—an Israeli businessman sentenced to nine years in Israeli prison after being similarly accused of spying for the

Soviet Union. Vogel approached Zichroni, who saw in it an opportunity not only to assist his client, Kalmanovich, but also to utilize his connections to help the staff of the captives and MIAs task force headed by Uri Lubrani, with whom Zichroni had had dealings in the past.

Following an assessment that demonstrated that it was possible to combine spy trade deals with the IDF captives and MIAs issue, Lubrani's staff and Shin Bet personnel—who were then in charge of handling the case of spies from the Eastern Bloc in Israel, including Marcus Klingberg—were introduced to the affair, in addition to certain members of the Mossad.

Attorney Vogel saw this as an opportunity to become involved in one of the most complex deals he'd ever been involved in, which included some of the highest-ranking spies in the region along with the IDF's captives and MIAs. The entire world of intelligence knew, of course, that the state of Israel was engaged in the matter and was very interested in resolving it. Vogel was not acting in the interest of promoting some kind of political ideology but, as stated, was in it simply for financial gain. It was, after all, his line of work.

The discussions with Vogel were strictly confidential at the time, since they involved spies; secret agents; prisoners of war and missing persons; Jonathan Pollard, the Israeli spy imprisoned in the United States; citizens of different nations in various prisons around the world; Jews in the Soviet Union; and defendants in pending criminal trials in the state of Israel. Dealing with this matter therefore proved to be unbelievably complex and convoluted.

This was one of the first affairs that I was also involved in, because by then, in 1988, I was preparing to receive the official appointment as special adviser to the defense minister after the conclusion of the process to receive the highest level of security clearance. By this stage, I'd already begun to be exposed to the most classified intelligence materials on the subject.

The intention was to gather intelligence relevant to all the captives and MIAs, including those missing in action in the Battle of Sultan Yacoub—Zachary Baumel, Yehuda Katz, and Zvi Feldman—as well as

Yossi Fink and Rahamim Alsheikh, Samir As'ad, and Ron Arad, and, of course, to make every effort to return them to Israel. Naturally, the negotiations continued for many months. During this time, I had already been officially assigned to be an adviser to the defense minister on captive and MIA affairs. Later, the name of Shabtai Kalmanovich was off the table, because the Russians were no longer interested in his extradition. The contacts between the parties included dozens of secret meetings around the world, attended by everyone involved in the subject, including Vogel, Lubrani, Zichroni, and me.

I particularly remember the meeting that took place in East Berlin when the wall still divided the city into two parts. Israeli citizens were not allowed into East Berlin back then, and I never agreed to travel anywhere with a false identity. I always wanted the table to stand on all four legs and stick to my true identity and intentions—that I was merely an Israeli lawyer helping with the efforts to bring home IDF captives and MIAs. For this reason, many foreign collaborators agreed to meet with me without fearing that I was part of some organizations or state agency with a hidden agenda. My transparency helped foster trust, even among elements hostile or ambivalent to Israel.

* * *

Meanwhile, in East Berlin, which was not friendly territory to Israeli nationals at the time, our relationship with Vogel continued. I was picked up by a car from West Berlin. After passing through one checkpoint, we moved from a modern and vibrant metropolis to a completely different world—a bleak, dark, slummy, and poverty-stricken city. I can only guess that the Stasi trailed us and were surveilling our moves every step of the way. I met Vogel, who was renowned in East Berlin, in a luxurious restaurant that had some very fine cuisine to offer. Only an extremely small minority of the locals could ever afford to have a meal there. During my visit I was also taken to a memorial site for fighters of the Soviet Union. Not much came out of this meeting, however, as is quite often the case in this area of work.

We continued to meet with Vogel in Paris, Geneva, and Zurich—large, neutral cities that allowed one to comfortably disappear in the crowd. On May 28, 1989, Vogel arrived in Israel, accompanied by his wife, to meet with Marcus Klingberg—a meeting that was important enough for the German lawyer to go to Israel for the first time in order to continue pursuing his interests. This visit was completely secret, of course. The Vogels were hosted at the Dan Hotel in Tel Aviv under a false identity, because Vogel's name and identity were known throughout the world from the Russian spy trade deals he was involved in, and also because Klingberg's imprisonment and, in fact, his very existence were still being kept secret. We went out to dinner with the Vogels during their visit to Israel at a restaurant that was closed the public. We entered, as always, through the back door.

Klingberg later described the meeting he had with Attorney Vogel in Israeli prison in the book he published:

> Early in the morning they had taken me to the Shin Bet wing of the prison. Zichroni was waiting for me in the room, and this time there were other people with him: an older gentleman and a beautiful woman, much younger than him. I didn't know either of them: the renowned attorney from East Germany, Wolfgang Vogel, and his wife. Zichroni emphasized that the meeting was highly secret and that no one in Israel knew about the couple's arrival.

> Before another word was spoken by anyone, Vogel came up to me, hugged and kissed me and it seemed that he was very moved by this encounter. His wife did the same. Then we sat down and started speaking in English, with Vogel's wife translating to German for him with the help of an English-German phrase book, a very novel concept in those days. I threw in a word or a phrase in German every once in a while, a language that I haven't used in many years.

Vogel told me that the deal was now in a very advanced phase, that it was just about to be finalized, and that he was there to tie up the last few loose ends. "Professor Klingberg, in the next few days you'll need to pack some suitcases. Based on the agreement, you'll be able to take only one suitcase with you, and Attorney Zichroni will go to Vienna or West Berlin, according to what we'll decide, and bring the rest of your luggage with him. I'll meet you there and bring your belongings to you, to the eastern part of town." I felt like I was floating on a cloud. It all seemed so close at hand. I have to start packing. In a few days I'll leave Ashkelon for good.

At the end of Vogel's visit to Israel, on May 31, 1989, a memorandum was signed by Attorney Vogel, Uri Lubrani, Amnon Zichroni, and myself. It was a secret agreement on a complicated global deal that included all the IDF's captives and MIAs in it—the details of which are still confidential. The framework agreement outlined the process in general terms, but no one knew how it would end and whether there'd be any results.

The quality most necessary in these kinds of contacts—beyond the wisdom of negotiating and knowing all the facts—is patience. It was a game of chess with some extremely sophisticated maneuvers on the board, one that requires carefully calculating the moves—both yours and your opponent's—to understand the interests that motivate the other players and to negotiate in a way that the other side understands that you don't just want the best-case scenario for yourself; you also want it for them.

Ultimately, this experience, which lasted almost a year, was unfortunately destined to end in great disappointment. Our efforts amounted to a big nothing. The spies were not traded; the American spy, Jonathan Pollard, remained incarcerated in America for over twenty more years; and Marcus Klingberg remained in his cell in Ashkelon until 1998.

And we couldn't get hold of any new information about any of our people.

* * *

During the years we dealt with the issue of captives and MIAs, we also met a lot of swindlers and crooks. Wolfgang Vogel was not one of them. He was a serious man with a proven record of success, a professional spy trader who could reach whomever he wanted, but in our case, even he couldn't do it.

I must admit that he was a man with a truly fascinating personality, at least to me. He was smart and experienced and possessed tremendous knowledge in negotiation and in delicate and complicated issues that require personal involvement. At the end of the day—even when you meet with people on painful and dangerous issues, and when the parties are motivated by economic or other interests—much of it boils down to the personal connection between the people involved in the deal. For me, the relationship with Vogel and the negotiations we held with him were extraordinarily fascinating. I was intrigued by him on a personal and professional level. We had a great relationship, and I often brought him a tie as a gift, after finding out that he was a tie lover. I can't really feel affection for a person who trades in human beings, but Wolfgang Vogel had a level of personal charm of otherworldly proportions.

For me, this affair was just another installment in the chain of the great many disappointments I've had to endure over the years as part of my endeavors in this area. I can't even count the number of times I was close to despair, and I also resigned twice because I felt like I was wasting my time and maybe even making a mistake by continuing to insist on being out in the field. I knew heartaches, it had a detrimental effect on my health, and I gave up a lot of money I could have earned working as a lawyer. I was only forty-four when I entered the field—at the time a successful lawyer who only aspired to take care of himself and his family. But I never really regretted the choice I made, even if it was hard for me.

In an occupation where the only test of success is the test of outcome, sometimes even the most heroic efforts are not enough. And the outcome in this case is sometimes the knowledge that a POW or MIA is no longer alive. This is a terrible thing to learn, obviously, but on the other hand, it also provides some consolation: it puts an end to the long, unbearable uncertainty one has to live with.

But even after suffering an untold number of disappointments, one mustn't let go. You have to carry on trying to find the way and the people, which can lead to information and maybe even a solution. It's a process that sometimes takes years, and most of the time, as it was in this case, you end up with absolutely nothing to show for it.

11

1991: A Year of Turmoil: MIAs

It was 1991 and we were deeply troubled by the fact that we knew nothing about the fate of seven Israeli MIAs: the soldiers from the Battle of Sultan Yacoub in 1982—Zvi Feldman, Zachary Baumel, and Yehuda Katz—the Druze soldier Samir As'ad, who disappeared in 1983; Israeli Air Force navigator Ron Arad, who was captured by Amal organization in 1986; and the soldiers Yossi Fink and Rahamim Alsheikh, who were captured in 1986 during an ambush in Lebanon Baka. We were constantly looking for any information that would shed light on their fate.

Rahamim Alsheikh, son of Shlomo and Saada from the city of Rosh Ha'Ayin, and Yossi Fink, son of Hadassah and Mordechai of Ra'anana, were both religious and enlisted in the IDF as part of the Hesder ("The Arrangement"). This required religious studies in a yeshiva or religious college in Israel in conjunction with up to two years of army service, normally in a combat unit. Both of them joined the IDF's Givati Brigade as combat infantry. They were abducted on February 17, 1986, when Hezbollah terrorists laid an ambush for an IDF patrol in Lebanon, which included an IED and a squad of armed gunmen lying in wait. A vicious firefight broke out, during which Fink and Alsheikh, who were sitting in the third vehicle in the IDF patrol convoy, were grabbed and placed into a Mercedes that had been prepared in advance and served as a getaway car. The car sped down an escape route, also prepared in advance by the enemy. We didn't know if the two soldiers were still alive and, if so, how badly they were injured. But it was clear to us, based on the evidence from the site, that they were gravely wounded during the attack.

Lebanon's media broadcast stations soon announced that hundreds of IDF soldiers—in tanks, armored personnel carriers, and assault helicopters—were scouring the entire area of Shi'ite villages north of the security zone on the border in search of the kidnapped soldiers. The next day, on Lebanese television, Hezbollah presented pictures of two people dressed in bandages from head to toe, claiming that they were the abducted IDF soldiers. The organization threatened that if Israel did not completely withdraw its armed forces from Lebanon, one of the soldiers would be executed. Later, personal items belonging to the soldiers were displayed on the CBS television network in Damascus. Members of Yossi Fink's family identified the kippah that was being displayed—the Jewish skullcap worn on the head by religious Jews—was indeed one that his mother had knitted for him. Later, the soldiers' names and IDF personal military numbers were also published. On February 21, 1986, another picture of Fink and Alsheikh appeared on the pages of *Al-Ahad*, a Beirut weekly paper published by Hezbollah, which purported that they were "hospitalized" at a local clinic. Their faces were completely obscured by bandages, and they could therefore not be identified. The Hezbollah clearly attempted to promote a narrative that they were still alive, even though we knew with almost complete certainly that that was not the case.

This trick was part of a campaign of brutal psychological warfare aimed at deceiving the state of Israel, especially the families of the soldiers. In the summer of 1989, the IDF captured Sheikh Abdel Karim Obeid, the spiritual leader of the Religious Amal Movement in Lebanon (no relation to the secular movement in Lebanon of the same name), who disclosed in his interrogation that Fink and Alsheikh were no longer alive. These facts were finally and officially confirmed only in September 1991, five years after the two were abducted.

At that time, there were also many non-Israeli hostages on Lebanese soil—foreigners from various Western countries who had been similarly abducted by Hezbollah. In 1991, UN Secretary-General Pérez de Cuéllar, together with his Italian aide Giandomenico Picco, began to mediate between Lebanese terrorist organizations and Western nations trying to find out what had happened to their missing people. Israel also joined these nations. The team who handled the issue on behalf of the Israeli government was headed by Uri Lubrani; former Israeli ambassador to the UN Yohanan Bein, who was acting on behalf of Israel's Foreign Ministry; and me.

Uri Lubrani worked for many years as a senior civil servant in the Ministry of Defense. Among his many other past roles, he was the Israeli ambassador to Iran, the coordinator of Israeli operations in Lebanon, and the head of the team investigating the fate of Israeli captives and MIAs. Uri was one of the most talented and educated people who worked in the civil service and was one of the people most connected with the Lebanese and Iranian world—possibly more than any other Israeli—as part of his duties but also thanks to his special personality and the nature of the tasks he performed. He was fluent in many languages and was personally acquainted with hundreds of Lebanese, Arab, and European government officials, businesspeople, media personalities, and others who had interests and connections in Lebanon.

In each of the conversations we had on the subject, we always talked about all our missing people, both in Lebanon and Syria. It's crucial to keep all the names and details of every one of the missing persons on the table and to keep discussing each one of them. There are practical reasons for this, but it primarily stems from an unwavering commitment to the families. This is especially true of my own personal commitment, being the only member of the team who has been in close contact with them on a personal and ongoing basis.

We were flying often to Europe and even to Lebanon at that time, for meetings with UN Secretary-General Pérez de Cuéllar and his aide, Italian Giandomenico Picco. In the book that Picco wrote after his term in office ended, he recounted his meetings with the other side, especially members of Hezbollah. The book has many descriptions of the hardships he endured while staying in Lebanon and touring Hezbollah strongholds—how, for example, they tied him, covered his eyes, and turned him around in circles—descriptions that sounded fanciful and almost absurd back then.

Disagreements sometimes arose between me and Lubrani during this period, who, by virtue of his role and status, always made sure to uphold the rules of courtesy and diplomacy, especially toward the UN secretary-general, the number one diplomat in the world. I was far less diplomatic and was, at times, a bit brash in my approach, but I saw it as a way of providing some balance in our relationship with the people involved, particularly with the most senior among them. The level of trust that I had in his abilities diminished with each consecutive time that I met him.

From the few meetings we had at a hotel on the shores of Lake Geneva, I got the impression that the secretary-general was very much motivated to secure the release of the Western hostages—an achievement that would obviously turn him into a globally celebrated diplomat and justify his endless self-aggrandizement. He was far less motivated to learn the actual details and facts about our missing people. Even now, review-ing our relationship many years later, I'm trying to employ very gra-cious, mild language here. I once had a personal clash with him for that background during one of our talks in Geneva, when I felt that he was just spewing rhetoric and beating about the bush. I told him then: "You know, I'm an attorney by trade. When I have to deal with the purchase of a property and I'm facing the lawyers representing the other party in the transaction, even before I find out what the status of the property is and what the price is, I try to answer a much more fundamental question: does the person sitting across the table from me have any access to the property or any rights regarding this asset? After all, there's no point in talking to the other party if they don't have ownership or knowledge of the asset. So I'm asking you a simple question, Your Excellency, Secretary-General: do you even have any access to the 'assets' we are seeking to retrieve here?"

De Cuéllar considered this an impudent question, especially due to the undiplomatic way in which I presented it. His undersecretary Picco, who was quite friendly toward me at the time, took me to the other room and said to me: "Ory, that's no way to talk to him." I told him with quite a bit of indignation and exasperation: "That's exactly how you talk to a Secretary-General who's got nothing to sell us." Admittedly, Uri Lubrani also commented, very gently, about my behavior. I told him: "You're right, but I couldn't help it."

I later regretted the way I expressed myself, but not the content of what I said. It was undiplomatic and even arrogant on my part, but the thing that burned in my bones was far beyond any guidelines of polite courtesy—a very real sense that our MIAs were not as important as they should have been to the UN secretary-general.

Later in the negotiations, Picco made many trips to Lebanon and brought us incontrovertible proof that Fink and Alsheikh were indeed no longer alive, something we referred to as "100 percent proven signs of death." In September 1991, in exchange for the release of ninety-one detainees from Al Khiam detention center in Lebanon, an envelope with photographs of Fink and Alsehikh was transferred to us via representatives from UNIFIL, the UN peacekeeping forces stationed in Lebanon since 1978. Their bodies were already embalmed, having been prepared for burial. I examined the photographs with the IDF's chief military rabbi, Gad Navon. The rabbi confirmed the death of one of the soldiers from the photographs and asked for additional photographs of the other body. When they arrived, and after reviewing transcripts from the interrogation of the aforementioned Sheikh Obeid, who also provided some information on the subject, the rabbi determined that both Fink and Alsheikh could be definitively declared to have been killed in action.

In order for the chief military rabbi to notify the parents that their son was no longer alive, the highest level of certainty had to be achieved so they could observe the seven days of mourning prescribed by Judaic tradition. Over the years, I've discovered how problematic and complicated this issue of "certainty" is, and how it troubled the religious leaders of the Jewish community as early as the war in Europe. For example, when they had to determine that a woman was no longer "Agunah": since her husband was confirmed to have died, she was no longer in wedlock and was now a widower, which meant that she was free to legally remarry and could also be finally rid of the unspeakable torment of the uncertainty involved. I had conversations with many rabbis who had to deal with the subject, and they admitted that sometimes mistakes were made, and occasionally a husband who'd been declared dead in the war suddenly reappeared. I've been bothered by this issue all of my thirty years in the field.

In the case of Fink and Alsheikh, the amount of proof available to us—not all of which can be discussed even today—stood at a full 100 percent. The military rabbi, Maj. Gen. Gad Navon, called me and Col. Varda Pomerantz, who was then acting as the IDF chief of casualties department, and told us that it was now possible to go to Ra'anana and Rosh Ha'Ayin and inform the families that, after five years, they could finally observe the seven days of mourning.

While we were preparing for the trip, Varda suddenly recalled that Tzivi, Yossi Fink's sister, was getting married the next day. The rabbi immediately told her that a wedding allows one to postpone bitter announcement to the families. Instead of going to Ra'anana and Rosh Ha'Ayin, Tamy, and I arrived at the jubilant wedding celebration in Bnei Brak. While there, I did my best to act like everyone else, and thought I managed to keep a straight face all through it and not betray the turmoil inside me.

The next day, we went to the families' homes and told them the news—bitter on the one hand but liberating on the other. I saw it as part of my role, together with Varda, to convey the message to the families that the identification had been completed. They didn't ask how we found out. When the Fink family asked me if I was sure, I simply answered with a "yes."

I apologized to Hadassah Fink for not telling her the previous day that I knew that Yossi was dead. "And do you think," she responded, "that I didn't see it on your face at the wedding last night?" My relationship with her and the rest of the family was so close that, despite all my attempts at concealment, there was something in my face that told her the whole truth.

Both families asked us to make sure that the efforts to recover their sons' bodies wouldn't impact the moves we were making on the cases of any other Israeli MIAs. "We will wait patiently," they said. It was truly noble of them. Eventually, after several bouts of negotiations, in 1996, we were able to return to Israel the bodies of Rahamim Alsheikh and Yossi Fink, and I'm going to tell you more about that later.

* * *

Long before that point in time, we learned that the president of Austria, Kurt Waldheim, was going to travel to Iran to meet with President Rafsanjani. Austria was among the few countries that still had formal relations with Iran in wake of the Islamic Revolution of 1979.

Like many other countries, Israel did not officially recognize Waldheim's presidency, and we replaced our ambassador to Austria with a representative who only had a semblance of official authority. This was in light of the reports about Waldheim's Nazi past. In various publications, it was claimed that during World War II, Waldheim was an intelligence officer in a German army unit affiliated with executions and the transfer of thousands of Serbians, Greeks, and Jews to Nazi extermination camps.

In this context, I met with President Haim Herzog. I suggested that we approach Waldheim with a rather crazy proposition to help him clear his name in exchange for information he could bring from Iran about IDF captives and MIAs. Herzog said it was a brilliant idea but added that he wasn't sure that the minister of defense, Yitzhak Rabin, could be part of such a move in his capacity as an Israeli official.

As mentioned, I was on very friendly terms with Yitzhak Rabin, and we'd had dozens of personal conversations on the topic of captives and MIAs. As a fighter and commander in the IDF, Rabin understood that the issue of captives and MIAs should be addressed with reverence but also by using unconventional strategies and methods. I met with him at his house and presented him with my proposal. Whenever someone told him something that he thought was wrong or inappropriate, he'd blush, and that's precisely what happened this time too. He said to me: "Uri, you've really gone out of your mind this time. That's out of the question."

I told him, completely understanding his response: "Then don't officially approve it, and I'll go there privately. I'm not a civil servant. If anybody finds out about it, it's on me."

"Listen," he replied, "I can't tell you not to make an effort on such an important task, but I want you to know that I'm opposed to it." The soft gaze in his compassionate eyes told me that he'd already given me his blessing, though he said nothing further.

I traveled to meet Waldheim at the Presidential Palace in Vienna, equipped with letters I received from the families of the missing soldiers; from Haim Herzog, who was in contact with the Austrian president after serving as the Israeli ambassador to the United Nations when Waldheim was secretary-general; and from my friend Aryeh "Lova" Eliav, who'd dealt with the issue of the MIAs in the past, especially with the Austrian authorities.

Waldheim welcomed me with the pomp and circumstance normally reserved for royalty. Apparently, meeting with an envoy of the Israeli people was very important to him in light of the problematic international situation he was in. I told him, "Mr. President, most of the people in the small group who know about our meeting were strongly against it." He claimed that he was being terribly wronged. I told him that this was a chance for him to somewhat remedy the situation. I presented him with my proposal and told him in return, he would receive the gratitude and appreciation of Israelis and of Jews all over the world—something that he was in dire need of, in terms of his public image and in practical terms.

Waldheim was very surprised. He didn't expect such an offer. He seemed happy with the possibility that, if he succeeded in his efforts, it might provide him with some kind of "certificate of good standing" from Israeli and Jewish elements, albeit unofficially.

I brought him documents related to our MIAs and some information on the Iranian connection to the affair. I had a strong conviction, and Waldheim even assured me of it, that he fully intended to make a serious effort on this subject. Deep down, I was hoping that his desire to be "purified" of the evils of the past would indeed make him move heaven and earth.

A few weeks later, Waldheim flew to Tehran. Several days after, in June 1991, he returned to Austria from his rendezvous in Iran. His military adjutant called me on the phone and told me that Waldheim had made a great effort and put a lot of pressure on Rafsanjani, but the Iranian president told him that he "knew nothing" about the subject—an answer that we would hear quite a few times later.

* * *

Samir As'ad, a member of the local Druze community in Israel and son of Mohammad and Afifa from the rural community of Beit Jann, enlisted in the IDF in 1979 and served in the Gaza Strip. After finishing his mandatory three-year service and signing on for a permanent commission in the army, he served as a translator at the military government house in Sidon. The military lost all trace of him in April 1983. According to the initial assessments, his abduction was related to a Druze girl from the Chouf Mountains in Lebanon, who was staying at the home of his friend in Israel and with whom he entered Lebanon when he made his way back to the army base. There's no doubt in my mind that if this was the case of an Israeli Jewish soldier, the fear that something bad might have happened to him would have been on the agenda a lot sooner. In the case of Samir As'ad, only speculation arose at first. In 1986, when I started working in my role and met with the wonderful As'ad family, I came to realize the problematic gap between the state of Israel and the Druze community.

It was not until December 1983 that Nayef Hawatmeh's Democratic Front for the Liberation of Palestine (DFLP) publicly announced that they were holding Samir As'ad. The terrorist organization knew about the sensitive relationship between the Druze community and the IDF and Israeli government. In a deliberate attempt to exploit this kind of sensitivity, they issued contradictory public announcements about the fate of Samir As'ad in order to create a crisis of loyalty among the Druze soldiers serving in the IDF. In April 1984, they released a video taken by a camera team from the NBC television network in which Samir spoke in Hebrew, said that he was captured by the DFLP, that he was in good health, was being treated properly, and that he hoped every effort would be made to secure his release. After a while, his family also received a letter from him through the International Red Cross.

In June 1984, the DFLP's spokesman in Syria announced that Samir As'ad was killed in an Israeli Air Force attack on Palm Island (sometimes known as Rabbit Island) near Tripoli along with his three guards when the structure in which he was held collapsed as a result of the bombing. The spokesman laid the responsibility for As'ad's death on Israel. The IDF spokesman denied these allegations and stated the terrorists had no base at all on the island and the accusation was therefore completely baseless and intended for the purposes of psychological warfare only.

We began to negotiate with the DFLP through dignitaries of the Druze community in Israel who left for Lebanon, but these contacts did not bear fruit. During 1986, several attempts at a dialogue were made through different organizations in Lebanon, both mediated by the Red Cross and directly with our government, but nothing came out of these endeavors either. Defense Minister Rabin visited the As'ad family home and stated that as far as the state of Israel was concerned, Samir As'ad would officially be considered alive as long as no reliable information could be obtained to contradict this.

A team that included Uri Lubrani, Reuven Erlich, and me held a negotiation with the DFLP through their representatives, usually on the soil of Lebanon. At the end of the negotiations, in 1991, we reached an agreement that stipulated that we would receive the body of Samir As'ad, and in exchange, the government of Israel would allow the DFLP terrorist "Ali" Abdullah Muhammad Abu Hilal to return to the Palestinian Territories. Abu Hilal was previously deported from the territories on the suspicion that he was recruiting young people locally for terrorist activities against Israeli targets. It was decided that the process would be carried out in Vienna, where the DFLP would bring the body. Once it was reliably identified, we were to return the terrorist to the territories on the same plane that would bring back the body.

The As'ad family wanted to meet with me before I left. They made several requests at our meeting: that we not allow ourselves to be deceived by the terrorists, that a Druze pathologist would be involved in the identification process, and that we would uncover beyond any doubt the circumstances in which their son was killed—whether in a bombing by the IDF, as claimed by the terrorist organization, or otherwise.

I returned with the family's requests to the security services, and we started looking for a Druze pathologist. We couldn't find anyone who fit that description, neither in the country nor anywhere else in the world. When I told this to the family, they asked that *I* be the "expert" on their behalf. I informed them that I had no relevant experience or knowledge of the subject, but the family insisted and asked me to take responsibility for these inquiries myself (of course, with the help of experts who *were* qualified).

We contacted every possible element dealing with the matter, and it was suggested that I take a dental specialist to confirm the identification of the body, as well as a pathologist, in case there was a chance to identify it using the bones. We decided to take their advice and traveled to Vienna with a dental expert and a pathologist.

The delegation consisted of Col. Reuven Ehrlich, then chief military rabbi at the time; Gad Navon, the highest authority for the purposes of identification; me; and security personnel. The Austrian government was in charge of the meeting and facilitating the exchange, but ultimately this was a meeting with known terrorist elements, and there was a great deal of suspicion about the potential for attempts to prevent the encounter or to disrupt it somehow. The terrorists informed us in advance that they were coming with a bag full of bones. They feared Israel's government would set up an "ambush" for them and not live up to its side of the deal, and we, for our part, received numerous security alerts, so there was a heavy security presence around us at all times.

The terrorists' representatives arrived at the morgue in the hospital in Vienna with a black nylon bag full of human bones, which were placed on the table and arranged just like a skeleton displayed to medical students in anatomy class. The tension in the air was immense. Everyone suspected everyone else.

The identification process was carried out pretty quickly. The dentist immediately recognized that this was Samir As'ad, according to the state of decay in his teeth, and the other medical expert identified the old signs of a sprained shoulder of Samir. The pathologist examined the bones and did not see any signs of shell fragments in them, demonstrating that it was not the Israeli Air Force, when it "bombed the Rabbit Island," that caused Samir's death. The pathologist had extensive experience in postmortem identification and a vast knowledge of the human body. He counted the bones in Samir's body and immediately found that one of the bones in the chest was missing, close to the heart. In his estimation, Samir had been killed by a single gunshot wound to the chest that struck the bone, and the terrorists made sure to remove it for that reason.

We therefore managed to meet the conditions set by the family, and rightly so.

We returned to Israel from Vienna, on an empty Boeing plane that belonged to the El Al airline. On one side of the plane solemnly stood the coffin of Samir As'ad, neatly wrapped with the flag of Israel, and on the other side, under close watch, sat Ali Abdullah Muhammad Abu Hilal, whom we'd brought back to the territories of Judea and Samaria, just as agreed upon.

*   *   *

We landed in Israel early the next morning. The As'ad family set up a mourning tent in Beit Jaan, as is common custom among Arab populations, and I arrived there together with Defense Minister Moshe Arens. The father asked Arens if Samir's body had been returned in its entirety. The minister looked at me. He had not yet received our report on the identification process, except for its final result.

I told him that there was one bone missing. "So," the father said to Arens, "you owe us." Minister Arens, who was, in my opinion, one of the finest ministers in any Israeli administration and a compassionate man and of the highest moral standing, told him, "You're right," and asked how they could compensate him. Mohammed replied without hesitation:

"More than twenty IDF fighters from Beit Jaan were killed in action, yet we still don't have a military cemetery in our community."

Shortly after, bulldozers arrived at Beit Jann and began building one of the most distinguished military cemeteries in the country.

12

The Grief of the As'ad Family: A Druze Family Whose Son Samir Was Abducted in Lebanon as an IDF Soldier and Murdered by His Captors

"This country can retrieve Iran's nuclear ar-
chive, but can't tell if my brother is alive."
—Yusef As'ad, brother of IDF soldier
Samir As'ad of Beit Jann

Samir was a happy and lively boy, my parents' fifth child out of nine children, and next in line right after me. He served in the army as an interpreter from Arabic just like me. I served as an interpreter at the Prosecutor's Office in the Gaza Strip, in the legal cases of some of the cruelest, most notorious of the terrorists, as well as the least of the street rioters. A serious and challenging role that requires good command of both Hebrew and Arabic and involves heavy responsibility. An error in translation could amend a judge's sentence. During his regular army service, Samir replaced me as an interpreter in Gaza and was later stationed in Sidon, Lebanon.

At the beginning of the Lebanon War, the border was pretty much wide open, and many Lebanese civilians could arrive at the border, present their passports for inspection, and enter Israel with their private cars. On the last Saturday that Samir spent at home, he brought home a friend of his, a reserve soldier from the village of Ussefiya, with a female friend from Lebanon. We hosted them, as is customary, with lavish generosity. Druze hospitality in all its glory.

On Saturday night, Samir and the Lebanese girl decided to spend the night in my student apartment in Kiryat Shmona—I was studying construction engineering at Tel-Hai College—so that they could be closer to the border and get to his base on time. The next day, March 3, 1983, at 9:50 a.m., I said goodbye to my brother in hugs near the student dormitory in Kiryat Shmona. It was the last time anyone in our family ever saw him.

Samir and the girl drove off in her Mercedes car. In retrospect, we found out that she was probably sent by terrorists to kidnap an IDF soldier. To this day, the main question that runs in my head is whether this girl really was a stone-cold spy sent to seduce him or she was one of the victims too. We tried to reach her later on all kinds of channels, without success. This question will probably always remain a mystery to me. I am more comfortable believing that she was a victim in this too. In our culture, it is unthinkable for someone to stay in your home, eat the food you serve them, and then act against you.

My mother is a very anxious woman, and Samir would always call her and say that he made it to the army base safely. When he didn't call that Sunday, Monday, and then Tuesday, she was very suspicious. We called Samir's base, and that's when we found out he hadn't arrived at all. Big question marks began to arise here, but it was a long time from the moment Samir failed to reach the base until they started looking for him. The army took two full weeks to realize that there was something wrong. I think lessons have been learned since then.

And so, two weeks after I last saw Samir, our journey of pain and agony began. It took another two months until the initial assessment that Samir was taken captive.

I was very angry about what happened. It just can't be that in such an advanced state like Israel, the border will be wide open like that, nor can it be that they waited so long before they started looking for Samir. I myself was investigated, and I told everything, down to the smallest details, to help the system, to make them realize that there was no earlier connection between Samir and that girl and that he wouldn't voluntarily go with someone else's girl. These are not the values we were brought up on.

For all the years that Samir was absent, I kept restraint, but deep down inside I was furious. I tried to play it like an Israeli, just like the families of the other missing soldiers, but I indirectly felt that as far as the establishment was concerned, I was something else. In meetings with other families, or whenever a senior official came from overseas, Kissinger and Carter, for example, I had a double mission: to explain that my family, despite its uniqueness, is just like the other families. A soldier is a soldier, and what does it matter if he's a Jew or a Druze? Samir is a soldier, just like any other soldier.

I had to deal with it alone; I didn't share these feelings with anyone. I wanted to feel that I was equal to the people sitting in front of me. After all, you'll get treated by others the same way you treat yourself. Coping with it wasn't simple. I tried to maintain the image of the state, as if it cares for its sons and doesn't abandon them, so that no one would take advantage of the situation between us and try to incite people from our community against the state and say that Samir was being treated differently because he was a Druze.

Meanwhile, thirty-four years have passed and nothing has changed. The demon, which was then hidden, has now come out of the bottle.

*   *   *

I was only twenty-four years old at the time, two years older than Samir who disappeared, but right from the start, I took it upon myself to take care of everything that was needed, including the relationships with the authorities. My mother is illiterate, and I didn't know if my father could get along with his Hebrew in front of all the official bodies and people involved. Besides, I wanted to ease their pain, to be able to be the filter for the information before it reached them, provide them with information that would only touch the edges of their nerves, but wouldn't leave them shaken.

My parents' mental health was important to me. We don't display strong emotions publicly in our community. My father always played the hero whenever he was around us, but I heard him cry at night, when he thought that no one could hear him. That's why to this day I admire him. I was looking for a way to strengthen my parents and give them hope.

When you're put in this position, you're ready to believe anything they tell you, and you examine every story and every possibility. You don't want to think that you're missing something and live out your life with your conscience tormenting you because you might not have done enough. That's the most terrible part of the uncertainty. Today, I can say with confidence, that it's better to lose what's dearest to you on the battlefield than to live with its absence, because not knowing is the most difficult situation. It makes you go around as if you were sleepwalking, drives you to madness. If Samir had been killed, we would be grieving for a while and then reconciled with his death. Instead, we went through eight and a half years of madness.

To bring some relief to my parents, I went with them to the fortune-teller in the village of Ghajar and then a priest in Shefar'am. The priest, trying to find where Samir was being held with magnets he placed on a map, was holding the map upside down and searched for him in the south, in the Negev instead of Lebanon. I kept silent as it went on and on, but I couldn't help it anymore. I said to him, "Mr. Priest, your map is upside down."

We lived on a swing made out of rumors, hanging between hope and despair, going through ups and downs. About eight months after Samir disappeared, Nayef Hwatme's "Democratic Front for the Liberation of Palestine" announced it was holding Samir. On April 5, 1984, one year and two days after I said goodbye to my brother in hugs, the organization released a videotape of Samir, which was the top story in the news on Israeli television. We saw Samir for the first time on television, giving his regards to our parents and asking the state to do everything in its power to bring him back. He looked unwell; I didn't like the shape of his mouth, which was obscured by the mustache, and there seemed to be a change in the shape of his head. But I disregarded the way he looked; the fact that he was alive was the only thing I cared about. The joy of Samir being alive was replaced with terrible frustration: What are we and the state supposed to do now to bring him back?

And after two months, we got shook up again. In June 1984, the organization announced that Samir had been killed in an Israeli Air Force bombing on Rabbit Island near Tripoli. To this day, I don't know what the truth is. Were the terrorists the ones who murdered Samir? It was right after a terrorist attack in King George Street in Jerusalem, where the perpetrators were killed, so maybe after that someone there went mad from the anger and killed Samir? And maybe it was all a mistake made by the Israeli Air Force? I don't want to be suspicious of the state of Israel, and I definitely didn't want to publicly challenge the perception that the state looks after its soldiers. I made sure to maintain my patriotism and didn't want to open a Pandora's box.

After receiving the news that Samir was taken captive, and after being provided proof that he was alive, we went into euphoria—I was even present on the arrival in the country of the Israeli prisoners who were returned in the Jibril deal, to experience this joy up close. And suddenly, uncertainty fell on us again.

Moving from knowing he was alive into doubts threw us into turmoil. The system tells you that as long as it has not been proven otherwise, he's alive, but this statement only made things more complicated for me. I believed in the power of the state, and I couldn't understand how it is that they didn't know what had happened to my brother. This country can retrieve Iran's nuclear archive, but can't tell if my brother Samir As'ad is alive?

* * *

And you have to deal with rumors all the time, especially in the state we were in, with total uncertainty about whether Samir was really murdered in captivity or was still alive. I don't wish on anyone this state of ignorance and helplessness. You think about your brother as if he were gone but then convince yourself that he might be still alive, and you try to think if he's eating and drinking and if they're torturing him. I tried as much as possible to repress the thoughts, not to ask myself too many questions. I was mostly busy trying to maintain my parents' sanity, find out what they were told and weren't told.

I had no way of defending myself. One day, one of the officers who accompanied us said to me, "Your brother was killed in action." Straight, just like that. I was stunned. I was very angry with her. Uncharacteristically, I was impolite to her and asked: "How can you talk to me that way? How can you be so cruel and inhumane? You tell me that my brother was killed in action; I want proof of this."

The good and intelligent people like Ory, people who inspired trust and respect, were like a ray of light in my life. Ory was always someone I could lean on. Thanks to his inner beauty, I became attached to him from the moment he entered our lives, and this connection is maintained to this day. He was my rock, a solid and human rock. Whoever picked him for this role couldn't have made a more successful choice.

An intimate relationship developed between us. Everything I couldn't say to the system, from the little things to the big ones, I could tell Ory directly and freely. Ory bridged effectively between all the bodies dealing with this loaded issue. It created chemistry and trust between us and the system. Thanks to Ory's unique personality and his integrity, I could believe everything he told us. He seemed to have a dictionary in his head, because he always knew how to pick the right words without offending the family but also knew how to tell it like it was. He never tried to embellish things.

Like Ory, defense ministers Yitzhak Rabin and Moshe Arens also treated the story of missing soldiers with reverence and deep respect. Arens was so attentive to us. In one of the discussions I attended, he told the IDF chief of staff that he was adopting my opinion, which was contrary to the position of the others in the discussion. Such people restored our confidence in the system.

* * *

Samir As'ad's body was returned to Israel on September 12, 1991.

When the negotiation for his return was being conducted and they asked for our opinion, I said: "If Samir is no longer alive, don't release anyone in exchange for him." I didn't want them to release terrorists for bones. For us Druze, there is no inherent value to the body, only to the soul.

I'll never be able to enter the mind of another family and learn their thoughts, and I wish with all my heart for the families who lost their sons and didn't get to bury them that they will get their children back tomorrow. My heart is strong. Everything I say is in my name only, and I have no criticism for anyone else.

The Jibril deal set a bar that I oppose. If Samir were alive, I wouldn't try to influence the negotiations. I would tell the policymakers: "You have the knowledge. The decision is yours." I wouldn't pressure them, go to the media, start a lobby group, start a nonprofit, or build protest encampments with tents. I would let the system do its job. Anyone attached emotionally cannot be involved, and it's impossible to involve emotions in professional considerations, because then the wrong decisions might be made. Hassan Nasrallah and the Hamas are playing with our national strength. We have become a weak people.

Ultimately, I found it vexing that they released Abu Hilal for Samir's bones. These inhumane people who murdered Samir while he was still alive, without any ability to defend himself, didn't deserve it. They should have paid the price for it. Even today, whenever the name of Yasser Abed Rabbo, the spokesman for the organization, is mentioned, I become furious.

The Druze always treated their prisoners of war with respect. When the Druze went to war against the Turkish Ottomans and the French mandate, when women were taken captive, they automatically became family members and were kept safe. So was the approach toward downed pilots. This is the tradition by which we were educated. How can you kill in cold blood a man who was held in your prisons, when you know that he can't possibly defend himself? I will never comprehend these cultural differences between us. They could have kept Samir alive and made a trade for him, just like Gilad Shalit was kept alive. So now we have to release a scumbag like Abu Hilal for a bag of bones?

*   *   *

After all our expectations and hopes that Samir would come back alive, losing flesh from our own flesh was very difficult for my family. And then the miracle suddenly happened: Samir was reincarnated and his soul rolled into a boy from a neighboring village. When the mother was pregnant, she dreamed that someone was walking toward her and telling her that his name was Samir and that one day he would come to her. Shortly after giving birth, she saw Samir's picture in the newspaper and recognized the man who appeared in her dream.

When my mother met the child, she felt like Samir suddenly came back to her. It comforted her. Today he is already married with children, and my parents treat him like their own son and his children like their own grandchildren. I think my mom talks about him more than she talks about the rest of her kids. He visits my parents once a week, and we have a competition on who spends more on him. It took away tons of pain and worry and helped us come back to life.

A year after we buried Samir, I married Rima. On our wedding day, I paid a special honor to Ory; they used his car to drive to her parents' house to bring the bride over to my house. I have lived with Rima for twenty-five years, she's an inseparable part of my life, and this is the first time we've ever told the whole story like this.

With Yitzhak Rabin at the prime minister's residence (photo by Shlomi Bochachio)

With President Shimon Peres, getting awarded the president's medal (photo by Yossef Avi, Yair Engel [Juha])

With Prime Minister Arik Sharon (right) at a function in the ministry of defense (photo by Sarah Davidovich)

At the Jabotinsky Award ceremony with families of MIAs. Standing from left to right: Yusaf As'ad, Ory and actor Haim Topol. Sitting from left to right: Hadassah Fink, Avraham and Pnina Feldman (photo from private collection)

The Lubrani team, Ory with Col. Rubke Ehrlich and Col. Yitzhak Tidhar (photo from private collection)

On a negotiations trip to Rome on the subject of captives and MIAs.
Right to left: Col. Kuti Mor, Ory, Uri Lubrani and Col. "Rubke" Ehrlich (photo from private collection)

With Maj. Gen. Amos Yaron, outside of the halls of the public inquiry committee investigating the events in the Lebanon War (Sabra and Shatila) (photo by Zoom 77)

Waiting for the coffins of deceased IDF soldiers Yossi Fink and Rahamim Alsheikh, returned to Israel from Lebanon. Right to left: Shin Bet director Ya'akov Peri, Mossad director Shabtai Shavit, Shin Bet officer Yossi Ginossar and Ory (photo by Michael Kramer)

With Maj. Gen. Itzik Mordechai (left) before my farewell parachute jump (photo by Yossi Roth)

At Red Square, on my "business trip" to Moscow (photo from private collection)

At Batya Arad's home, with Tammy Arad (middle) (photo from private collection)

The one Israeli pound note Batya Arad insisted on giving me

Col. Varda Pomerantz with Yonah Baumel, father of Zechariah Baumel from the Battle of Sultan Yacoub
(photo from private collection)

My portrait, painted by Avraham Feldman, father of MIA Zvika Feldman from the Battle of Sultan Yacoub

With Mohammad, father of IDF captive Samir As'ad from Beit Jann (photo from private collection)

With Tammy (far left), Rima and Yusaf As'ad, the family members of Samir As'ad from Beit Jann, at our meeting in preparation for the writing of this book (photo from private collection)

With Karnit Goldwasser (right) and Israeli State Attorney and Supreme Court Justice Dorit Beinisch
at the Israeli Bar Association's Award ceremony (photo courtesy of the Israeli Bar Association)

With Sa'ada and Shlomo Alsheikh, parents of MIA Rahamim Alsheikh
at a family event (photo from private collection)

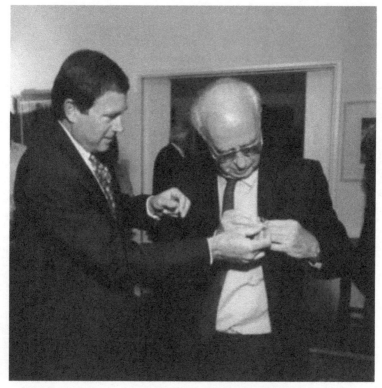

With the late Rabin. "I told him I had a breakthrough offer about Ron
Arad, but it is a bit unusual. Rabin listened and confirmed it "

Mustafa Dirani

13

Operation Dirani Brothers

Thursday, June 7, 2018

At the entrance to a hotel in Copenhagen, Denmark, two older men warmly embrace. They hadn't seen each other in twenty-six years. As is customary in such meetings, they exclaim: "Incredible, you haven't changed at all," even though the time that has gone by had left its traces here and there. But the Danish lawyer's face remained mostly as it had been, with the only addition being a white beard.

I had gone all the way to Denmark to receive his blessing to tell this story.

Prior to our meeting, I reviewed the operation portfolio—with the approval of the Mossad and with the assistance of its operatives—including documentation lists and reports made both by my friends and by me. I spoke with my collaborators at the time, who will be mentioned later. They all gave me their enthusiastic support to write this story. But I knew that if the Danish lawyer vetoed this move, my story would never be told.

I carefully cultivated my renewed relationship with the Danish attorney, who will be referred to simply as "The Lawyer." I had written to him via email that I was coming to Copenhagen with my wife, Tamy, and that I would be glad to meet up with him. I didn't mention my desire to write about this subject at this stage. The Lawyer replied that he and his wife would be very happy to spend time with us in Copenhagen. We didn't discuss details, but we both knew very well what we were going to be talking about.

Our first meeting in the hotel lobby took much longer than we had planned. We talked about our professional lives, our families. The Lawyer asked about our Israeli friends who had participated in the operation. As he spoke openly and proudly about our mutual efforts back then, and how happy he was to have taken part in the events, it raised the opportunity for me to ask him the question. To my surprise, not only did he give me the blessing I had hoped for, he also provided me with some new information.

We spent three wonderful days together in Copenhagen with our wives. When I returned to Israel, The Lawyer sent me an excited email. He wrote:

> *Our cooperation at that time was very important for the persons involved, and for me it was an opportunity to confirm my Jewish identification doing something of importance to others. I was happy that I got the possibility. I did my best and I'm sure that you did it too.*

So now I can tell a story that has never before been revealed. When in Copenhagen, I met with Mohammed Hassan Dib Dirani and Subhi Hasan Dib Dirani, the brothers of Mustafa Dib Mara'i Dirani. These meetings were part of an effort to obtain information about the fate of Ron Arad, as well as any other possible leads about IDF captives and MIAs.

But first, I have to go back to the beginning of 1992.

One of the objectives in the effort to rescue the captives and MIAs was to try to reach those who were holding them, or at least those who could reach the ones holding them. To this end, all the different bodies involved in such affairs used all the means at their disposal, including assistance from human being resources, without any reservation or deliberation. I took part in these operations often, and some were my own initiatives.

In early 1992, in conjunction with my work on captives and MIAs, I was deeply engaged in a very large trial involving Israel's banks. At a very early stage of the trial, I was called to attend an urgent meeting at the Mossad with "Y," the head of the POW/MIA team (who requested that his full name not be published here), and with Arale Scherf, the head of "Tevel," the division that serves, among other roles, as a kind of foreign ministry in the Mossad that maintains contacts with counterparts in the field of secret service worldwide. At the head of the pyramid was the head of the Mossad at the time, Shabtai Shavit, who was appointed to coordinate the captives and MIAs department of the Mossad by his predecessor, Nahum Admoni. It's worth noting here that the involvement of all senior members on the issue of captives and MIAs, from the head of the Mossad on down, conveyed the message that this was a highly important and relevant endeavor. Shavit spared no effort or expense on this operation, which will be detailed here.

I was still unaware at that point of the urgent subject for which I'd been invited to the meeting, but as always, I didn't ask lots of questions. My friends, Arale Scherf and Y, knew very well that they were pulling me out of the big trial that had shaken the whole country in those days. The first question they asked me was whether I would be available for a mission that could take several months. I had no way of knowing at the time that "a few months" would become nearly a year, in which I would be occupied with a radically different task than the one I was dealing with in the Jerusalem District Court. I couldn't even begin to imagine at the time who I would be facing instead of the honorable Justice Miriam Naor.

As the Mossad meeting drew on, it began to dawn on me that I would have to make a difficult decision: whether to abandon the biggest trial of my life—a "once in a lifetime" case. If I agreed, I would first have to confer with my fellow litigator in the trial, Israel Cantor, and with our client, Leumi Bank CEO Mordechai Einhorn, without being able to tell them even an inkling of what the mission was about. At that point, I barely knew anything about it myself.

Indeed, it was not an easy task to contact them and ask for their permission to be absent for an extended period of several months, which

meant, in all likelihood, that I would have to retire from my appointment as legal defense in the case. These were not simple conversations to
have, especially as I could not divulge anything more than that it was
something important regarding the captives and MIAs—an issue that
they knew I was involved in. This new situation was particularly difficult
to accept for Mordechai Einhorn, with whom I'd had interactions that
were very close and frequent. Beyond our attorney-client relationship, I
served as a shoulder to lean on for him, and he talked to me a lot about
his own personal predicament—being a senior executive who suddenly
finds himself a defendant in court. I assured him that on a personal level I
would continue to be available to him as much as I could on the weekends
that I would spend in Israel. Since the decision to leave the "trial of the
century" was pitted against my involvement with the captives and MIAs,
ultimately, I managed to justify my decision to Einhorn, to Cantor, and
especially to myself.

Of course, I also consulted with Tamy, who was a full partner in the
decision to give up this major professional achievement and the tremendous financial gain it entailed in order to invest all my time and effort in
something completely different, and at a time when I was still unaware
how truly "different" it could be.

But even today, looking back, I do not regret my decision for a
split second.

* * *

I went back to my meetings at the Mossad where gradually, piece by
piece, I began to understand the complexity of the operation that would
be conducted in a foreign country, in accordance with local laws and
standards, and during which I would encounter some people who were
not—to say the least—great lovers of the land of Zion. It is important
for me to emphasize again, that not only was I not a Mossad agent, but
I made sure to use my full name and my true identity at every forum
or meeting around the world. "Truth is also an option, and being transparent can be a serious advantage in the intelligence world too," veteran
intelligence official Zvika Malkin once taught me. I was already quite

well known in the country by then, and my pictures were published here and there in the context of my professional practice.

Moreover, in this operation—as my friends explained to me—my participation with my full identity was an unconditional request of the government in the nation where the meetings were to take place. They demanded that the mission not be conducted by intelligence personnel with false or borrowed identities, but by a person approved by the local authorities, once his personal details and identity had been thoroughly vetted.

The people who attended that first meeting were, as mentioned, Arale Scherf, the head of the Tevel division, and Y, a senior official in the Mossad who served in many different positions, including the head of the captives and MIAs team. Arale—a tall, impressive gentleman with a thick mane of hair that, despite his advanced age, would look great even on a young man—was one of the organization's true veterans. A wise man with a great wealth of knowledge. He was drafted into the General Security Service (Shin Bet) by Rafael Eitan in the late 1950s and served as a personal bodyguard for Israel's first prime minister, David Ben-Gurion, for about two years. At his request, Eitan transferred Arale to the Mossad, where he was accepted by the head of "Tzomet" (Junction)—the department that operates agent recruitment and the Mossad's global network of agents—reportedly saying: "At least this one has the face of a goy." Over the years, Arale fulfilled numerous roles at the Mossad, both in operational and management positions, until he reached the very top, at the point where our paths intersected when he was in the role associated with the captives and MIAs. Our families also became friends later. Arale didn't share with us the exact details about his role in the organization but told us many amusing stories about David Ben-Gurion and his wife, Paula, who was a very special prime minister's wife, while taking care not to infringe on their privacy.

Y was also an impressive man who served in many different senior organizational, operational, and managerial positions at the Mossad. During our years of joint activity, I got to know him and his family and discovered a person with great love for life who was also a professional sailing aficionado (especially on transoceanic yacht trips). To the best of my recollection, during our acquaintance, he crossed the Atlantic in a sailboat more than once. He was also a very well-informed wine connoisseur. A brave and charismatic man, he had excellent abilities at recruiting and persuading people to join his cause. At one of our first meetings in my office, after he'd started working in the field of captives and MIAs, I told him, "Keep in mind that everyone who works in the field, searching for IDF captives and MIAs will find that his life has completely changed."

He told me a long time later, "Your words have proven to be very true for me as well."

Another person who took part in the affair was Shimshon Yitzhaki, also a senior member of the Mossad, who, like Scherf and Y, has since retired. Shimshon Yitzhaki, who is also an expert on Islamic terrorism and the author of a book on this subject (and another about the arch-terrorist Osama bin Laden), served as the chief of state affairs in the research department of the Military Intelligence Directorate (AMAN) and from there moved to the Mossad. At the time of the operation, he was the head of the Northern Europe subdivision and was living in Copenhagen with his wife, Nora. All through the operation, they hosted me and everyone else who took part in the mission; they were the initiators and took the responsibility for nearly every detail. Shimshon was tasked with maintaining the connection with the local state security services and the authorities vis-à-vis the state of Israel. With his knowledge and experience, he was also the most suitable person to prepare me for the complexities of this operation.

Even after I had met Shimshon and knew that the operation was going to take place in Denmark, I was still not provided with the precise details. Danish security services had to authorize my participation in the operation first, especially considering that I was supposed to meet with the targets whom we wanted to make contact with personally. The reason for the conditions posed by the Danish authorities was that the people I was going to meet with were of Lebanese origin—guests in Denmark—who had temporary resident or refugee status. Many European countries have granted refugee status to people who escaped from their countries of origin due to direct threats or persecution, and many of them came from the Middle East, including Lebanon. The Danish were very conscious about safeguarding their rights and made sure that anyone they were going to meet was not a "secret agent," security personnel, or a foreign intelligence service agent of some kind.

In order to prove that I was indeed a private individual and a lawyer who participated voluntarily to help the families of captives and MIAs, I was invited to a meeting with the woman who headed the Danish intelligence service, Hanna Beck Hansen. Prior to the meeting, she received a file with a considerable amount of press clippings about my legal practice and the legal affairs I was involved in. I later learned from Shimshon Yitzhaki that, upon his first meeting with her, when he explained the humanitarian nature of the mission, she was very suspicious and initially asked to meet in private with the Danish attorney who was collaborating with us.

Around February or March of 1992, I flew for the first time to Copenhagen to meet with Hansen. I arrived at the meeting, accompanied by Shimshon Yitzhaki. Hansen was already well acquainted with my résumé. The conversation was quite relaxed and warm, and she was quite assured of the veracity of my identity. She asked me what motivated me to take part in such an operation, and I told her that it was my life's mission alongside all my other professional pursuits.

By this point, I had already been briefed about all the secret details— or more accurately, most of them, since, in retrospect, I discovered that there were many more details unknown to me at the time. Perhaps I was better off that way. It turned out that I was supposed to meet with Mohammad Hassan Dib Dirani, brother of Mustafa Dirani, the man who abducted Ron Arad in Lebanon. Mohammad, I was told, was staying in Denmark as a temporary resident, having been injured in Lebanon, and his health was severely compromised. I was also told that he agreed to meet with me knowing my true identity and the voluntary nature of my humanitarian activities. My business card read as follows: "Ory Slonim—Advocate." The phone numbers listed on the card belonged to the office I was renting. It was the same year that I had also begun my activities with the Variety Israel organization.

I returned to Israel and met with people from all possible agencies and bodies who knew anything about the Dirani family without, of course, disclosing the reasons for my interest. Eventually, after two trips to Copenhagen, the local security apparatus approved my participation in the operation. Hansen told Shimshon that she felt a kinship with me due to our mutual legal backgrounds, as well as on a personal level. However, she set two conditions: no Mossad personnel should attend the meetings with Dirani, and security would be provided by her people in coordination with Shimshon. An additional condition, from the Dirani side, was that the meetings would, under no circumstances, be recorded.

At this point, the Danish lawyer entered the picture. He assigned me a room in his office where the meetings were going to take place. The Lawyer was a Jew whose family had lived in Denmark for many generations and an attorney who had dealings with cases pertaining to refugees and immigrants, but his main area of expertise was actually legal representation of local clinics and medical facilities. I knew at the time that The Lawyer was in direct contact with the brothers Mohammed and Subhi Dirani, but I didn't have any relevant details about his connection with them. I learned the full picture only in my last meeting with him in Denmark in 2018: The Lawyer accepted Shimshon Yitzhaki's request to contact Mohammad Dirani, with the understanding that our intentions were on a humanitarian basis only. The aim was to use Dirani to obtain information about Ron Arad and other missing IDF soldiers who had been taken captive in Lebanon—and perhaps even to get them back home—in exchange for help with the rehabilitation of his health. The Lawyer received all the details and also received the approval of the local authorities for creating the connection between me and Dirani.

The Lawyer was excited about the opportunity to help us and told me that he had helped Jewish people in Russia at a time when they were forbidden from having any contact with the state of Israel, let alone immigrating there. As one dealing with various humanitarian issues, The Lawyer was associated with different nonprofits whose mission was to promote these issues in European countries. "There's a warm place in my heart for Jews around the world and for the country they founded," he told me at our first meeting, "and if there's anything I can do to help the families of Israelis whose loved ones are missing, as you've been doing for years, then I'll be happy to assist you."

Preparations for my first meeting with Mohammad Dirani were progressing. I must admit, I was quite apprehensive about what was to occur: a meeting in a foreign country, alone with the brother of the man who'd kidnapped Ron Arad and held him in captivity, when I didn't know anything about the intentions of the man who would stand before me. Never before had I arrived at a meeting armed, and I certainly wasn't going to do so in my meetings with Dirani. My partners on this mission assured me that I would be monitored and guarded at all times. I had long conversations with Tamy about the operation, having received permission to share all the details with her. After all, it was near impossible to deal with all my fears and concerns without getting true emotional support from home—perhaps the most important kind of support. Tamy was, and remains to this day, after fifty-four years together, my most powerful source of support and encouragement.

Y, who was involved in every stage of the operation except the actual meetings, was another source of assurance for me. Knowing that he was in an adjacent room while I was meeting with Dirani alone instilled in me great confidence. I really wanted him to be by my side, not only so that I wasn't physically alone but also to have someone hear from me exactly what I'd heard, right after the meeting.

When we met recently in the course of my work on the book, Y told me how complex and unusual the operation was for members of the Mossad: having someone who was not "one of their own" meeting with relatives of a known terrorist on their behalf, and being worried for my safety security. He told me, "Because of the risks you were exposed to during the mission, this move was met with a great deal of concern for your fate. Shabtai Shavit himself had great reservations about a non-professional being involved in operational activities, but I assured him that I would guard you closely. I had complete trust in you. Against the Mossad's deliberations about whether it was right or wrong to involve external people in field activity stood the fact that we acted without any restriction in these missions. That was also what the logic was behind the decision to involve you in field activity.

"The entire headquarters staff and myself, as the commanding officer in the field, were terribly fearful that when you disclosed your identity to Mohammad Dirani as an Israeli national, he would be recruited upon his return to Lebanon by his brother Mustafa to harm you in some way. We must not forget that Mustafa Dirani was still an active member in a terrorist organization in Lebanon at that time, and that was our main concern during the mission. The Danish security services established a covert security network all around your activities. We managed to identify them, but to my knowledge, they did not succeed in discovering our presence."

Shimshon added: "We had serious doubts about both your safety and that of the Danish attorney. Y and I thought that The Lawyer was less exposed to risk, given that he was a Danish citizen, and Mohammad Dirani would not want to jeopardize his status as an asylum seeker in Denmark. The problem was with your security. That's why it was determined that Y would stay in the next room in addition to the undercover security provided by the Danish services, the details of which you were completely unaware."

All the fears that preceded the operation were, of course, insignificant in the face of hope. For me, they faded away completely after the first meeting with Mohammed Dirani, when I saw the person standing in front of me, and because of the confidence inspired in me by my partners in the operation.

* * *

Many long years have passed and many events have occurred since then, so it's difficult for me to accurately recall what was said in those meetings in Copenhagen, fateful though they were. Thankfully, my reports about the meetings—which I'd written in real time and are now found in the Mossad's files—allow me to go back with the greatest clarity to the six meetings I conducted with Mohammad Dirani in Copenhagen, at the office of The Lawyer, between July and November of 1992.

The first meeting was on July 6, 1992. I saw Mohammad arrive at the meeting with another person. I didn't know who it was. I found out later that it was his brother Subhi, who was seeking asylum in Norway. I requested to meet with only one person, as planned. The two went upstairs to the office together, but only Mohammad entered the room. Subhi waited in the lobby.

The meeting at The Lawyer's office, like all other meetings, was conducted in English, which Mohammad spoke pretty well. The Lawyer introduced us to each other and left the room. I had mixed feelings about this. On one hand, I was standing in front of someone whose family was engaged in terrorist activity, the brother of the man who'd abducted Ron Arad, but on the other hand, this person might be able to help me achieve the goal that we'd all been laboring so hard for.

We shook hands, and I introduced myself. Mohammad knew that I was acting on behalf of the foundation displayed on my business card. I told him about the foundation and its purposes. I informed him that it dealt only in humanitarian affairs, helping those who'd been harmed in times of armed conflict and whose relatives had disappeared. We spent some time engaged in small talk. I asked him to tell me about his own personal condition and that of his family. Mohammad told me that he was about to leave for Lebanon because his father had just had a stroke, and he feared that it could be the last time he would ever get to see him. I told him that the foundation could help fund his trip and also assist his father, if possible, to come to Europe to receive medical treatment locally.

I told Mohammad that I was helping families in Israel, and when I mentioned the name of the Arad family, he jumped up like a spring. I was very polite and courteous. I told him that I knew his brother Mustafa would be able to help and that we could help them as well. Mohammad's first response was that his relations with his brother were not "as good as they used to be," because Mustafa objected to him leaving for Denmark.

Mohammad told me a lot about his family. He told me of another brother who'd been killed in an Israeli air raid and that his family relative, Ghassan Dirani, was in an Israeli prison together with hundreds of Shi'ite Muslim prisoners. He asked if I was familiar with the subject of the Lebanese Shi'ite prisoners in Israeli jail. I told him that I had general knowledge of the issue and that if we made progress, I might be able to assist in this matter as well. I also told him that I could give his regards to his relative in prison, but he did not respond to the offer at this stage. When I hinted that the foundation could assist his family financially, he said, "You can't use money to atone for the blood of my brothers spilled in Lebanon."

"Let's talk man-to-man and keep it civil," I replied.

Mohammad asked me if I thought Israel would agree to release all the Shi'ite prisoners in Lebanon in exchange for Ron's release from captivity. I told him that I was not negotiating, but as far as I knew, Israel had officially stated in the past that, in return for the release of captives and MIAs, including Ron Arad, it would be prepared, pending negotiations, to release Shi'ite prisoners.

The conversation took a sharp turn at this point. Mohammad inquired for the first time about my nationality. I told him that I was an Israeli citizen who was born in Israel, seventh generation in the land, with all the generations that preceded me being natives of Hebron. Mohammad smiled. "In that case, you are a Khalili ibn Khalili."

I felt that Mohammad was quite relieved after this exchange. He told me that he'd feared his involvement in this affair would create the impression that his brother Mustafa was solely responsible for the imprisonment of Ron Arad and that he (Mohammad) had read in the Israeli press that his brother was indeed regarded as responsible. I told him that, to my knowledge, the state of Israel also held the Iranians responsible for Arad's fate and that his brother Mustafa might be able, at this stage, to provide assistance with information and perhaps even the return of Ron Arad to Israel.

I gave Mohammad my business card and told him he could contact me anytime, both through The Lawyer and the phone numbers listed on the card. He asked me if I was going to condition the humanitarian aid that was being offered to him with the request that his brother help us. "Absolutely not," I replied. I added that if the subject of Ron Arad or any Israeli captives or MIAs could be promoted by the family—anything from basic signs of life and up to their ultimate release—we would be talking about extremely large sums of money. Mohammad told me that he had been approached in the past by a Christian family in Denmark acting on behalf of the "Amnesty" NGO, but he disregarded them.

The meeting, which lasted a full seventy minutes, was concluded in good spirits. Mohammad promised to speak to his brother Mustafa and do the best he could. Those were the words he used in conversation both with me and with The Lawyer, when they spoke after our meeting. The Lawyer told us that the message I relayed to Mohammad was indeed received, but he was scared that his brother would be angry at him, both because large amounts of money were involved and because he'd made contact with an Israeli national. Mohammad also told The Lawyer that my "Palestinian" identity, the fact I was "Khalili ibn Khalili," played a crucial role in his decision to talk to me.

I returned to Israel. I reported the meeting, including all that followed, to the minister of defense, Itzhak Rabin, and was also invited, naturally, to meetings and briefings on the subject at Mossad HQ.

The second meeting took place on September 16, 1992. Mohammad had requested in advance through The Lawyer that his brother Subhi, who had come from Oslo and had been asked to wait outside last time, be allowed to join the meeting. We agreed to this request. I had the hunch that Subhi was there to watch me closely and to try to get a better idea of who I was.

The meeting was shorter this time, lasting only thirty minutes. It required me to behave a little differently: a discussion with multiple sides is different from a dialogue. The two brothers spoke simultaneously, saying that Mustafa told them to pass us the message: "When it comes to humanitarian affairs, we all want to help. He is also willing to help search for Ron, though since the time he left the Amal organization in 1987/88, he had no more contact or information regarding the affair. However, he is prepared to assist as best he can."

After returning to the hotel, The Lawyer called me and told me that the brothers wanted to meet me again. Apparently Subhi had approved of me. I went back to the office immediately. This conversation was similarly relaxed and calm. The brothers told me more about their father, who was very ill, and their meeting with him in Lebanon. Mohammad told me that between our first and our second meetings, he himself had undergone surgery due to his injuries in Lebanon.

Mohammed and Subhi came with a clear message from their brother to me, which they read aloud: "For the past four or five years, Mustafa has had no contact with Ron. Our brother has left Amal, and since then, he had no control over the affair. However, since this is a humanitarian issue, he is prepared to help." While this was nothing more than a repetition of the message that they had already given me earlier, this time it was read off the page.

At this meeting, since I had promised to help them with the surgery, I gave Mohammad 1,500 US dollars through The Lawyer, who was waiting right outside. I insisted that I always deliver the money to them physically by The Lawyer.

I sensed at this point that the brothers Mohammad and Subhi had full confidence in the foundation, its goals, and in me as its representative.

The fourth meeting, which was preceded as always by analysis and briefings, took place on October 30, 1992. Before the meeting, the idea was raised that Y might join me this time. In our preparations, which took place the day before the meeting with the brothers (and with the participation of both The Lawyer and the Danish authorities), some reservations were expressed about someone else on our side joining the meeting, contrary to the initial agreement. Obviously, we had to comply. While it was only natural that Y—who had chaperoned the entire operation from start to finish—would like to attend, he immediately understood not only their reservations but also how the addition of another person could undermine the trust formed between the brothers and me. I therefore continued attending the meetings alone.

Only Mohammad attended the fourth meeting. It lasted for ninety-five minutes, with almost an hour of it in discussion about his health. Mohammad said they had implanted in his body a device that transmits electrical currents that massage his muscles from the inside and that he was taking large amounts of painkillers. I offered him the help of my fellow European doctors, who have no connection with Israel, and told him that sometimes it's better to use private doctors and not rely only on government institutions. I intended to take him to private doctors to whom I had access in Switzerland.

I made sure to separate the offer of financial aid for his medical care and that of his family members from my requests on negotiations at all times. I proposed that Mohammad go to Lebanon again to give a special message to his brother from us. I assured him that I would finance the trip. At this point, he suggested we involve the Red Cross. I told him that I was receiving help from the Red Cross separately and that it was better that our contact be direct, as it would make it easier for me to help them in a way that wouldn't be possible through the Red Cross.

It was a very intimate conversation. Mohammad was very open to sharing with me the story of his family and the hardship they had to endure in Europe. He told me that his wife was six months pregnant. Mohammad even lifted his shirt and showed me the scars on his body from the many surgeries he had undergone. I had a feeling that his trust in me had grown stronger. I showed him an envelope with some cash in it. I didn't give it to him right away. I told him that when he decided he was ready to go to Lebanon again, I would hand over the money to The Lawyer so he could buy the flight tickets.

It was agreed that he would give me a reply about the trip on November 6, 1992, a few days after the medical treatment he was about to receive. Upon receiving the reply from The Lawyer that Mohammad was ready to leave for Lebanon, I flew again to Copenhagen.

The fifth meeting with Mohammad Dirani took place on November 11, 1992, and lasted for about an hour. As always, the first part was devoted to his precarious health, which had not improved in the interim. I reiterated my offer to take him to my friends' clinic in Europe. Mohammad told me he was about to leave for Lebanon. I gave him 5,000 US dollars on the spot in an envelope, through The Lawyer. I told Mohammad that he could count the money. He replied that there was no need to do so. Mohammed also said he did not speak to Mustafa over the phone for security reasons and that he did not involve Subhi either on the financial issues or my request that he make the trip.

The details of my request for proof of life were as follows: a personal letter in Ron's handwriting, including special details that only he and his family would know about; a recent photograph of him holding a well-known newspaper with the date clearly visible; and if a video tape was added to all this, we would pay the family, through The Lawyer, the sum of 100,000 dollars—but of course, only after we had verified the details.

I informed Mohammed that if this "sign of life" was somehow made public, we wouldn't disclose where it had come from. At the same time, we would continue with the negotiations for the release of detainees from Al Khiam prison in exchange for the return of Ron Arad and other IDF captives and MIAs, including the bodies of any deceased captives.

I also told Mohammad that if he wanted to meet with me during his stay in Lebanon, we could meet in Cyprus, Athens, or Rome, if he left me a message to that effect at the foundation's offices, and that I would go anywhere, anytime he asked. Mohammad made sure to mention repeatedly, that his friends were "imprisoned despite having committed no wrongdoing." He emphasized and declared several times that he was just a messenger and he wasn't responsible for the outcome of our conversations on a personal level. His desire not to take responsibility and to only be the messenger was expressed frequently. He wanted to know what assurances he had that the money would be paid if he fulfilled my request. I told him that the money would be deposited by The Lawyer in a trust fund and that if he succeeded in getting what I asked for, he would get the money from The Lawyer. Mohammad agreed.

Mohammad flew to Lebanon on Friday morning, November 13, 1992, by direct flight.

The sixth and final meeting between us took place in Copenhagen on November 23, 1992. Needless to say, I came to the meeting knowing that there were only two options: the first, that maybe this time our mission would succeed; and the second, for which I was also prepared, that we were, yet again, setting ourselves up for disappointment. To my terrible dismay, the second option was the one that materialized.

Mohammad returned from Lebanon nervous and depressed. He told me about his hard experiences in Lebanon, including the fact that his passport had been confiscated for several days. The state of his health had deteriorated even further. When he'd met Mustafa in Baalbek, his brother's response was extremely harsh and unambiguous. Mustafa claimed he had no information about Ron Arad, that he couldn't do anything to help, and that if he had any more information, he would turn it over to the Red Cross. He also said he did not consent to his brother's involvement in this matter, if only because of his health condition.

Mohammad was terribly upset by his brother's reaction. He announced that he was unwilling to receive any medical assistance and symbolically returned a few hundred dollars he had received from us for the trip. To my questions about the change in his brother's attitude, he said his brother was terse in his speech, angry, and more aggravated than usual, so he (Mohammad) had to follow his instructions. Mohammad said there were problems in the family and that he no longer wanted to be in contact with me, despite the help I had given him. When I asked him again if his brother knew whom he had met with in Denmark, Mohammad only noted that he had given his brother my business card. Mohammad told me once again that he emigrated from Lebanon against his brother's wishes and that his brother's anger with him only increased as time went by.

Mohammad Dirani also recounted this same story to The Lawyer and then severed the connection between us. On my last visit to Copenhagen, I was surprised to learn that The Lawyer hadn't seen Mohammad Dirani since that meeting either. At the time, I mistakenly thought that he had continued to represent him afterwards. I did not know that he'd cultivated this relationship with the Dirani brothers solely for the purpose of this mission.

To my great chagrin, a nearly yearlong operation with many ups and downs and contact with the person directly responsible for Ron Arad's captivity, along with the organizations that had information about him and other missing persons, ended with absolutely no result whatsoever. Despite the fervent hope (we all, of course, operated under the assumption that Ron Arad was alive), I was protected by the self-defense mechanisms that I have developed over the years. I knew my chances of success were quite slim, but even a small chance justified everything we did. I didn't feel an ounce of regret for this operation, not for one second. It was part of our immense effort to do everything we could, even if it involved many difficulties, as was the case with this operation as well.

A year and a half later, on May 21, 1994, the elite IDF unit "Sayeret Matkal" kidnapped Mustafa Dirani from his home in southern Lebanon. During his interrogation, he mentioned that his brother Mohammad had appealed to him to disclose information about Ron Arad after meeting in Denmark with an Israeli lawyer—that is, with yours truly. Mustafa Dirani attempted to use this as leverage with his investigators and claimed that if he'd known anything about Ron Arad, he wouldn't have hesitated to pass on the information to me at that time. Dirani was held in Israel for six years, until his release as part of a prisoner exchange deal with Hezbollah.

Twenty-six years later
Copenhagen, June 2018

During the three days we spent together, the Danish-Jewish lawyer and his non-Jewish wife told us that they observe the Jewish traditions of the Passover Seder and Yom Kippur—that they light the Shabbat candles on every Saturday and eat only kosher meat products. The Lawyer told us that he goes to the local synagogue occasionally on Saturdays. We made a highly emotional visit to the Jewish Museum in Copenhagen together and enjoyed wonderful exhibits that illustrate the special connection between Denmark's history and Judaism. We ended our visit on Saturday, right in front of the synagogue in Copenhagen. The sounds of prayer could be heard from within.

* * *

It was a very moving ending to a connection between two people who'd met twenty-six years earlier when they were in their late forties. When they finally met again, they brought the circle to a close and understood much more than they realized about the sanctity of the mission they struggled to fulfill together—the redemption of captives.

14

Every Available Pipeline

O ur attempts to create any kind of connection with the Iranian authorities—if not in the political arena, then perhaps through the
business sphere—obligated us to exert every ounce of imagination and
creativity we had and leave no avenue unexplored and take advantage of
every available channel or pipeline. In this case, it was a pipeline in the
most literal sense of the word.

For the purpose of our operations, I sometimes found it necessary to
call on my clients for assistance in the 1980s and 1990s. Among them
were some who had partnerships in international business ventures and
connections with oil-exporting countries. Iran, which was one of the
world's largest producers of crude oil, was one of these countries. I had
plenty of clients overseas during my forty-eight-year career as a lawyer.
My firm would advise on (among other things) risk management, a crucial global field of research with internationally adopted principles. The
field has become one of my firm's key areas of expertise over the years,
which allowed me to advise businesses and companies abroad.

Coincidentally, I was contacted by the CEO and owner of a large
European corporation, a person whom I'd never met and who reached
out to me through another client of mine. This person expressed interest in the Eilat-Ashkelon Pipeline, also known as the Trans-Israel
Pipeline, or the Tipline for short. The line was a joint venture between

the governments of Israel and Iran. It was established in 1968 to transfer Iranian crude oil from the seaport in Eilat, the city on the Red Sea, to another Israeli seaport on the shore of the Mediterranean Sea, in the city of Ashkelon. He asked for my professional help to try to set up an international business venture that would acquire the rights of the two former partners in the pipeline—Israel and Iran—or lease them for several decades. The aim was to circumvent the problematic nature of the failed partnership between Israeli corporation and Iranian corporation, allowing both sides to benefit from the arrangement as they did before.

I knew very little about the oil business back then, but I saw huge potential and quite a bit of logic in this plan, and much beyond that—it didn't take more than one conversation with the man for the idea to suddenly materialize in my mind that it was possible the people involved in the deal might develop important relationships with Iranian nationals, which could also benefit us in our endeavors regarding IDF captives and MIAs. Iran played a role in at least some of their cases, after all.

I shared the proposed program with a senior official in the Israeli economic world who gave me his blessing. Later, I also met with his successor—I happened to know him and his wife—and got his opinion on the business venture. His eyes lit up immediately. He had been a successful businessman and, as such, recognized the great potential of the plan along with the possibility of ending an intractable international conflict that demanded ongoing arbitration. It might also resolve Israel's energy problems. He saw the plan in all its different aspects, business and political alike, as a worthy undertaking. We began to hold preliminary talks with the client and even traveled together to meet with him in Europe.

I must point out that the client does not wish for his personal details to be disclosed in this publication, despite the excellent relationship that has been maintained between us for more than thirty-five years, due to the chain of events that followed.

As we grew closer, I shared with him my thoughts about the potential opportunity to help the IDF captives and MIAs. I refrained, obviously, from pointing to the Iranians as the party responsible for the plight of our missing people. I only cited their role as "collaborators." I decided to be completely honest with our client, since we'd developed a warm personal connection over the years, and although he is neither Israeli nor a Jew and has never dealt with any issues remotely related to captives and MIAs, he agreed to help.

In parallel, we continued to advance the pipeline project, which was to be a deal of global magnitude. As an attorney, I made sure not to turn the humanitarian issue I was promoting into something that might somehow bother the client, personally harm him, or sabotage the essential nature of client-attorney relations. However, later, especially during the times when we dined together or took a short break from doing business, I often talked to him about the significance of the captives and MIAs in my life.

During one of the client's business trips to Israel, I invited him to dinner at my home—something I'd never done with any of my other clients—and showed him a picture of a missing person's family that I had in my house. The photo shows casualties officer Ita Tamari together with Yonah Baumel, father of Zachary Baumel, the IDF soldier who has been missing since the 1982 Battle of Sultan Yacoub; Hadassah and Mordechai Fink, the parents of Yossi Fink who was missing in action in Lebanon; and Yusaf As'ad, Samir's brother, who was then still considered missing in action in Lebanon. I shared the story of each of the families with the client. I felt that I was able to convey to him the sense of terrible uncertainty that they must endure each day of their lives. In this case, too, as in many others where I was able to get people to join some kind of activity on the subject, I felt that my attempts at "recruitment" were successful.

We continued to promote the oil pipeline deal at the same time. An indirect negotiation began between the different parties—Iranian and Israeli—through intermediaries. One of the people involved in the deal was the Jewish tycoon Marc Rich, who is the founder of the international trading company Marc Rich & Co. AG (today Glencore International AG). Rich also did business with regimes that were under an embargo by Western nations, and his trading company earned billions of dollars thanks to oil deals with the Iranian Ayatollah regime. In the 1980s, he was indicted in the United States for tax evasion, fraud, and trading with the enemy, and he escaped with his partner, Pinky Green, to Switzerland.

My client introduced us to each other, an introduction that helped me immensely, since Rich, who was very connected to Israel and to his Jewish identity, provided me with a way to contact the Iranians. In September 1990, I went with my client to the city of Zug in Switzerland to meet Rich and his partner. The purpose of the meeting was strictly business at this point.

On September 30, 1990, after the meeting, I sent a detailed letter about the progress we'd made to an interest holder in the deal. This is what I wrote to him:

> The core of this issue is a renewal of the operation of the Eilat-Ashkelon oil pipeline in large output by moving oil imported from Iran and other producing countries and transporting it to European parties who will receive it in Ashkelon. For the purpose of this project, I approached one of the relevant potential partners and, following my inquiry, an envoy met on his behalf with one of the parties who have strong ties with the National Iranian Oil Company (NIOC) which has a financial interest in a European corporation. After my meeting with you, I received a proposal from this European element. Naturally, and due to the sensitivity of the issue, all parties operate by anonymous companies serving as proxies, but the companies involved are very large firms dealing with the subject of oil production vis-à-vis Iran and other producing countries.

> After accepting the abovementioned proposal, I initiated a meeting last week in Switzerland between the European element and Marc Rich, where it was decided to establish a joint body comprising the European company and Marc Rich, to suggest the matter to the Iranians and to the Eilat-Ashkelon pipeline company. Since I am the one facilitating this initiative, the advancement of which seems to me very favorable, I would be grateful if

you give me your blessing for the continuation of this initiative, which I will coordinate with you while using all required discretion and confidentiality.

On October 24, 1990, I received the following letter: "I wish to hereby confirm in writing, per your request, that we are interested in promoting the initiative discussed in your last message. My letter does not constitute consent to the details of said proposal, which will need to be formulated at a later date."

I told Uri Lubrani, the former Israeli ambassador to Iran and then coordinator of operations in Lebanon, about this chain of events. I reiterated my idea to try and use the connection created with the Iranians through my clients—in light of their strong motivation to promote the deal—on the issue of captives and MIAs. I added that my clients had agreed to help me on the condition that it would not interfere with any of their other business ventures and that their identities would not be publicly disclosed, a condition that I have been careful to observe since then and I continue to honor to this day.

In the end, despite the great efforts and the connections that we used in the process, the oil pipeline deal did not come to fruition. Incidentally, Marc Rich later received a formal pardon from US President Bill Clinton. President Clinton said that one of the reasons for his decision to pardon Rich was the requests made by senior Israeli officials to repay Rich for his extensive and long-standing contribution to the state of Israel, including through assistance in matters related to intelligence.

* * *

I continued to serve as legal counsel to the clients related to the oil pipeline deal for many years, and I continued to implore them to move heaven and earth in an effort to make contact with any Iranian entities about the humanitarian causes I was promoting at the time. Due to the highly sensitive nature of this subject, and because of my desire to avoid jeopardizing and entangling people who helped or tried to help our unremitting efforts to obtain information about the captives and MIAs,

I must be extremely judicious and can only provide a description using very general terms.

These clients, businessmen based in Europe, had close relationships with key persons and leaders in the topmost echelons of the Iranian regime. The business relations that we established were focused not only on oil but also in other areas, including agriculture and one of Iran's most important and iconic exports—Aleppo pistachios—in an attempt to promote it in global markets. Thanks to those connections, I managed to meet senior Iranian public figures, with the intercession of my clients and in their presence. I was asked not to publicly disclose their names, and I respect this request even twenty-three years after those meetings.

Of course, I reported the meetings to all those involved in the issue in Israel, including Defense Minister Rabin and his military secretary Danny Yatom, through Yossi Ginossar, who was the coordinator of the captives and MIAs mission, and to officials in the various Israeli security apparatuses. At this point in time—the period leading up to the Iranian elections campaign in 1997, in which President Ali Rafsanjani was replaced with President Mohammad Khatami—Iran experienced bitter struggles for power between various political parties, the leaders who headed them, and the different groups involved in that highly entangled elections campaign.

At a long meeting lasting eighty minutes that took place in 1995, in the presence of one of the directors of the international companies I represented, I met someone who was very close to one of the contenders for the upcoming elections. He told me, among other things, that during the years before our mutual acquaintance, he was involved with several other people in negotiations to release people who had been abducted and held hostage in Lebanon. He further said that he was still in contact with representatives of countries involved in various attempts to liberate the captives, including the release of Iranian citizens who were accused of criminal activity in Europe. During those negotiations, a request was also made by the French to obtain information from the Iranians about Ron Arad.

My companion added that he was directly linked to elements who'd helped to secure the release of hostages, including the British pastor Terry Waite, held captive for over four years in Lebanon, as part of the negotiations conducted with the mediation of UN Secretary-General Pérez de Cuéllar and his aide Giandomenico Picco. Because I was personally involved in these negotiations at the time together with Uri Lubrani, I was very much aware of all the details. In that negotiation in 1991, the only information that the UN secretary-general managed to bring us was "death signs," proof of the deaths of Yossi Fink and Rahamim Alsheikh.

The details my companion provided me gave me reason to believe that he was indeed in contact with the foreign elements dealing with these matters and was very close to the regime in Iran. When I asked him about his motives for meeting with us, he replied without hesitation: "I know that resolving the issue of the IDF's captives and the issue of Ron Arad will improve the general international atmosphere with regards to Iran." He added that he was well aware that there could be the promise of an additional reward for his efforts, of a more practical nature, in the areas of business and finance. Because he was a businessman, these motives were, in all likelihood, no less important to him. He stressed to me several times, without being sanctimonious about it, that he did not act out of any love for Israel or out of personal affection for me, but in the interest of resolving humanitarian issues, which would benefit Iran, the firm he was a member of, and also him personally. He flew to Tehran after our meeting, and we all kept the matter in complete secrecy.

On October 5, 1995, at a meeting with the prime minister, Defense Minister Rabin, and his military secretary, Maj. Gen. Danny Yatom, the minister was personally updated on the meeting with the man. At the conclusion of the meeting in the Ministry of Defense, I was authorized by the minister to continue my contacts with my companion and to meet with him alone.

After the aforementioned person returned from Tehran, we met again, this time in Germany. He told me that he'd tried to get more information during the time he spent in Tehran but was unable to do so. He also told me that during his visit there, additional Israeli elements were beginning to engage with him in regard to this issue. He said he feared for his life and asked to discontinue the connection with me. He was very polite about it, but he looked scared, startled by the sudden multitude of different channels of communication, so he probably got cold feet. And so, this intervention from another Israeli element put an end to the dialogue in the channel that I created.

The question of whether or not I believed the explanations the man gave me at the time is irrelevant. This is a well-known phenomenon that characterizes many relationships as people move from the stage of casual acquaintance and exploration of the connection to the more advanced stages, especially when those connections are formed in their own home field. At these stages, concerns, threats, and risks become far more difficult to deal with and much more daunting.

* * *

At the same time, and in a completely different arena, certain contacts were being made between Israel and Syria on the possibility of reaching a peace agreement. I asked Prime Minister Rabin to tell Syria that any information they had about the POWs and MIAs would need to be shared as part of the agreement.

For the purpose of advancing the issue, I met with two of the jurists involved in the contacts: Dr. Yoel Singer, then attorney general for the Israeli Foreign Ministry, and Military Attorney General Gen. Ilan Schiff. In June 1995, Singer drafted an explicit clause (originally in English), at my request.

The return of missing in action, prisoners of war, and bodies of dead soldiers

1. Each side undertakes to return to the other side all prisoners of war, missing in action soldiers, and bodies of dead soldiers and their remains belonging to the other side, that have not yet been returned (hereinafter "missing in action soldiers").

2. To the extent that such missing in action soldiers are not held by or under the control of either side, and without derogating from the responsibility of any third party who may hold such soldier—whether a state, an organization, or a group—to return such soldiers, the two sides undertake to cooperate by assisting each other in their efforts, whether unilateral or joint, to provide information about, locate, and return these in action soldiers.

3. The cooperation referred to in paragraph 2 above may include, among other things, the involvement of an agreed third party that will be given the task of taking all measures necessary to collect information and conduct searches for the missing in action soldiers.

4. In order to facilitate the implementation of the provisions of this Article, each side shall provide the other side with a list of the names of its missing in action soldiers.

5. The two sides will establish a joint ad-hoc working group in order to coordinate all the necessary activities in implementation of this Article.

6. Recognizing the supreme humanitarian importance of the Article, the two sides shall commence its implementation immediately upon the signing of this agreement with the goal of concluding the implementation expeditiously.

A full partner in dealing with the subject was the IDF chief of staff, Maj. Gen. Amnon Lipkin-Shahak, who received all the information and correspondence and was involved in the captives and MIAs issue and aware of all the relevant details. Lipkin-Shahak is regarded—by me and many others—as one of the great paragons of the entire country, an IDF commander of the highest standing.

We first met when I was a young parachute jump instructor at the IDF's School for Parachuting Training and Commando Warfare. Amnon arrived at the school with the rest of his class from a military boarding school that all enlisted in the IDF together at the same time. They were a wonderful bunch that included many people who later became top military and state officials. Together with my good friend, Shlomo "Tully" Toledano, I instructed both groups of jumpers formed out of their class of boarding school graduates, and that's how I met Amnon. His family also originated from Hebron, and we discovered that there was a connection between the Slonim and Lipkin families in early twentieth-century Hebron. Amnon and I became and remained true friends until the day he died. He was a faithful partner in my many years of activity searching for captives and MIAs and also a confidant who listened whenever I faced adversity and problems.

On November 4, 1995, Prime Minister and Defense Minister Yitzhak Rabin was assassinated.

Unfortunately, the peace treaty with Syria was never signed, and the contacts with the Iranians have not matured to produce any actionable knowledge that will end the uncertainty regarding our missing people.

15

From Russia to Africa, and a Short Stay in New York City

Shipments of tanning lotion, a bizarre visit to the circus, a surprise encounter at an airport in the remote parts of Kenya, an urgent meeting with an American pastor—and one worried wife who didn't understand where her husband had gone during a Broadway show. These were all a small part of the extraordinary experiences that came my way during the global campaign to try to obtain in every possible way—wild, original, and hazy though it may be—even the smallest amount of information about the fate of the Israeli captives and MIAs.

Over the years, as part of the search for information and contacts with agents that might be able to help, hundreds of meetings have been held, and numerous attempts have been made to reach every body or person in the world—including intelligence and security services—who might have had any relations or contact with Syria, Iran, and Lebanon. My attempts to obtain information about the missing soldiers from the Battle of Sultan Yacoub—Zachary Baumel, Yehuda Katz, and Zvika Feldman—also led me to Moscow. An IDF tank was displayed at a museum in the Russian capital at the time, which was recovered from that very same battle.

As part of my activities with my colleagues in the various teams working on the issue of captives and MIAs, both in the Shin Bet and in the Mossad, I was trying to reach elements in the Soviet Union that might be able to help indirectly in some manner, though generally the relations between the heads of the two countries' intelligence organizations were very good. A friend of mine who worked for one of the Israeli security services introduced me to a senior member of a secret service in the Soviet Union. He introduced me as a lawyer who was helping the MIAs' families and the state on a voluntary basis and from a humanitarian standpoint only. Through this senior Russian official—whose name I'll never be at liberty to disclose—I was hoping to reach that Israeli tank and try to figure out how it managed to roll into Moscow, of all places.

The Russian intelligence man invited me to be his guest in Moscow and promised to try to help me. The visit was arranged, and I flew to Moscow. The trip was known to all the relevant parties in Israel who gave me their approval and their blessing and assisted me with plenty of guidance and direction.

Upon arriving in Moscow, I was greeted at the airport by Misha, a representative of the Intourist travel agency. I knew that this wasn't a private travel agency, but rather an official state agency, just as I knew for sure that Misha—a handsome and very well-built fellow who introduced himself as the agency's representative—was a Russian secret service man. I arrived in Moscow with clear instructions on how to conduct myself, and knew I would be under surveillance at all times.

At the airport, I noticed a man who wouldn't stop staring at me. I ignored him. Many years later, in Israel, I encountered that same person, Yasha Kazkov, or in his Hebrew name: Yaakov Kedmi. Kedmi served as the head of Nativ, also known as Lishkat Ha'Kesher (Liaison Bureau), the body that acted as a unit of trust in the Prime Minister's Office—covertly, initially—in order to reach Soviet Jews and encourage their affiliation with Judaism, Zionism, and the state of Israel. Kedmi told me that he'd recognized me at the airport back then and was simply attempting to greet me with his gaze.

After arriving at the hotel sometime in the afternoon, I went down to the bar to have a drink with Misha, while being careful not to become intoxicated. To my surprise—these were pre-Google days—Misha showed incredible knowledge about my résumé. He certainly did his research on me, the kind that only a professional in the field of intelligence can do. Misha even quoted from the summaries I submitted to the Kahan Committee, which dealt with the massacre in the Sabra and Shatila refugee camps, where I represented IDF commander Amos Yaron.

Misha asked me what I would like to see in Moscow. The instructions I received in advance were to spend as little time as possible on leisure activities, but since I wanted to be polite and also actively promote the subject for which I arrived, I told Misha that I wanted to see a live performance at the Bolshoi Theater. Misha said the theater troupe was on a world tour right then. I said that I loved the Red Army Choir too. They, too, it turned out, were traveling around the world. "Do you like the circus?" Misha asked. With no choice, I answered in the affirmative, and we went to the circus.

We got to the circus, and it was a full house. Misha asked where I wanted to sit. I replied sheepishly, "We'll sit wherever you bought tickets," knowing full well that Misha was a person who didn't need to buy tickets to anything, anywhere. Misha asked again where I wanted to sit. I said that it didn't matter to me. But he kept on pressing me. I finally relented and said, "Let's sit in the center." Misha then approached two people who were sitting in the central row, placed his hand on their shoulders, and without saying a single word, the two immediately left their seats and exited the hall. "In my tourism office, when I put a hand on someone's shoulder, they stand up," he explained. I did not enjoy the circus performance, obviously. Besides, my head was in a completely different place.

The next day, I arrived at a hotel in Moscow for a tête-à-tête with the man who invited me, which turned out to be a meeting with an additional "tête." My host introduced me to his lady friend—a beautiful girl who was at least twenty years younger than him and spoke excellent English. The most striking thing about her appearance was her exceptionally tanned skin, like someone who spent most of their time exposed to the sun in the swimming pool or by the sea.

After a long talk about the purpose of my visit, which included many details and documents I'd received at home to give to my hosts, a personal conversation developed between the three of us. I told the woman that I came from a country with a very sunny climate, but thankfully we had Dr. Fischer, who was kind enough to develop some sunscreen products for us. She became very animated upon hearing this and asked me where she might be able to purchase such products. I promised to deal with the matter when I got back home.

When I returned to Israel, I contacted my good friend Asher Havkin, who had also been injured in the terrorist attack at the cinema in Tel Aviv in the 1970s. Havkin, who happened to be a friend of Dr. Fischer, helped me get a package of some of the company's sunscreen products, which I sent to the Russian intelligence man and his lover.

All the details of the meetings were reported to the Shin Bet. They requested that I be accompanied by a person whom I would present as "my assistant" on my next trip to Moscow. And sure enough, I did travel with "my assistant" on my next trip—a senior Shin Bet official who dealt with Soviet-related matters routinely but had never been to the country. When we met in Moscow with the Russian intelligence man, I was the king of the world to him—thanks to Dr. Fischer's product package, of course. I had endeared myself to him and, apparently, the entire staff in his organization, who spared no effort to reach out to any elements who might be able to assist us in our mission.

* * *

My long journey on the trail of the Israeli captives and MIAs led me to Africa too. My companion on this trip was my good friend David "Dave" Kimche.

Dave, who by the end of the 1980s was a private businessman, used to be one of the most senior intelligence men to serve the state of Israel and acted in this capacity for many long years. A very special and color-ful figure, he was an educated man with several academic degrees from

Israel and the Sorbonne in Paris. His dissertation for a doctorate's degree in international relations focused on the Afro-Asian Movement, and he was quite well-known internationally.

Kimche served in the Mossad starting in 1953, including in the Tzomet division (the one responsible for human intelligence) and later as the head of the Tevel division, which oversees intelligence and diplomatic ties with foreign elements. During his years of service at the Mossad, he went on covert missions in Africa, Asia, and Europe and worked under various assumed identities. After a service with many notable accomplishments in the Mossad, he was appointed director-general of the Israeli Foreign Ministry in 1980 and served in this role until 1986. He was involved in many political events in the state—including the First Lebanon War and the Israeli involvement in the Iran-Contra Scandal (dubbed in Israel, as in other places, as the Irangate Affair)—and fulfilled many different special tasks. He was a member of the Israeli delegation to the 1991 Madrid Conference, which was a joint American-Russian attempt to advance an Israeli-Palestinian peace agreement, and was also among the people who drafted the 2003 Geneva Initiative, which proposed a two-state solution to the Israeli-Palestinian conflict.

Dave later turned to the business world, where he engaged in extensive activities, including in Africa. For me, Dave was a kind of secret consultant with rich experience in the many worlds he inhabited and engaged with—the intelligence world, the world of statesmanship, the business world, and his vast knowledge about Africa and Iran. He was one of the smartest intelligence agents and statesmen I ever met, and he served me, personally, as a friend and advisor, one of the best I could wish for.

Dave had good relations with many African leaders, including the president of Kenya at the time—the dictator Daniel arap Moi, who was the ruler of the country from 1978 to 2002. In one of our many conversations, Dave and I raised the idea of meeting with the president of Kenya, who had very close ties with the Iranian leadership. I submitted the proposal to Defense Minister Yitzhak Rabin, and it was decided that Dave and I would travel to Kenya and have a meeting with Daniel arap Moi to deliver an official request from the state of Israel to assist in making contact with the Iranian regime on the subject of captives and MIAs. Seeing that the mission was highly secret, and given that Dave Kimche was world famous, it was determined that we would arrive in Kenya on a long and winding road full of different stops rather than a regular direct jet flight.

After a great deal of preparation, we received the planned route, the last stop of which was a very remote airport in Kenya. Dave and I, who were already very friendly with each other at this point embarked on the arduous journey in which we passed the time with long and fascinating conversations. At some point in our journey, we boarded a flight in a certain African capital on a light aircraft with one engine, which took us to the aforementioned remote airport. There, an official vehicle of the Kenyan government was supposed to be waiting for us to drive us to the president's summer residence.

All through the flight, for an hour and a half, the small plane experienced constant turbulence due to bad weather and was endlessly shaking, jerking from side to side, and rattling. We were very grateful to safely land at the airport, which had only one runway, at the end of which stood the "terminal"—a shabby tin building with three wooden benches in it. Dave, who, together with all his other virtues, was a very polite and courteous person, did not stop apologizing to me for having to go through these nine divisions of shaking hell just because he was a "famous and highly exposed person in this world."

While we were waiting alone in the "terminal" for the vehicle to come and take us to our destination, a young man with a thick beard entered the hall and sat with his back to us. Naturally, we completely ignored him. Suddenly I heard a whisper: "Ory?" I ignored the whisper too—I thought I mistakenly heard a name that was similar to my own—but after a few seconds, I heard again: "Ory?" I told Dave that the guy was whispering my name. Dave completely dismissed this. He might have thought that I was getting hazy due to the heat.

But then the guy turned to me and said to me with a clear voice and in a perfect Hebrew: "Ory, it's me, Nachi Elkin, your friend from Ha'Biktah." Ha'Biktah (The Cabin) was a restaurant in Tel Aviv where I used to spend many years with my fellow paratroopers, and that's where I had met Nachi. Only when I saw him standing right in front of me, and despite this huge beard on his face, did I recognize him. We embraced for a long time in front of Dave's incredulous face, which Nachi instantly recognized.

Nachi told us that he'd come to Africa as part of his business as a crocodile breeder and also to set up a pharmaceutical factory in the area. I politely dodged his questions on how and why we arrived in this desolate airport terminal. We all had a lovely conversation until the car finally arrived to pick up Dave and me.

Dave and I spent the rest of the trip laughing about how, at the end of this winding journey that was meant to cover the tracks of the "famous and exposed person," I was actually the one who'd been recognized.

The meeting with the Kenyan president took place at his private residence, over a hearty and heavily laden dinner table, with a fascinating conversation about Israel's technological and agricultural innovations, some of which Kenya happily availed itself. When we got to the main topic, which was the purpose of our visit, I was the main speaker. I told, as I usually do, about what happens to a family whose loved ones have disappeared or were taken captive by the enemy, while knowing almost nothing about their loved ones' condition. I showed the president pictures of the parents of MIAs, among them some Holocaust survivors who started families in Israel with a strong desire to open a new page in their lives, and a picture of Yuval Arad, the little girl who hadn't seen her father, Ron Arad, since she was a baby. I went on to describe the terrible hardship of a life of uncertainty, which involves enduring these torments for many years.

Dave went on to tell the president about my service in the army as a parachute jump instructor who had launched into the air some family members of African rulers—trainees in parachute jumping courses in Israel—and about my volunteering activities on the captives and MIAs front. Dave, who, as I've mentioned, was an expert on both Iran and Africa, told the Kenyan president that he might be able to help us make contact with the rulers of the Iranian regime and explained the benefits of such a mutual relationship. The president was very attentive but also very much realistic in his approach, yet he promised to try and help.

In this case, too, the efforts did not bear fruit. After a short period, it became clear to us that the answers Mr. arap Moi received from his colleagues in Iran were the same ones they used with everyone else who made inquiries in this area: that they knew nothing about the whereabouts or fate of our captives and MIAs.

And Nachi? He returned to Israel a few years later, opened a successful restaurant called Nachi and Betty Cook in Moshav Ramot in the Golan Heights. He later closed it and opened another restaurant in Tel Aviv. Many years after our surprising reunion in Africa, Nachi reminded me of this historic encounter. By then I was at liberty to tell him what Dave Kimche and I were doing at that godforsaken airport and how the entire state security apparatus had rigorously designed a near-perfect secret path for our journey but failed to take into account the bearded Israeli guy who would suddenly hug me at my destination.

* * *

In the early '90s, Tamy and I were on a private vacation in New York. While we were there, a member of the captives and MIAs team rang me and said that a cleric from the Anglican Church lived in one of the suburbs nearby. He was a close friend of Terry Waite, the Anglican priest released from captivity in Lebanon just a short time earlier. Waite, who'd been held by members of Hezbollah for 1,763 days, was released along with other hostages from Western countries thanks to the efforts of UN Secretary-General Pérez de Cuéllar. I was also told by the person who called me that this same cleric, Waite's friend, was willing to meet with me. We wanted to get his input about the conditions in which Waite had been held.

It was noontime. Tamy and I had tickets for a Broadway show that evening. I told Tamy that I had to go on an urgent meeting and that I would come back in time for the show.

I drove to the cleric's house, less than an hour's drive from New York City. The meeting extended beyond my expectations because it opened with a relatively long bout of unnecessary small talk. The preliminary part of the conversation was interesting in itself, but for me it was mainly intended to inspire trust—a very important part of the job. We shared stories about our lives and lineage. I felt that we started our mutual relationship on good terms just because of my prestigious pedigree. The fact that I wasn't a complete nonbeliever and that I was descended from several generations of rabbis did much to get him to show openness later on as well.

I asked Waite's friend every possible question I could think of: Where was Waite held? How many people watched over him? How often did they change shifts? Were those who guarded him also the ones who served him food, and did they ever talk to him? Was he tied up, or was he occasionally freed from his bindings? In this kind of meeting, you have to ask any question that comes to mind, even if it seems strange or trivial, to gain an understanding of the conditions that foreign hostages are held in. Even the most marginal detail can prove to be useful information, certainly when it comes to the identity of the guards and their scheduled duties.

He told me about the difficult conditions Waite had to endure when he was held in captivity. Some were things we'd already found out from other sources. Among other things, he said that most of the time Waite's hands and legs were tied and that his guards were changed often so that a personal relationship between the captives and the guards could not be formed.

The meeting with the cleric was getting protracted. I didn't tell him that my wife was waiting for me so he would feel comfortable and speak freely. And besides, I must admit: I was so immersed in the conversation that I completely forgot about the tickets to the show.

Meanwhile, at the hotel in New York, when Tamy saw that I wasn't coming back or making contact, she started to worry. Neither of us had mobile phones at the time. She called a friend of ours in New York, hoping he might know something, but he didn't know where I was either. I was acting in an irresponsible and uncharacteristic manner, which caused Tamy unnecessary woes in this case.

I returned to the hotel late in the evening, long after the show we were meant to see had already started. So, Tamy missed a Broadway show, but she earned an interesting story from her husband. She forgave me, of course. She never got angry about anything that had to do with my work with the captives and MIAs. After so many years together, she is my full partner in this endeavor and has shared all my experiences during every moment of our happy lives together.

16

Fink and Alsheikh: Return of the Righteous

O ne of the greatest challenges I faced when handling these cases was entering into the lives of people who were going through the worst and knowing my limits. Trying to get the correct sense of when they needed me to be there and when it was time to let go of them. Accepting—with pain but also with love—that you might become a punching bag for them, even when your intentions are good and entirely pure.

I arrived at the home of each of the MIAs' families after learning everything that was possible to learn about their personal background and the circumstances of their children's abductions. In this endeavor, I had help from members of the IDF Manpower Directorate's unit for detecting missing soldiers: Varda Pomerantz, Yonah Tillman, Ita Tamari, Itamar Barnea, Tzila Neumann, Orly Cohen-Geffen, Gabi Almashali, Shlomit Carmi, and the rest of the men and women of the IDF cadre of officers who worked alongside them. Another partner was Nissim Barda, who was appointed as the commander of the EITAN General Staff Unit in the IDF for detecting missing persons. I would visit the families as part of a daily routine and my ongoing relationships with them, even when I didn't have anything particular to report or say to them. We talked about current affairs, shared life stories with each other, and sometimes we even gossiped. Whenever I had something new to say, I would do it carefully, without letting them develop any expectations. This mission required me, certainly in the first phases of my role, to put a great deal of thought into every word that came out of my mouth, which sometimes made contact difficult. It's hard to have a warm, close relationship with a person when you know that you have to be careful all the time, because every word you say can cause anticipation, disappointment, disillusion, and even anger.

With the experience I gained and as the years went by, I have learned new things that have equipped me with the knowledge, tools, and sensibilities that a person in such a position needs to have in order to deal with families who live in a state of constant uncertainty. The connection with people who live daily in such distress is unlike any other connection. Beyond the need to be careful with your choice of words at all times, you have to learn to feel out, in the first few minutes of the encounter, what kind of disposition or attitude the family currently has. It will not always be reflected in the things they'll say to you. Sometimes you can feel it in their body language, and sometimes I received the information in advance from someone that a family was feeling terrible distress and that I should pay them a visit.

I was often called to meet with the families on short notice, without having the chance to get a deep look into what the cause of their distress was. Sometimes it was some mindless rumor they heard somewhere, and sometimes there was no particular reason and it was just a bad day, one of many in the course of the hellish existence the family was going through. My job was to be ready for it when I got there, even when I didn't know what was bothering the family, and to try to calm everybody down. This required the development of a technique that first and foremost protected the families but also protected me from the possibility that I'd make a mistake that would leave the members of the family in an even more difficult situation after I said goodbye.

I always spent a lot of time preparing for the first encounter with the family of a captive or MIA, but what actually happened was almost never like I'd anticipated. As soon as you walk through the door, they want to know who you are, what you are, why you're there, and why you are even helping them. The level of suspicion and skepticism is usually very high, and it takes time to build trust.

* * *

This was not the case when I made first contact with the family of the late Yossi Fink, who was abducted together with Rahamim Alsheikh by Hezbollah terrorists in the Security Belt—the area under Israel's control in southern Lebanon on February 17, 1986. Only five years later, in September 1991, we were informed that our missing IDF soldiers were no longer among the living, and it took another five years before their bodies could be brought back to Israel for a proper burial.

My entry into the Fink family's lives was, in relative terms, one of the least complex experiences for me. Mordechai and Hadassah Fink, along with their daughters Tzivi, Raichi, and Ossi, made me feel like I was part of the family right from the first moment. In my relationships with other families, I had experienced terrible ambivalence and mental conflict, heartaches and discouragement. I was told things that would be hard for anyone to hear. In the Fink's home, on the other hand, I never feared even for a second that I was going to be used as a punching bag.

Perhaps this is due to the family's British background. Hadassah was born in Hungary. Her father, Attorney Yossef Bernstein, was taken by the Nazis in 1945, and his fate is unknown to this day. His grandson Yossi was named after him. It was the family's hope that the name would bring good fortune to the newborn, in contrast to the fate of his grandfather. When our relationship was just forming, I told them that I went to Manchester once, having been invited by my dear friend Haim Topol to the premiere of *The Fiddler on the Roof*. Much later, Topol invited Hadassah and Mordechai themselves to see the theater show when they visited London in the framework of the advocacy work to have their son returned. When I found out that Hadassah was working with her mother, Ethel, in a small fabric store in Nahalat Binyamin Street in Tel Aviv, I told her that I spent my childhood years in that part of town. We enjoyed a relaxed and rather warm connection after these first few conversations.

In the Fink family home, which is warmly furnished and full of pictures, the picture of Yossi surrounded by his three sisters stood out. There was also a calendar marked with the days of Yossi's absence. At the entrance to the house, there was a picture of him in uniform, his face coated by a handsome beard. That was the same smiling face, whose features I could remember even in my sleep, that I would have to identify when the day came.

The Fink family lived on Mendele Street, a quiet street in Ra'anana, the city that was then also my own home. On one of my visits there, I happened to run into the neighbor, Nachman Tal, one of the senior officials of the Shin Bet, who lived in the house across the street. We'd been working together for many years on the issues of captives and MIAs of the IDF. Tal invited me to his house and gave me more details about the neighbors across the street. If my memory serves me correctly, they had never run into each other and did not know each other personally. This is the kind of thing that can only happen in our country: on the same small street, living opposite each other, are the family of a kidnapped IDF soldier and a senior Shin Bet officer trying to find him, and then there's me, standing in the middle, someone who knows both sides.

In the first meeting with a family whose loved one was kidnapped and is being held captive by the enemy, the amount of available information on the case is extremely low. This means that the expectations from those who, like me, represent the supreme executive authority in the country, are much higher than those who makes contact with the family on a daily basis. From the moment I recognized this, I made it clear to them that I didn't yet have any new information, but my colleagues and I were doing everything that we could and staying positive.

It was not easy to explain this to the family, because as part of my role I could meet with anyone from the prime minister to the Mossad to the military, and I had to do my best to get the families to lower their expectations and avoid giving them the impression that I knew more than I was letting on or that I might be hiding something. Of course, new facts and details certainly emerged from time to time, but there was no point in sharing them with the family as long as they were in the preliminary stage and not yet verified.

This task was particularly difficult in my meetings with the Fink and Alsheikh families. In this case, we knew with absolute certainty who was holding Yossi and Rahamim and the region they were in. The

Hezbollah terrorist organization instigated a relentless and crushing campaign of psychological warfare, which certainly affected the families and also anyone who tried to help them. Every couple of days, the families would hear something, read some article in the news, or receive information and all kinds of mixed messages from friends or various "knowledgeable sources." I myself received dozens of phone calls from these "knowledgeable sources" and advisors, none of whom were real professionals with relevant experience or knowledge, who had something to say and advice to give. These people obviously made phone calls to the families too. As someone who was particularly close to the family, I had to navigate through this swirling maelstrom of useless information to try and filter it for them, to calm them down, and to help them extract the relevant details from an immense jumble of mindless rumors and hearsay.

I soon learned that the Fink family had one of the most important assets human beings can possess: a wealth of friends, most of them traditional or practicing Jews. For the first time working in the field, I witnessed firsthand how real friends and a community that provides authentic support can help people who are going through such a traumatic event. There's no doubt in my mind that the fact the Fink family is a traditional family surrounded by traditional friends had a great positive impact on their ability to cope. As a secular person, I've always thought that it's a good thing for a person to have a rabbi, practice traditions, have a faith, a community, a synagogue they go to every Friday and Saturday… and certainly all of these must have special significance in such difficult times. I'm not suggesting under any circumstances that secular people don't have a shell of protection and support, but the framework I discovered in the religious families was more powerful.

I visited the Fink family's house almost every week. Mordechai and Hadassah are hiking enthusiasts, like me, and we used to talk about their trips. The Fink family acted with restraint and nobility, making life easier for everyone in contact with them. They never talked about other families in the same predicament; they didn't draw comparisons. They didn't argue with me and had no issues with why things were done a certain way, and even if they did make such a claim, it was expressed with an air of restraint that was more powerful than any outcry or public protest.

* * *

Shlomo and Sa'ada Alsheikh, humble and very hospitable people, also acted with restraint that inspired awe and was quite astonishing sometimes. Their quiet conduct made it even more difficult for me to deal with our inability to quickly find a way to bring back their son, Rahamim, to them. I really liked this special couple. The Alsheikh family was surrounded by the supportive and embracing community of Rosh Ha'Ayin, who waited with them for the return of Rahamim and Yossi. Through them, I got to know another social segment of the beautiful and good people of Israel.

I never had a shred of criticism, not even the slightest bit, to a family who preferred to behave in a different way and chose to cry out, protest, get angry, or go talk to the media. It's a perfectly legitimate response, and sometimes it's the right thing to do. If at any point in time, their public activity hindered our efforts, we just handled it. That's what I did with the Shalit family several times, during critical moments of the negotiations. I arrived at the tent they set up in front of the prime minister's residence in Jerusalem, which they'd inhabited for over a year while holding constant public protests, and invited them to an apartment across the street. There, over a cup of coffee and some cake, I asked them to lower the flames for a few days. A family can accept this request—to lower the flames slightly for a time—or reject it. But I never presented this as a condition for continuing my work. I thought, as I still do today, that it's the family's right to cry out and demonstrate as much as they want.

* * *

I never met Yossi Fink personally. I heard many stories about him. I knew what he liked. I knew his smile. All these stood before me when I was asked by his family—ten years after we first met—to identify his body. The bodies of Yossi and Rahamim, which were already embalmed

218

and prepared for burial, arrived in Israel in July 1996 in exchange for the release of forty Lebanese terrorists imprisoned in Israel and the return of 123 bodies of terrorists, a deal that was reached with the help of German mediation. I saw Yossi's and Rahamim's faces, and they looked exactly like they did in the pictures in their families' homes. These were the bodies of the righteous. When Hadassah asked me later: "What did he look like?" I replied: "I can only hope that I and everyone that's dear to me look like he did, ten years after our deaths."

Throughout the years and to this day, I have been in contact with the Fink family in times of both joy and sadness. Like other families, Mordechai and Hadassah became an inseparable part of my life. They accompanied me when my younger brother, Gili, was fighting cancer and when he passed away, and they shared in my happiness at my children's weddings. Even today, when Hadassah and Mordechai inform me of the time and date for Yossi's memorial, they always make a point of saying: "You don't have to be there. We're just letting you know." I came to the memorial services several times, and at some of them, I also talked about Yossi and his family. I've also spoken to the young IDF fighters from his unit—the Givati brigade—who were still little children when Yossi was kidnapped.

If I am ever approached by a psychologist who wants to do a dissertation for his doctorate's degree on the subject of dealing with uncertainty, I would recommend that he speak to the Fink family. They made the courageous choice to go on with their lives. It's the right choice to make but also probably the hardest one. The Fink family chose life, both in their years of uncertainty and after Yossi was buried in his hometown. They managed to keep their dignity and faith without getting angry at the world while continuing to smile and keep their friends close. It takes a lot of mental strength to do this.

17

From Hell A to Hell B: The Tormented World of Hadassah Fink, Mother to Yossi Fink, Abducted in Lebanon in 1986 and Then Murdered

For ten years we lived in uncertainty.

I was four years old when my father disappeared. We do not know to this day where he was buried. We thought we'd already paid the price, but apparently, we didn't pay enough.

When we were told that our son was "missing," we didn't understand what the word meant. What do you mean "missing"? How do you lose track of a soldier? We had great faith in the military; we believed that if you send your child to enlist in the IDF, they will come back home. It took us a while to realize what it means to be parents to a son who was missing in action.

We were in shock at first. We thought that Yossi would be back in a matter of days, because the Hezbollah communicated their conditions for the release of Yossi and Rahamim and also displayed some of their belongings, and I recognized the Kippah I knit for him. We would sit together in front of the TV with the people who came to see and wait to see what they were asking for in return for his release. But time passed, another day and another day, and nothing happened. Nothing was moving, and we were given instructions not to talk so that nothing we said could be taken advantage of. That, too, was just a guess. No one really knew what the right or wrong thing to do was.

There were two people who gave me strength in the early days: Nathan Sharansky and Yonah Baumel. Sharansky, a prisoner of Zion, was released from prison in the Soviet Union just days before Yossi and Rahamim were kidnapped. When they showed him on TV, I said to myself, "After everything he's been through, he still looks normal." Yonah Baumel, the father of Zachary, from the soldiers who were missing in the Battle of Sultan Yacoub, arrived at our house on Friday about a week after the abduction, holding the hand of a little girl with curly hair, and talked to us. After he left, I thought: "Here, it's been a few years since his son was kidnapped, and they've moved on. They're functioning. They lead a normal life."

How can you live a normal life when things are not normal? There are only two options: continue to move forward or fall. I remember on the eve of Israel's Memorial Day, when I heard a conversation on a radio show with the brothers of the fallen soldiers who paid the price, I thought to myself that the brothers shouldn't have to pay this price, which is constantly trying to keep your family from falling apart.

And that's what we did. I allowed the girls to stay home only on the day after the abduction, and then they went back to school. I sent Mordechai to work after one week, and I also went back to work in the fabric store with my mother. A person needs a purpose in life. If we kept sitting at home, we would end up in a mental institution. I forced the girls to continue their activities in the Bnei Akiva youth organization. When they went away on trips sometimes, I got angry, because they might have already forgotten the situation that we're in, and Mordechai told me: "But that's what you wanted, that they go on with their lives, and now you're angry?"

People didn't know how to behave around us. There were some occasions when family members got as far as the door to our house and turned back, as they had no mental strength to enter the house. There were people who crossed to the other side of the street when they saw us. Our friends came over in groups; they were afraid to come alone. We weren't big conversationalists before and definitely didn't enjoy standing in front of an audience, and suddenly, we had to talk all the time so that a conversation would develop and people wouldn't be feeling awkward.

We didn't build a work plan on how to go about it; we just lived our lives. We forced the girls to do what was necessary and forced ourselves too. When we went to meetings abroad, Ory said, "If you're already there, go watch a theater show as well." There are always feelings of guilt. Why should I enjoy myself instead of using the time to talk to someone? It's hard to enjoy yourself when you don't know where your son is and what he's going through. But if our group went out, we joined them because we didn't want to spoil it for the others. We were surrounded by so many friends; we kept getting wedding invitations, even from Yossi's friends. It was very difficult. If I went to a wedding and kept my distance, it was fine, but sometimes I broke down during the ceremony—it happened to me twice. And still, we didn't give up on going to weddings. I told myself that if I was invited, then it's a sign that they wanted me to come. Sometimes we went to three weddings a week.

Religion also gave us strength. We don't make our own fate—someone else did that for us. There are many questions and sometimes there's anger, but it is what it is. You accept your fate.

It was very difficult, of course. The Hezbollah was constantly playing with us. Apparently, that was their weapon. In the first five years, we received information that Yossi was alive. The army, too, told us occasionally that there were signs that Yossi was alive. Sometimes, the army rang to tell us that tomorrow there would be an article in the newspaper about the kidnapped soldiers and that we should know that it wasn't true and that nothing new had happened. The news was published, and all our friends called us; they were happy: It's written so and so in the paper, how could it not be true? We didn't want to spoil their day with the information we had, and the truth is, we also wanted to get carried away and believe it was true.

The Baumels were like a raging storm, and sometimes they got angry at us, said that we weren't making enough noise. Mordechai is an Englishman who originally comes from Manchester, completely different from Yonah, who came from New York, and it was hard for me to shout, too, even though I'm a spicy Hungarian woman. Sometimes they'd give us a bunch of advice before we went on a meeting with Rabin: "Shout about it; make him fight with all his tanks and warplanes," and I thought, "How can I go and tell Rabin to use force to release our sons, if it means ten others are killed? So that other mothers would have to go through something ten times worse than what I'm going through? Absolutely not. Thank God we don't have to be in Rabin's shoes and have to make that decision."

And in the meantime, I didn't know what to pray for or what to ask. Should I pray and hope that my boy is still alive? But what if he's seriously injured and going through terrible tortures? I wanted him to come back alive, the same boy he was before. I couldn't imagine what it'd be like to have a child coming back home after being tortured. I dreamed about Yossi only once during all these years. I dreamed he was back home, and I said to him, "Let me see you," and I was checking to see that everything was fine with him, that nothing happened to him.

We always used Yossi's room, but I didn't take his clothes out of the closet. I wanted him to see that everything stayed just as it was when he came back, including us. I wanted him to see that we kept our part of the deal: we kept hanging on, same way he did.

It's very difficult to live in this kind of uncertainty. I went to a meeting with the head of the IDF Manpower Directorate and told him: "Give me something, even something small, just something to hold on to." He had nothing to give me. I felt like they weren't sharing with us what they knew. In the middle of all that, in all the chaos around us, Ory was the most reliable source for us. Everything he told us was, as far as we were concerned, like Moses coming down from Mt. Sinai with god's word. We didn't always believe other people—we thought they had their own reasons for saying things and maybe were not always be accurate about it—but we believed everything Ory said. He told us everything he could tell.

Ory chose, along with the others, not to tell us in September 1991 that the bodies of Yossi and Rahamim were positively identified, so as not to spoil the joy of our daughter Tzivi's wedding. At the wedding, I saw on his face that he was going through something, but I was glad that he stayed until the end of the night and didn't come just for the sake of politeness and leave after ten minutes. The Alsheikh family had already been told and started the Shiv'a, and people told us that it might mean that Yossi was still alive, but we were waiting for the blow to come, and it did. The day after the wedding, Rabbi Navon told us that we could now sit for the seven days of mourning, if we wanted. We stayed home that week, but we didn't count it as the Shiv'a. Eventually, when they brought Yossi and Rahamim to burial—five years later—suddenly some cousin of ours announced out of his own initiative that there wasn't going to be a Shiv'a. Although we were staying at home now, too, people didn't know it was possible to come and console us.

Mordechai immediately accepted it when they told us that Yossi had definitely died. Ory saw that it was harder for me to accept it, that I was hesitant. He told me that the rabbi

Navon was very strict in his judgment, that he'd been given more than enough signs to rule in this case and determine my son's death, but I didn't want to accept it. After all, my own mindset hadn't changed since yesterday. I had nothing to hold on to. Maybe it was some kind of an escape. But subconsciously, I did realize that Yossi was no longer alive.

When they returned the bodies of Yossi and Rahamim in July 1996, there was a relief in this, in the sense that we now knew where our son was buried, and nobody could do anything more to harm him. It's the end of an era; there's a grave now. So now we're in Hell B, compared to those who were still in Hell A. My best friend, a childhood friend, told me, "It's over." And I said, "What do you mean 'it's over'? It just started. We haven't mourned Yossi yet." Even this girl, who was my best friend, didn't realize that we weren't mourning all this time.

After Ory identified Yossi, I realized that I had to accept his death. Ory also said that to me. Despite all the years that have passed since—thirty-two years—Ory remains a part of our lives. Every Friday, at 7:30 a.m., we receive a greeting from him before the Sabbath.

At first, we thought of burying Yossi in Jerusalem, but in the end, we decided to bury him near us, in Ra'anana. We don't leave an empty space for him at the dinner table. I find it to be a terrible thing when they do that; it won't let you carry on with your life. Our grandchildren tell their classmates about Yossi, their uncle, at their schools. It makes me glad to know that, thanks to them, he won't be forgotten, and we never even had to ask them to do it.

When our oldest grandson was about to enlist in the army, I was feeling pressure. Are we going to have to face all the fears again? But the truth is, if I had another son and he wanted me to sign a permit so he could enlist and serve in a combat unit, I would sign it. Is there any other choice? You never know in which direction luck might take someone.

18

The 1982 Battle of Sultan Yacoub:
The Two Who Are Yet to Return

The battle that took place in the area of Sultan Yacoub in Lebanon on June 11, 1982, during the early days of the Lebanon War, was a swift and bitter clash between the IDF and Syrian army units that were then occupying different parts of Lebanon. It is a battle that haunts us to this day. The results were dire: twenty IDF soldiers were killed in action, forty were wounded, two men were captured—Hezi Shai and Ariel "Arik" Lieberman, who were later returned to Israel in prisoner exchange deals—and three other soldiers who went missing in action—Zachary Baumel, Yehuda Katz, and Zvi Feldman. Their fate is unknown to date. For nearly forty years, their three families have had to live with the uncertainty of the fate of the son and brother who were sent to the army, never to return. After the publication of my book in Hebrew in 2019, Zachary Baumel's remains were returned to Israel and he was buried in Jerusalem after twenty-seven years of being missing—the only American citizen among our MIAs.

The preoccupation with this battle stemmed from the complexity of the subject and its various aspects: the problematic management, the harsh results, the war of versions waged in its wake, the fatalities, the wounded, the global efforts to determine the fate of the captives and MIAs and bring them back home, and the captives whom we did manage to return—among them Hezi Shai, who for a long time, was believed to have died in battle. All these different considerations left a deep scar in the lives of everyone involved and the life of our country as a whole. I would like to address my own part in this affair—my relationship with three special families that I met as soon as I took up my position in 1986.

* * *

The tremendous amount of research into the battle and its consequences revolved in large part around the study of the truth. I am very familiar with this subject—not only from a philosophical point of view but also from a practical angle—from the many years that I've dealt with the issue of captives and MIAs and from almost half a century working as an attorney. The years and experience have taught me that there are very few cases in which one can say that they know the absolute and indisputable truth about something—one's birth and death and simple facts like dates, which can be verified, for example. In almost every other case, attempts to establish the facts and findings are far more complex. I am even more skeptical than my counterparts in the EITAN unit—the IDF's detection unit for missing persons, where I now officially do my service in the reserves—because my work as a lawyer taught me how easily one can get lost among the myriad different versions of "how it really happened."

In a mock public trial that was aired as part of the Israeli television show *The Defendant Is Long Dead*, I served as defense counsel for Yossef Ben Matityahu, also known as Flavius Josephus, who is considered one of the few historians to write in real time about the Second Temple period in the first century CE. During the investigation I did for my part in the show, I met many people who said that you couldn't rely on what he wrote, because he was a prisoner of war held captive by the Romans (albeit in a gilded cage) in the city of Rome and therefore was completely biased in his analysis. I, too, was brought up on the notion that Josephus was historically a traitor. It took thousands of years of research to prove when Josephus got it right and when he was wrong. Either way, at the end of the program, he was acquitted by the honorable panel of judges: the chief justice on the show was former Knesset Chairman Yitzhak

Berman. Defending Josephus in court was one of the greatest intellectual challenges of my life. It taught me to be cautious and never take things at face value. Human memory is, in the end, a function of the work of agents of memory.

Let me give you a completely fictional example: three soldiers are sent to a terrible battle. One of them is mortally wounded on the battlefield and appears to be dying; another is lightly injured and can escape the battlefield but needs someone to help him; the third one remains completely uninjured and manages to help the soldier who was only lightly injured. When the hostilities finally come to an end, only the last two return to base. They are destined to carry with them the baggage of pain, guilt, and doubt for the remainder of their lives, and no one on earth could know the full truth: Was the badly wounded soldier truly about to die when they left him? What if they were wrong in their assessment as they rushed to extricate themselves from the battle? Or maybe saying they couldn't save him was just a bald-faced excuse that they told themselves and others, as an understandable mechanism of self-justification? The one who wasn't injured at all would have been able to carry only one of the wounded on his back. Like I said, this story is pure fiction, but I know very similar cases from my own experience in wartime. The conclusion that arises from this story, at least for me, is clear: there is no single truth in existence.

Hence my desire to obtain incontrovertible evidence—the closest thing to the truth that I can possibly reach. I've seen innocent people convicted of crimes they did not commit, and I've seen people acquitted and went scot-free, though there was absolutely no doubt that they were guilty of a criminal offense. Therefore, I am at the most cautious and skeptical point on the scale, the one that demands 101 percent proof. Nothing less will do.

This worldview was reinforced by several orders of magnitude after I learned the details of the Jibril prisoner exchange deal, which happened before I received the appointment for my position. As part of the deal, 1,500 prisoners and detainees imprisoned in Israel were released in exchange for three IDF soldiers—Hezi Shai, Nissim Salem, and Yosef

Groff. I was caught up for many years in Hezi Shai's incredible story, which served as the subject of many books and research papers. Hezi and his wife, Iris, both of whom I knew personally, were senior employees at Bank Leumi—the same bank that I represented in court for many years as an attorney. They are a symbol for me of how captives and their families handle the terrible trials of life in captivity.

I saw with my own eyes the intelligence reports—very serious and as supported by the evidence as can be—which stated: "It is estimated that Hezi is no longer alive." As Ronen Bergman tells in his book *By Any Means Necessary*, Iris Shai informed the IDF that she did not accept this determination. She said she knew he was alive, that the responsibility for his fate rested upon the Israeli government, and that she was going to knit him a sweater that would be waiting for him upon his return. The analysts at the intelligence bureau, Bergman goes on to tell, completely missed an interview with one of the senior operatives in Jibril's terrorist organization, Mustafa Khamis, which had been published in a Jordanian newspaper on July 9, 1982. In the interview, Khamis said that shortly after the battle, his men took an Israeli soldier captive, whose name was "Tessie Shai." Another year went by until additional information led to this interview again. Significant pressure was exerted all around the world and produced the long-awaited result: On July 5, 1984, two years after the battle, it was announced that Hezi was alive and included in a prisoner swap deal. Almost a year later, on May 21, 1985, he returned to his family.

* * *

This story and the deep feelings it stirred in me were faithful companions for me every step of the way during the years I spent with the three families whose loved ones did not return from the battle, and I keep in touch with them to this day. Despite all the attempts to end the affair—including the intention of the system to officially declare Zachary Baumel, Yehuda Katz, and Zvi Feldman as soldiers killed in action whose place of burial is unknown (a move vehemently rejected by the families)—I never gave my consent for any of them without clear and conclusive evidence.

* * *

Zachary is the youngest child of Yonah and Miriam, brother of Shimon and Osna. He was born in Brooklyn, New York, and up to the age of ten, attended the Jewish school in Borough Park. His father told me that Zachary—Zack, as they called him—was not very enthusiastic about the family's decision to fulfill the Zionist dream and immigrate to Israel. He wanted to stay with his friends in New York. Ultimately, the Baumel family immigrated to Israel in 1970 and settled in Kiryat Haim. After graduating from high school, Zachary chose to serve in the IDF as part of the aforementioned "Hesder" program for soldiers from religious families. He divided his time between his studies at the Har Etzion Yeshiva in the settlement Alon Shvut and his combat service in the IDF's Armored Corps, where he later became a tank commander. When he went to the war from which he has not yet returned, he was nearing the end of his military service. He was already admitted to study at the Hebrew University of Jerusalem and planned to study psychology.

His father, Yonah, devoted all of his life, energy, and dwindling fortune to the efforts to rescue the son who didn't want to immigrate to Israel in the first place, then learned to love the country and went to war on its behalf. I had the privilege of getting to know this extraordinary person; the least I could do for Yonah Baumel was to be at his side and support his efforts as much as I could.

I met with Yonah Baumel dozens and maybe even hundreds of times. I really liked him personally. Not only because of his relentless determination and tenacity but because he was truly a very special man. In one of our first calls, Yonah told me, "I don't really understand why you're doing this. I don't understand why you insist on getting your head into this hellish subject, but I'm glad you're with us." He then revealed to me that he had conversations with President Haim Herzog, the man by whose recommendation I was appointed to this role. Herzog told him that anyone who entered this world "must be different, couldn't be a normal person, and Ory is not normal in a positive way." Yonah also told me: "We're going to get angry with you, and occasionally we'll tell you things that will be difficult to hear because as far as we are concerned you are the representative of the kingdom. We're going to be trading jabs sometimes, but you have to understand that it's nothing personal."

In September 2008, a few months before he died, Yonah sent me a personal email, the last one he wrote to me, with very harsh criticism directed at pretty much everyone. But the warm words he used with regard to me in his letter softened the blows.

In that email, which was very moving for me, Yonah wrote that he wanted to offer my name as a candidate for the Israel Prize. I rejected the offer. I have received many awards in my life, but for me, his letter was one of the biggest awards I could ever receive. Yonah was the true flag bearer of the families of the captives and MIAs. He used polite terms, but the message was bitter and sharp. Yonah claimed, among other things, that nothing was being done, that his son had been forgotten, that the establishment showed preference to the "fresh MIAs" over the "veterans," and that everyone wanted to forget that battle. I agreed with all his claims, of course, though his statements were sometimes not factually accurate. And I'm not saying that just because one shouldn't judge a man in his time of grief. In my view, these parents are allowed to say everything, to get angry, to make accusations—so long as the state does not fulfil the duty it had from the day it recruited the son or daughter to the armed forces: to return him to his family, dead or alive.

And yet, despite that, the families are not aware of all the efforts that are being made—efforts that enlist the entire array of the state's security apparatus, military, and political system—to bring the soldiers back home from captivity. Almost all government ministries and policy makers in the country are directly involved in these efforts, not to mention the tremendous efforts made in the military and intelligence sector. The names of the MIAs are raised in almost every official meeting of Israel's prime minister and government ministers with foreign powers and various other parties all around the world.

On October 28, 1993, I wrote the following message to Yitzhak Rabin: "I find it appropriate once again to request from you that the subject of the captives and missing soldiers—both the necessary information with regards to their fate and the efforts to return them home—be properly defined and given special priority when discussing these issues with negotiators in the process of recognition and peace as a 'Special Issue on the Agenda,' as I believe that defining the issue in this way is of the utmost importance—in addition to the effort in itself."

After I sent this letter, Danny Yatom, who was then Rabin's military secretary, wrote: "Prime Minister and Minister of Defense Rabin has noted that the issue of the soldiers who are missing in action in the Battle of Sultan Yacoub is handled in collaboration with the most senior Palestinian officials, and he has distributed new guidelines which state that the captives and missing soldiers issue enter immediately and formally into the agenda of the negotiations with the Palestinians. The subject will be addressed in other channels of the negotiations as well."

Since Zachary Baumel was an American citizen, I approached almost every senator and house representative and also reached out to the US vice president at the time, Al Gore, and Yonah was also busy: he met with thousands of people in Israel and all around the world. Thanks to his great efforts, in November 1999, US President Bill Clinton signed the Israeli MIA Act, H.R. 1175—"To Locate and Secure the Return of Zachary Baumel and other Israeli Soldiers Missing In Action." The bill was approved in the US Congress by an overwhelming majority. It requires the American administration to raise the issue of Israeli soldiers missing in action in any official contacts made with Syria, Lebanon, the Palestinian Authority, and any other party in the region that may be able to help in the efforts to locate the missing soldiers and secure their return home.

There was no politician in the world who ever made contact with Israel and was not approached through every possible avenue, both open and secretive. The issue of the missing soldiers kept so many people occupied, but unfortunately these efforts have produced little in the way of results. The families appealed to anyone they managed to contact, and I always tried to do my best to accommodate them in terms of approaching different people. When their requests could not be implemented for various reasons—sometimes I, as the envoy, was the one who took the heat for it. And despite that, it's still my strongest conviction that these families have every right to be angry, because the only thing that's important is the outcome, and in that respect, we have failed.

Where one's efforts do not meet with success, there's a place for people like Yonah Baumel, who devoted his entire life to the subject and was a one-man foreign office and intelligence bureau. His widow, Miriam, tells me occasionally: "I'm not like Yonah. I didn't choose my words carefully, and I was always angry."

I replied, "You were perfectly fine, just like everyone else. But sometimes, it's even more poignant when you speak softly and with a civil tongue in head, like Yonah did."

* * *

Yehuda Katz, born in Ramat Gan, the son of Yossi and Sarah Katz and brother to Farhiya and Avi, also chose to enlist in the army as part of the "Hesder." In conjunction with his service in the IDF's Armored Corps, he studied at the "Kerem B'Yavneh" yeshiva. Yehuda intended to work in the field of education in the future.

His parents, Yossi and Sarah Katz, Holocaust survivors, were very special. As religious people, they had a strong bond with the rabbis of their community, and the fact that I was descended from a great rabbi's family was one of the topics in our many conversations. Yossi often told me that I was a "lost son." He also had many conversations with me about basketball and the Maccabi Tel Aviv team—it was during the same time when we started doing the ceremonies for the Variety children as part of the Maccabi basketball games—and he was quite knowledgeable about the sport. Sarah was a noble woman, and not just for the fact that she was milder in her manner than some others but because of the way she expressed herself. Whenever we had a meeting, she always made sure to take interest in me and ask me how I was doing first thing. The sister, Farhiya, was, and still is, active in a dominant and very respectable way in the efforts to bring her brother back home. After the death of her parents, she took upon herself this sacred mission, to continue to deal with the matter until Yehuda returns.

One could learn about the nobleness of this family from the way in which Yehuda's father, Yossi, described in the book *Where Art Thou* the moments when they were informed that Yehuda was missing in action:

The small delegation from the city's IDF Civilian Liaison unit came with a doctor, but no one in our family collapsed or felt faint. I think I even said "thank you very much." I recited a chapter from the book of Psalms and briefly called everyone who needed to know on the phone. We didn't need to take any sedative pills or anything like that, Sarah and I. I'm no Superman, and I can't really explain it, but not a single crack formed in my wall of faith, not even in those terrible hours. And then, when everybody gathered, something wonderful happened, that holds us together with steely, unbreakable bonds: we looked straight at each other, I looked at Sarah—the delicate mask of her face which even the signs of shock and grief could not hope to crumble—and Sarah looked at me, and we both looked at Avi and Farhiya, and they looked at us, and then at each other, and we knew. There was no need to say anything, only the hearts were relaying messages to each other: we're not giving up, under any circumstances. We're going to fight for Yehuda.

Zvika (Zvi) Feldman, the eldest of four children, was born in Tel Aviv to Avraham, who lost his entire family in the Holocaust, and Pnina, who immigrated to Israel from Morocco. Zvika is named after his grandfather Zvi, who was murdered by the Nazis. After completing his mandatory military service, he worked as a nature and sciences class guide in high schools and had been accepted just before the war broke out into the fall semester in university. He also planned to marry his girlfriend at the time.

In Tel Aviv's Kiryat Shalom neighborhood, I met a couple of modest people. At our first meeting, Avraham told me how he had come to Israel full of faith, wishing to turn a new page, how he met his wife here, and he joked about the trials of a meek Yiddish-speaking Ashkenazi Jew from Europe marrying a fiery immigrant from North Africa. From his childhood, he told me, he knew how to sing and loved very much the cantorial performances of verses from the Jewish scripture and from medieval Jewish music. He even sang for me a chapter from the scripture in a clear and very melodious and pleasant voice. It only took half an hour for me to fall in love with this couple. I came to visit the house of people who didn't know what had happened to their son, and instead of bombarding me with questions, they took a long time to get to know me and ensure that we were well acquainted and fond of each other. Only toward the end of the meeting did they ask, almost in a whisper, if I knew anything new about Zvika. I told them I didn't know any more than they did.

I became very attached to the Feldman family, far beyond the mission I was attempting to accomplish. Over the years, I visited their home almost every week. There was always a wonderful meal waiting for me there, Pnina's handiwork. In a small shed near his house, Avraham was producing homemade bath sponges out of the ropes he got made of loofah plant fibers, in order to preserve his father's tradition of producing handmade ropes. In addition, he was a painter and created engraved art in copper with incredible talent and is considered an expert in the field. During one of our meetings, Avraham asked to draw me. I have the beautiful painting in my home today, of course.

Avraham later passed away, and Pnina became gravely ill. Even when she was already having trouble identifying people close to her, whenever I called her on Friday to wish her a good Sabbath, as was my habit, she would immediately recognize my voice, ask how I and the Mrs. were doing, and ask if there was any news with regard to Zvika.

I spoke to many people about Avraham and Pnina Feldman, whose story is the quintessence of the Israeli story of hope and sadness in this country: a man who lost his entire family in the Holocaust, entered the land of Israel as a penniless immigrant, and met a girl who came from Morocco via the youth immigration organizations. Together they turned to a new page in life and history, and in 1982 their new world was suddenly ravaged by a terrible calamity. They didn't know that there was no hope for the problem to be resolved in their lifetimes.

When Zvika was a high school student, he wrote "I Am Here," a song about life in captivity, not knowing that he was writing of his own future life:

I am here, yes it's me
The last of the last
It's been a long time since then
More than just a few years
I did not fall alone
Of course not
But a pity that so many others did
The best of the best.

"Until Proven Otherwise, My Brother Is Alive!" The Words of Anat Cohen, Sister of Zvika Feldman, Missing Since the Battle of Sultan Yacoub on June 11, 1982

Maybe it's a cliché to say of someone who never returned from the war that he was special and perfect, that he was the salt of the earth, but I'm Zvika's sister, so I'm allowed to do that, and in any case—I'm telling the truth. Zvika really was those things.

From my childhood, I admired my brother, who was six years older than me. A Zionist political idealist, a leader in the local scouts, who loved his country and the land. Smart, charismatic—when Zvika entered the room, people would go silent. His appearance would speak for itself. They said he was tough sometimes because he didn't smile much, though he had a crazy sense of humor. He was a real bookworm, with a talent for writing and drawing. When we were children, Zvika always made sure we spoke proper Hebrew. It mattered to him because we grew up with parents who came from the diaspora—a father with a prominent Polish accent and a mother who came from Morocco.

Our parents, Avraham and Pnina, are the source of all the good values that Zvika and the rest of us absorbed. Dad lost his entire family in the Holocaust, about a hundred people in all, and he himself was saved just because of his talent for painting. My grandfather, his father, knew what was going to happen after the Germans entered Poland and his daughter's fiancé was shot. He filled my father's pockets with money and told him to run away and go to his brother Yitzhak's house on the Russian-Polish border. When my father got there, he was captured by Russian troops. My father knew how to draw and sing very well, and he was also fluent in several languages. He spoke to the Russians in Russian, and they sent him to a brutal work camp in northern Russia, where people often died at night in their sleep in the cold weather. They asked him if he knew how to do anything, and he said: "I can draw." The camp commander gave him pictures of different people, including Russian leaders, and asked him to draw them. The commander threatened him that, if he failed, he would be shot to death. My father, who was unrivaled at painting portraits, asked for a charcoal pencil and some paper. The commander was amazed by his paintings and made him the camp painter. My father was very resourceful; he shared the food he received with the criminals and murderers interned at the camp, and that's how he managed to survive.

My father arrived in Israel as a soldier in the Polish Anders' Army. Here, he took a British officer's uniform without permission, forged an official stamp to arrange himself a pass to leave the army camp, and without knowing a word in either Hebrew or English, got on a bus and traveled to a family relative who lived at Kibbutz Giv'at Brenner. In this way, he defected from his army unit and remained in Israel. Dad had crazy optimism, which saved his life and later helped him deal with the disaster that had befallen him.

Mom immigrated from Morocco with the help of the Aliyat Ha'Noar (The Youth Immigration) organization. She lived at Beit Ha'Halutzot (the home for female pioneers) on King George Street in Tel Aviv and met Dad at a party in town. He was a regular Don Juan who was thirteen years her senior but looked much younger than his true age, and she was captivated by his charm.

My parents had four children with exactly three years between each birth, and we all got named after members of my dad's family who perished in the Holocaust. Zvika, the eldest, is named after Hershel Zvi, Dad's father. I was named after my grandmother, Yentl. After I was born, Mom and Dad didn't know how to transform the name Yentl into a Hebrew-sounding name and kept arguing about it. A nurse who happened to be there overheard the argument and offered them the name Anat. Dad still kept calling me "my little Yentl," until he got sick with Alzheimer's and no longer remembered that he called me that. Itzik and Shlomi are named after dad's brothers, Yitzhak and Shlomo.

Zvika inherited dad's painting talent and sense for music. He played the harmonica, and when we were little, he painted pictures from Walt Disney films for us. And then he drew pictures of us. He also used to go folk dancing. He always said: "I dance on Sunday, Monday, Tuesday, Wednesday, Thursday, Friday, Saturday." Zvika was the life of the party in the dancers' group. We all started going dancing because of him and went together with the guys from the dance clubs on hiking trips across the country.

Zvika planned to be a tour guide. He took an Israel studies course at the Yad Ben Zvi college and research institute in Jerusalem and taught a class on "Shelakh" (Hebrew abbreviation for Nature, Nation, Society) at the Hadash High School in Tel Aviv. Zvika enrolled in archeology studies in the Beit Berl College. The letter that said he was admitted to the college for his studies came when he was already officially classified as missing in action.

* * *

I have very accurate memories, not only of the events of that terrible day, but also the days that preceded it.

On Saturday, we were all at our home, and there was a very pleasant atmosphere in the house. Music was playing in the background. Zvika particularly liked the old-timer's songs of Israel and was also crazy about The Beatles. Suddenly, there was a knock on the door. My brother Itzik who was a military police officer, was called on duty by the IDF during the 1982 war by Directive 8 and joined a paratrooper unit. He was then stationed in Lebanon, at the IDF outpost in the city of Tyre. My parents were in total state of shock. I served as a bureau clerk in the IDF's Ordnance Corps at the Nathan Military Camp in Be'er Sheva, and I was supposed to be on my last leave before getting discharged. They asked me to return to base the next day, early in the morning. Zvika was scheduled to leave the next day for reserve service in the Tze'elim army base down south. Shlomi was still a high schooler.

Zvika went to the place where we kept our large duffel bags at home and asked me: "Which bag do you want, the orange one or the military one?"

Mom asked him, "What are you doing?"

"I'm packing my bag," he answered. He knew he wasn't going to Tze'elim anymore. Zvika put his two mandatory items in the bag: a large orange candle, which would function as a bonfire if there were no wooden planks around, and the harmonica.

The next day, Sunday morning, Zvika and I left the house together. Mother ran after Zvika and told him: "You didn't tell me which Saturday you're coming back on."

Zvika turned around and answered her, "I don't know which Saturday I'll be back on," and kept going. That was the last sentence that Mom ever heard from him, and she could never forget it.

That night Mom had a dream that a delegation from the city's IDF liaison officer's unit came to our street and knocked on the neighbors' door, the Falcon family. Rina Falcon told them: "The Feldman family lives in the house opposite. What happened?"

"We need to announce to the Feldman family," they answer.

"But what happened to them"? Rina shouts after them, and they knock on our door and announce that Zvika is missing in action.

Mom woke up scared and told Dad about the dream. Dad tried to calm her down, told her everything's going to be fine. But Mom's dream came true: a few days later, when the announcers came to our house in the early hours of the morning, my parents were still in bed and heard the knock on the Falcon family door and the conversation with Rina the neighbor. When the delegation reached our door, my mother opened the door and said: "I know, Zvika is missing."

But even before the announcers came to us, I was going through very difficult days at the army base. I felt distressed, suffocated, felt like something was about to happen, and not just because I was busy with recruiting soldiers who were going to be sent to war. My parents constantly stood in front of my eyes. I heard my mother scream in my head.

One night I dreamed that Zvika was sitting on a tank on a bright sunny day, waving at me with his hand. Despite the sun in the dream, the feeling was that something bad was about to happen. I woke up with a heavy heart and went to the bureau. I arrived very early. Only the lieutenant-commander of the battalion was in the office. As soon as I got in, I saw a light flicker on the switchboard. I picked up the phone. From the other side, I heard the voice of my mother's boss at work: "Hello, can I talk to Anat Feldman's commander?"

I threw the receiver away, ran out of the office like crazy, and I shouted, "Something happened to Zvika."

The lieutenant-commander picked up the phone and heard that Zvika was missing in action. He ran after me, grabbed me, hugged me, and tried to calm me down: "He wasn't killed, he's just missing."

But I didn't relax. I cried out to heaven, to God: "What have you done to me?!" Someone came from the clinic, they gave me something to calm me down, put me on a Rom Carmel military vehicle, and drove me home. The drive from Be'er Sheva to my parents' home in Tel Aviv just wouldn't end. It was the longest car ride in my entire life.

To this day, I have the image that I saw when I entered the house carved into my mind: Dad was hugging in his arms a picture where Zvika painted himself, his eyes were swollen from the tears, and he kept mumbling "my Zvika'le, my Zvika'le." Dad was very sensitive. He knew how to be joyful, and then he also knew how to cry. For him, Zvika, his firstborn, was like a victory over Hitler. My mother sat on the couch and was completely devastated. Itzik and Shlomi were quietly lying somewhere in the house. I ran over to Mom, put my head over her, and curled around her body. I wanted to be like a fetus at that moment; I wanted to become absorbed into her body and be the little girl who didn't understand anything. At this point, we already knew that Zvika's entire tank crew had disappeared in the terrible Battle of Sultan Yacoub and that nobody knew what had happened to him.

Mom's sisters soon started to arrive one by one and made some food for us, so we could at least have something to put in our mouths. We had a small mixed black dog called Teddy that Zvika took care of. It got under Zvika's bed, started howling, and refused to come out. Mom asked my aunts to make him something tasty to eat, but he wouldn't budge. The dog just didn't want to eat. It's as if he felt that something bad had happened to Zvika.

The house was filled with army representatives. The one who was our main source of hope and air to breathe was the IDF chief of casualties, Varda Pomerantz. It was only after many years that we learned that she actually saved Shlomi. When he enlisted in the IDF, she occasionally summoned him to come to her bureau; she had conversations with him and acted as his psychologist. She managed to extract all the evil that was clawing at his soul.

A new life began, a difficult routine, in which my mother set the tone. She was the strongest person in the house and had the final say on every matter. My mother was full of hope. She came from a traditional Moroccan house. Her late father was a well-known practitioner of Kabballah traditions, a very wise and righteous man. She saw him in a dream standing in front of her wearing a white robe, all shining with bright light, promising her that all will be well. I later traveled with my mother to a meeting with the king of Morocco, who received us with great honor and promised to try to help get Zvika back home. He promised Mom that if Zvika returned, he would hold a big party in his honor and asked her to pray for his own sake at the synagogue. The gift the king gave her, an ornate Moroccan tray with a little jug for tea, Mom gave to Ory.

Mother kept saying to us, "Zvika is alive," and when she said, "Zvika is alive," the whole house felt it and decided that Zvika was still alive. Whenever any of us started to feel bad about it, Mom said, "Zvika is alive." My parents would always leave the door of the house wide open just in case Zvika might come back one day, and they always kept an empty chair for him at the dinner table on the holidays and put a plate and silverware in his spot.

Dad always said that Zvika's Holocaust is more difficult for him than the Holocaust in which he lost his entire family, because back then he didn't have anyone to turn to, and today he has a state, and his son went to battle on behalf of that state and never came back home.

I didn't agree to get discharged from the army because I knew that Zvika wouldn't want me to do it. We did everything we could to learn what happened to him. Throughout the years we always felt that we were being sidelined, that we didn't matter to anyone. Everybody else's case got taken care of, and ours didn't. The people we met with just repeated the same rhetoric they always used: "We've done everything, we are doing everything, and we will do everything we can to find out what happened to the missing persons. Don't think for a moment that we gave up on it."

Of all the public figures we met, I was impressed by two, who I really felt cared about us and haven't forgotten about the boys: the late Menachem Begin and the late Yitzhak Rabin. At his meeting with us, Begin took off his glasses to wipe his eyes which had tears in them. He truly felt our pain. At one of our meetings with Rabin, we were speaking very furiously. I said to him harshly: "One day you're going to stick your heads in the sand with shame for not doing enough." Rabin looked at me and said in his quiet voice: "I wish that the day would come when I'd have to bury my head in the sand from the shame and say we were wrong, but I would also know on that day what happened to them."

We continued living our lives with sorrow and pain deeply embedded in our souls, but we never stopped living. Mom always said, "We have to keep living, we won't give up until Zvika returns." When Shlomi went to the folk dances for the first time, they stopped the music out of the shock when he came in. Shlomi looks very much like Zvika. Our parents wouldn't let us fall into the abyss. Over the years we got married, bringing them grandchildren and joy. To this day we are a very warm family, and we are all connected to each other.

* * *

Ory entered our new life too, and has not left it to this day. Even Zvika's friends have disappeared over the years—except for one friend who has been in contact with us to this day—but Ory never left us, no matter if he was in an official role or not. His role is at the human and moral level. A thread of grace has continued to run in his family throughout the ages. They don't call him Ory ("my light") for nothing: he is a truly enlightened human being.

As far as we were concerned, Ory wasn't just a representative of the system, the same system we didn't like, that we were angry with, that we bad-mouthed. We took him out of this equation. He was part of the house; he belonged to our side.

For my parents, Ory was a dear man with an attentive ear. My mom consulted him about everything. She knew he would help her with everything. When my brother Itzik got divorced, Ory sent a lawyer to help, who didn't want to take any money from us. My mother refused to not pay the fees, so Ory said, "Donate the money to the Variety charity."

I received some help from him too. I had to give a speech once at some conference on the subject of the soldiers who were missing in action. I called Ory to read him the speech I had written, in which I attacked the system, even though he was supposedly part of that same system. For me, he was already a family member, and I even dared to ask him if the speech was strong enough. Ory listened to the speech and asked: "And what about the people you need to say thank you to?"

I said, "You're right," I hung up the phone and added his name, even though that was really not what he meant for me to do. When I gave my speech, I attacked everyone, without taking my eyes off them, and finally said, "I want to say thank you to a dear man, Ory Slonim." And he wasn't even in the crowd.

When my father passed away, Ory was here for the Shiv'a, and when we had a memorial service held at the synagogue, he also arrived with his wife, Tamy. I remember people asking me who they were, because it was clear that they weren't family.

How do you know that a person is truly great? It's the small things where you get to see the greatness of a person. When Ory's mother passed away, I went with Itzik and my mother to pay our respects. Ory is connected to world leaders and other dignitaries, and we are just a little family from Kiryat Shalom. We saw Ory surrounded by people and sat down somewhere at the edge of the room. As soon as Ory noticed us, he left everyone and came over to us. He asked my mother: "Pnina, what are you doing sitting in the corner like that?" And he started bringing over all the important people who were there. He didn't take Mom to meet them—he brought them to meet her and introduced them to her. It's impossible to wrap your mind around what he did for this humble, shy woman, how he honored her. I remember how elated she was. When we left, my mom said, "Wow, what an honor he gave me."

Ory's connection to our family is something that's truly rare. Mom suffers from Alzheimer's today and no longer remembers those closest to her, but she remembers those who've been burned into her soul, and Ory is included in this group. I told Ory that he can stop calling Mom because she didn't remember anyone anyway, but he insisted on continuing to do it and claimed that she remembered him. I couldn't believe him—Mom couldn't even remember her own sisters anymore—but Mom herself told me: "Ory called me."

* * *

It's been thirty-six years, and Zvika is still missing.

I don't go to any of the ceremonies on Memorial Day. I don't want to be officially part of the family of the bereaved. I just want to stay quietly in my own corner, so I sit in front of the TV, and I can't stop crying. Everything floats again and rises back to the surface, into my consciousness. I'm inside of this, whether I want it or not, and for me it's not over yet.

On the first day of the First Lebanon War, the cousin of a good friend of mine was killed in action, and I went with that friend to console his mother, the friend's aunt. A few days later, when that same aunt found out that our Zvika went missing in action, she told me: "I envy your mother, because your mother has hope." A few years later she said to me: "I take back what I said. I don't envy your mother; I feel sorry for her. At least I have a grave to cry on, and your mother doesn't have even that."

We traveled all over the world; we even reached the pope. We tried, we ran around, we did our best—and the result is zero. After all these years, we're exactly at the same starting point, back to square one, the place where we started from the moment Zvika went missing. All these years, we wanted to believe for Mom's sake that Zvika was alive. Only in recent years have I been saying to myself: *I just want my brother any way he is. After all, if he's still alive, what's possibly left of him?*

There's no one who wants this story to end more than we do, but we won't agree for the story to end without us having proof about what happened to them—to Zvika, to Yehuda, and to Zachary—even if it's a pain in the neck for someone. Rabin was the one who said, "They are alive until proven otherwise," and these words follow us to this day.

20

At Batya Arad's Garden

For many years, Tammy Arad has been keeping a diary in which the entries are addressed to her missing husband, Israeli Air Force navigator Ron Arad. Excerpts from it were published in her book, *Al Hut Ha'Sa'ara* (*Hanging by a Thread*). On October 15, 1988, Tammy wrote about her first encounter with me: "Rabin appointed Attorney Ory Slonim to be his advisor on your case. We met him in his office. Impressive man, highly motivated, connections. Let's hope he can succeed where others have failed."

About two months later, on December 7, 1988, she wrote: "Ory Slonim recruited some Corsican to be the negotiator in the exchange of the French hostages. Sounds amazing, because he knows Berri personally, as well as Dirani, and is willing to mediate. Rabin approved. Meanwhile, there are no free lunches. The Israeli government is supposed to show support for the right-wing in France now (I have no idea in what way) because that Corsican guy is right-wing, Jacques Chirac is involved in it. The deal is that you will be photographed by Dirani with that day's newspaper and with a threat on your life that if the state of Israel continues in its bombing campaign, they're going to kill you. I didn't really understand the logic here. So far nothing actually happened, and according to my calculations, tomorrow is the last day. That Corsican was talking about 10 to 15 days starting from 24.11.

"In addition, Ory Slonim, who was appointed by Rabin, has requested re-organization of the system that deals with your case. The
treatment should go from the IDF Manpower Directorate to a group that
will consist of Shin Bet, Mossad, and IDF Military Intelligence (AMAN)
personnel to inject a stimulant and move things along."

Tammy has another entry later in the diary: "Your mother contacted
a witch from Beit Jann and I joined her for one round. Don't laugh. I'm
desperate. The witch says you've gained a little weight (won't hurt you)
and also that you said you love me. I don't really believe in witches and
hope to hear that you love me in person and not through a witch. A long
and hazy story that will be told to you with all the specifics when you
come back. I'm picturing your face when you read this, and I'm not sure
you want me to go into detail."

Batya Arad didn't stop at getting help from the witch of Beit Jann.
Her burning desire to learn her son's fate led her, among others, to a
fortune-teller in Ramallah. When she told me at one of our many meetings about her intention to meet with her, I told her I didn't believe in it
and tried to convince her to change her plans. "Maybe you're right," she
replied, "but I still want to meet her." When she returned from Ramallah,
she told me that the fortune-teller had placed a basin of water in front of
her and asked her to peer into it. "You can say whatever you want," Batya
told me, "but I saw Ron's face in the water."

* * *

Two years had passed from the day that Ron Arad plunged with his
parachute into a life in captivity in Lebanon until I first met the family,
in October 1988. As I later learned, those who were handling the affair
at the time believed that there was a chance that Ron could be returned
to Israel very soon, so there was no need to include me in the picture.
During those two years, it was clear that Ron was alive, as letters were
received from him.

In the Arad family there are a wife and daughter, Tammy and Yuval;
a mother and her life partner, Batya and Moshe Aroeti; brothers and their
spouses, Chen and Likki, Dudu and Merav. When an IDF soldier went

missing in action, sometimes not everyone in the family was involved in the cause. There were families where the children were very young; there were those where, for various reasons, one of the family members chose to coordinate all the activities; and there were also parents who wanted their children to just go on with their lives, and they took on the bulk of the responsibility for handling the issue. In this case, Ron's was a family in which everyone was involved in his or her own special way depending on their personality, ability, wishes, experience, and background, and I was in contact with each and every one of them.

Chen was an exceptional partner and colleague for me. At first, I had a very hard time with how cynical he was—a trait I find difficult to deal with—but when I got to know him, I discovered a special, kindhearted man whose cynicism may have been part of his defense mechanism. I'd met Likki and her family many years before: her mother was one of my older sister Naomi's best friends. Likki, who served in the IDF as an officer, was one of Tammy's most reliable and rational supporters, stable as a stone pillar. Dudu, the youngest of the boys, met Merav during his military service. Merav was serving at the IDF's Manpower Directorate and was actually part of the team that handled Ron Arad's case. They got married and started a beautiful family and were very much involved in all the family's endeavors.

The relationship with this beautiful and close-knit family required me to be particularly sensitive and alert. In terms of caring for the family, there's a difference in the way you regard the mother and father, the brothers, the wife. I am very careful about making comparisons, but if we know anything about the world of bereavement, we know that a mother who loses her son will live with the loss for the rest of her life. There is no substitute for the fruit of her loins getting killed. A widow can marry again, bring into the world children, and live another life alongside the grief, even if it accompanies her for the rest of her days. The sorrow and pain are different. There is no measure for the grief and the pain; they are huge for everyone. The emphasis here is on the word *different*; it can't be gauged. The siblings will probably be able to continue with their lives better than the parents. Hadassah Fink, the mother of the deceased Yossi

Fink, tells in this book that she urged her daughters to go on with their lives. In the first few years, while they were still very young girls, they did indeed manage to do this while, at the same time, providing help and support for the parents, who devoted themselves to the efforts of recovering their missing son.

In Ron's family, I sometimes had to face everyone together, and I sometimes faced them individually. I have no doubt that I occasionally said the wrong thing or behaved the wrong way—even my body language may have given the wrong impression. Mistakes are almost inevitable in such a sensitive situation.

There are no clear and uniform codes of conduct that are right for every situation. Every family was a whole world to me, and there was hardly anything I could learn from one family that I could successfully implement in the case of another. But with every family, however wonderful, there are a variety of possible responses that you can expect, which require you to be sensitive to the topic itself and to the relationships between different family members. What happens, for example, when you return from a trip abroad that was related to investigating the case of one of the MIAs or negotiating for the release of a POW, who will be the first person you're going to tell about it, and who else will be present at the meeting? How, exactly, will you say what you have to say? Sometimes I felt like I hardly knew anything, although I was learning all the time.

*   *   *

I had a particularly close relationship with Batya Arad. We had hundreds of hours of conversation at Batya and Moshe's warm and lovely home in Magdiel, in the large garden with the trees and saplings that they cultivated with such admirable skill. Batya was a very clever, sober, and practical woman with two legs planted firmly on the ground. She was opinionated and never tried to hide her views; she always spoke her mind, using the most unambiguous terms. It was clear who Batya Arad liked and didn't. If there were any misunderstandings between us over the years, it was just around the issue of cigarettes: I abhor smoking, while Batya seemed to use the butt of every cigarette she ever smoked to light the next one. As much as she tried to avoid smoking while I was in their home, especially when we were having some hard conversations, she found it difficult to resist the temptation sometimes and had to step outside to smoke in the yard.

And Moshe Aroeti was always there, carrying around his coffee pot in which he used to roast the most special kind of coffee for us. If they ever ask me what's the most important thing a person needs in times of trouble, my response will be: having someone like Moshe Aroeti around.

During my time as a parachute jump instructor, one of the cadets asked me to give him a ride to our hometown, Ra'anana. Along the way, he introduced himself: "Yossi Aroeti, Moshe and Batya's nephew." He told me about his warm Bulgarian family, people who love life, know how to rejoice and eat well, but also have a sensitive side to their character. That's just what Moshe Aroeti was like; his ability to remain in the background was true art. It's a simple thing to butt in and ask questions, especially when it comes to your spouse and more so when her son is a soldier who's missing in action and whose name regularly appears in the newspaper headlines. Moshe was present at all our meetings but never interfered. If there was any tension in the meeting, by the very fact of his being present—without even saying or doing anything special—he managed to dispel it. I was happy for Batya, who had lived through the worst of all, but at least she had a life partner like Moshe who was always there for her.

I've been involved in their lives on almost every subject. Batya was already retired and started working at the local nursery in Magdiel at some point. Almost every morning on my way to work, I stopped by at the nursery. When Yossi, the nursery manager, saw me, he quickly motioned everyone to get away so as not to disturb us. Batya and I would have a conversation for about fifteen minutes—sometimes about Ron, sometimes just idle chatter—and then I would continue on my way to work. Many of our conversations were about current affairs. We could talk for a whole hour without mentioning Ron when nothing new had happened in the meantime.

The duality of my role was not simple to handle. On the one hand, I was almost like family for Batya, and yet I was also the representative of the system that completely disappointed her, *and* the one who conveyed her anger to the defense minister or the foreign minister. Despite this, and although Batya was a very outspoken woman who would say almost anything that was on her mind, she was always careful not to offend me.

As time went by, I began to notice that Batya and Moshe barely had a life outside of the preoccupation with Ron's return home. I suggested that they go abroad. Batya rejected my suggestions, offering a variety of reasons and excuses: she wasn't in the mood, what if Ron were to come back just when she's abroad, what would people say if they saw the mother of a missing IDF soldier having the time of her life, and why would she spend money on something that wouldn't make her happy anyway.

Among my clients as an attorney there were also airlines and travel agents. I contacted one of them, I asked him to find an organized trip to a destination that was relatively near, with people who were close to Batya and Moshe's age, and to also give her a big discount—not because Batya needed it, but so the price could no longer be used as a reason for turning down the trip. The perfect destination was selected—a trip to Yugoslavia. I spoke with the group's guide, who promised me that he would make sure no one bothered Batya or pestered her with unnecessary questions. Then it was time to convince Batya. I pulled out the ace: I promised her that if Ron returned, I would send a private jet to pick her up and bring her back before he reached Israel. Batya and Moshe traveled to Yugoslavia, and lo, they saw that it was good. They later made some very enjoyable trips to other destinations.

My frequent encounters with Batya posed complex challenges because she knew almost every day where I was going to be and when I was traveling abroad. So even if she didn't know that I was going to Denmark to meet the Dirani brothers—the brothers of the person responsible for the abduction of her son—she still knew that I went to Europe, and she naturally had questions after every trip. Batya didn't like it when people played with words, and she didn't appreciate it when people were busting her balls instead of giving her straight answers.

The way in which one must respond in such complex and delicate circumstances is an art unto itself. I would sometimes practice this with Itamar Barnea, the former head of the IDF casualties department, and not just for the purposes of meeting with Batya Arad. Unfortunately, in this case, I was not at liberty to give any reports to the family. The most I could say was, "There's nothing new at the moment." That was the only way to avoid getting into hot water. I stuck to my guns and remained true to my principles; as I said, I never used words that might instill illusion or unnecessarily get someone's hopes up. And unfortunately, in all the years I accompanied the Arad family, I never had any news to deliver to Batya.

A shadow of constant stress was cast on Batya Arad's life, sleepless nights and anger at the system for not raising hell to bring her son back. The family of an MIA cannot take comfort in knowing that "efforts are being made." Without results, there is no consolation. Batya would often tell me that she dreamed of Ron. We also never had any conversations with regard to where Ron was located or what his condition was, and we hardly ever talked about Ron himself. I, too, have my own defense mechanisms. I didn't want to miss someone whom I didn't know. I just wanted to bring that person home. Period.

* * *

I learned something from every family I went through this process with. Some of the people I met along the way have given me a thousand times more than anything I could hope to give to them. Tammy Arad was one of those people.

In the first phases of my relationship with the family, Tammy didn't really understand what my role was. Since I was closer to Batya and Moshe in age, the relationship with them formed more quickly. Tammy and I became close friends with time, and we remain such to this day. I tried to be open with her as much as I could.

Tammy is a very special woman. The way she coped was a life lesson for me. With all my background and experience, Tammy taught me a lot more than I could teach her. Tammy has lived through these difficult years with a strength that I have not encountered, even among people who had to face much simpler crises.

The role of "the wife of..." (a very exposed wife), whose actions and behavior were subjected to scrutiny by the whole country and whose business everyone stuck their noses into, robs someone of almost every part of their private life. Tammy's ability to handle this challenge deserves every conceivable form of praise. Tammy is a powerful, strong-willed, and intelligent woman, and all these qualities have only been pushed into center stage and intensified over the years due to the situation she's been in.

* * *

One particularly sad evening, Batya called me and told me she was diagnosed with cancer. She wanted to consult me about a doctor. I made some inquiries and got the best expert I could find to see her. Prior to her hospitalization, Batya wanted to be in a room where she would have a measure of privacy, if at all possible, despite it being a public hospital. I asked the hospital manager to make arrangements for it. That was to be the last thing I ever did for Batya Arad.

At one of our meetings, Batya gave Tamy and me a huge bottle of red wine as a gift. When we refused to accept it, she insisted: "Save the wine and drink it when Ron comes back." At another meeting, in 1994, Batya wondered why I was doing my work on a volunteer basis, and I implored her not to bother herself with such questions, as she was already burdened with enough concerns of her own. Batya pulled out an old one Israeli pound note, which she apparently kept around as a souvenir and told me: "Keep this note and give it back to me when Ron comes back."

We never did drink the wine, and it seems I will have to keep the note forever, the last memento from this extraordinary woman.

21

The One Who Took to Heart: The Voice of Tammy Arad, Wife of Navigator Ron Arad, Taken Captive on October 16, 1986, Not Yet Returned

O ry appeared in the life of our family several years after Ron was taken captive. It was not an easy time. We had gone from one disappointment to another, had our share of frustrations, and we'd already learned a thing or two about the fairy tales people tell about life in captivity and did not allow ourselves to happily fall into the arms of new government officials each time someone was appointed into office, especially when we saw how they come and go—and Ron isn't coming back.

In one of our conversations, Ory reminded me that I wasn't being very nice to him at the beginning of our journey together, and in all honesty, I wasn't surprised, even if it's hard for me to recall the details about why he got a sour face from me, which he absorbed with such patience. He probably wasn't the only one to get a big dose of my anger and frustration, but he took it to heart. As a side note, I'd like to point out that those were the days when we still had no doubt that Ron would return, because just a few months after he was taken captive, we received life signs from Ron—pictures and letters that came through various intermediaries involved in the case. The question was when exactly Ron was going to return, and how can we get him back home as quickly as possible.

Until that day, October 16, 1986, we were a young family living on base in a housing unit for families at the Israeli Air Force base in Ramat David. We took our first steps walking down the path of life with lots of dreams and aspirations, and the kind of huge love young people have (twenty-eight, twenty-five, and a one-year-old baby), only to suddenly be torn apart. From that day, the extended Arad family's journey into the world of captivity began, and the constant wait for a sign of life was nerve-racking and accompanied by endless anxiety and worries. Our concern was that someone might hurt Ron, even though we heard day and night from people in the system and from former prisoners of war that the letters and pictures were Ron's insurance policy. Captives come back, everyone kept assuring us.

But we were worried, and we missed him. He was alone in harsh conditions, and we were over here, with nothing but a feeling of helplessness. After about a year and a few months, the letters from Ron stopped coming; the pipelines were completely clogged. The language of "pipelines" was the language used by those who reported to us on behalf of the system handling the case, and for us it became the official language and the oxygen tank from which we received the doses that allowed us to maintain our hope.

In my estimation, Ory came into the picture at a time when Prime Minister and Defense Minister Yitzhak Rabin felt a certain emotional connection to the family's sense of despair and realized that the attempts that had been made up to that point in time had come to a dead end. The staff on the handling team was replaced, freshened up, in order to come up with new methods of action, and indeed Ory worked in concert with the system but as an independent channel. Ory was introduced to the family as a successful lawyer who volunteered to help. I couldn't help but wonder to myself why he was getting into all of this, a cause that was all but lost. In retrospect, I can understand the motives, as well as the prices that Ory feels he had to pay.

In the interest of setting the historical record straight, I'll say that the initial relationship was not created between me and Ory but between Ory and Batya and Moshe (Ron's mother and her life partner), a relationship that became a very personal affair and later even turned into a daily routine. I tried to remember the time when the connection was actually made, but I just couldn't recall. Ory is the kind of person you meet and you get the feeling that you've known him for years. At times, it seemed to me that Ory was a permanent fixture, sitting in Batya and Moshe's green garden since the dawn of time. Next to the old swing upholstered with that brown faux leather, in the shade of the pecan trees, the brightly colored begonias and petunias, Ory, or sometimes Ory together with his wife, Tamy, was sitting with Batya and Moshe, drinking black coffee that Moshe was roasting. The copper jug stood on the white ceramic tiled table, the steaming black liquid poured into small china glasses, and the conversations flowed, or were sometimes replaced by an oppressive silence.

Batya took Ory's advice. She trusted him and shared with him her most secret thoughts and rewarded him with a special closeness in one of the most difficult times in her life, if not the hardest of them all. Ory visited Batya and Moshe many times, escorted by Tamy, the woman who was his indispensable companion. Always accompanying him, listening, hardly ever talking. The little wife, or so we thought. In retrospect, we learned that Tamy was an opinionated woman and herself a highly successful lawyer—the manager of a large legal firm with her own team of lawyers who worked under her, but in the relationship with us, she seemed to choose to be a stand-in at her husband's show. Looking back, it can be said that she served as a perfect aide at his side, and her support was critical, especially during the times when any details about his work were very obscure and he had to return to us from his travels around the world empty-handed.

In retrospect, Ory told me about the difficulties he experienced in these meetings with us, the younger generation, and, in contrast, the memories that I formed at those meetings is visual and emotional and touches not on the content of the meetings, but on the imagery of their relationship. The way that Tamy was quietly sitting beside him—the support she gave him—made me think all sorts of thoughts and even feel jealousy about how lucky he was to have a woman like her. We later became acquainted with Ory's children, who, in their own way, also gave Ory their blessing to do his best for Ron's sake, at their expense to some degree, and we learned that the eldest son, Erez, was actually not far from our own age.

One episode from a meeting overseas that was conducted by Ory is particularly memorable for me, not because it was really important but due to a few comic and truly hilarious moments, rare for those days. The meeting was held in one of the capital of a European nation with one of the UN secretary-general's deputies. The name of the man was Giandomenico Picco, a name with an unforgettable continental flavor. Ory managed to recruit him for the benefit of our cause, a short time before he was going to retire from his official position at the United Nations, with the hopes that he could use his good relations with Iranian figures and officials in other Middle-Eastern countries to find out what happened to Ron and perhaps even start a pipeline through which some information might be funneled. In those days, the different avenues of information were intermittently opening and closing, and we longed and prayed for any source of information, even if it had to come in a small trickle.

The meeting was held in a hotel suite, and as befits such a luxurious suite, next to the armchairs and large dining table, there was a very large double bed. Yuval, who was just a young girl in those years and always fidgeting about, took off her shoes as soon as she noticed the huge trampoline that came her way. She started jumping on the high-quality mattress and giggled in rolling trumpeting sounds with each leap that carried her higher and closer to the ceiling of the room—the sky as far as she was concerned—while rolling our guest's name on her tongue, as if playing with a funny new rhyme. Ory's face, sitting in the armchair by the bedside, became ashen. I assumed that it was just a panic attack and not a full-blown heart attack, because Ory couldn't hide his fears about Yuval's gymnastics performance. I was trying to calm him down, but got caught with Yuval's contagious laughter, as did my sister-in-law Likki, who joined me on most trips abroad, and we all three got dragged into a laughing attack, which made Ory even more anxious.

Just minutes before Picco arrived, when Ory's sweat was already pouring profusely down his face, I managed to regain the right composure for such occasions. I explained to Ory that Yuval already had plenty of official meetings on her belt, and as soon as Picco arrived, we would pull out the painting kit, and the girl would draw for the guest a house with a red roof and a blossoming flower garden; the sun will rise on the white paper and butterflies will fly, and if Mr. Picco would be nice, maybe even a colorful rainbow would be added to the rays of sunlight. But Ory couldn't relax. He remained frozen, fearing that Yuval wouldn't be able to resist the temptation and during the official meeting she would take off her shoes, climb onto the mattress, and continue to jump to her heart's delight and to his horror.

The meeting, if my memory serves me correct, was held while adhering to all the accepted standards. Yuval kept a very calm countenance and drew a spring painting for the guest in recognition of his agreeing to meet with us, and I, as far as I could, endeavored to persuade Mr. Picco to comply with Ory's request. The results, as you can guess, were not very exciting, but after many years of examining nothing but the results, I learned to appreciate the efforts and especially the goodwill of the people who showed up in our lives. Israelis and foreigners, volunteers and appointed officials.

Chen, Ron's brother, divided the office holders whom we ran across into two main categories. Those who played a role and those who took to the heart, including those who kept in touch with the family years later. Ory and Tamy were together with Batya during her last months at home and in the hospital and, after her death, kept in touch regularly with Moshe. They gave Ron and us a place in their hearts and were among those who came into our lives and stayed there to this day.

22

The Two Grieving Wives from Nahariya

O n Wednesday morning, July 12, 2006, a squad of Hezbollah ter-rorists launched antitank guided missiles at two IDF Humvees that were on a routine patrol mission at the perimeter fence on the border between Israel and Lebanon. One of the Humvees sustained a direct hit, and the three servicemen riding in it were killed instantly. Two soldiers in the other Humvee survived the attack, and two others—SFC Ehud Goldwasser and S.Sgt. Eldad Regev, both reserve soldiers—were kid-napped by the terrorists, who breached the perimeter fence and entered Israel's sovereignty for that purpose.

That same morning, the Hezbollah launched a heavy artillery bom-bardment of Israeli communities on the northern frontier. Israel launched a massive assault of its own in retaliation, from the air and later also using ground forces. Dubbed "Operation Change of Direction," the attack became, after its conclusion, "the Second Lebanon War."

Two days after the abduction, on Friday, July 14, Tamy and I went out with our son Erez and our granddaughter Shira for lunch at a restau-rant in Herzliya. While we were at the table, an unidentified number appeared on my cell phone's monitor. On the other side of the line, I heard a female voice that I didn't recognize, which I would later come to know well. "My name is Karnit," said the young woman, "and I am the wife of Udi Goldwasser, the soldier who was kidnapped two days ago in Lebanon."

From that very first conversation, I learned of the special character and determination of the woman who embarked on a relentless struggle to rescue her husband. "I would really want to meet you as soon as possible," said Karnit.

"Where do you live?" I asked.

"In Nahariya."

"I'll drop by sometime in the middle of next week," I promised.

"Can you do it a little earlier?"

"I'll try earlier that week."

"Can it be sooner?"

"Would Sunday be okay?"

"Ory, how about a little push?"

"Do you observe the Sabbath?"

"No."

"So maybe Saturday morning?"

"Would it be possible today?"

"When?"

"Now," she answered without any trace of tremors in her voice.

Karnit left me no choice. "I'll be there," I promised.

Karnit later described this conversation from her own viewpoint in her book *The Way to You*, which describes everything she went through from the moment she received the news that her husband, Udi, was missing in action after a clash with Hezbollah terrorists on the northern border until the moment he was brought back to Israel in a coffin: "The third phone call I made was to Ory Slonim. My friends gave me the number. Everyone knows that Slonim deals with captives and MIAs, that he knows everything there is to know about it. When his name came up, I said, 'Sure, come on, here we go,' and on this phone call, I met a person who became one of the most important people in my life. I had no second thoughts about making this call."

＊　＊　＊

I told my family about the conversation and apologized to them for leaving in the middle of our family lunch, but I must head straight for Nahariya. On that same day, in those very moments, the city was under a barrage of "Katyusha" rockets launched by the Hezbollah, and local residents were in bomb shelters. Tamy immediately told me that she was joining me. She knew full well that if she was with me, I would seek refuge at a shelter in the event of an alarm, which I wouldn't bother to do if I were alone. At the entrance to Nahariya, right next to the local hospital, the alarm sounded, and a rocket immediately fell very close by. There was nowhere to run.

Karnit greeted us with great enthusiasm at the home of her mother, Daniella. It was a private house in a quiet neighborhood, the complete antithesis to the storm raging inside of it and the roar of the exploding rockets that landed in the area. The house was teeming with close friends and family who'd came to offer their support to Karnit. At the same time, Mickey and Shlomo Goldwasser—Udi's parents—were making their way back to Israel from South Africa.

We had our first conversation there—one of several hundred that we were going to have over the course of the next two years, until the bodies of Udi and Eldad arrived in the country. But already at this meeting, I discovered a strong, purpose-focused woman. Karnit did not appear fragile, frightened, or agitated, as one might expect from a woman whose world was turned on its head and where a new world, alien and menacing, was now waiting for her. She had a mission to accomplish.

My first meeting with Karnit was unlike any first meeting I had with the families of other captives and MIAs. I'd come to each of those meetings having prepared in advance. I knew a great deal about the people who made up the family, their character traits, their life's circumstances, and of course, the circumstances surrounding the missing soldiers. When I met Karnit, it was hurriedly and at extremely short notice as she requested, without having been able to learn anything about her, the rest of the family, or any details regarding the abduction. In addition, we had very little time, because Udi's parents were about to walk in through the front door at any moment, so I wanted to learn from Karnit as much as possible about the family.

It was important for me to use the little time we had available to hear from Karnit about herself, Udi, and the rest of the family, and to gather information from her that would help me to prepare for what comes next. I learned that Shlomo was a seaman—the former captain of a naval vessel who held management positions at a shipping company. As a fellow seafarer, I already had something in common with him, which would soon allow me to make our first conversation a bit more relaxed.

On top of that, I also had some things to say to Karnit. She wanted to know how to best prepare for dealing with this situation. Just a few days earlier, she had a reservist husband whom she'd occasionally receive messages from while he was at the front. Now, suddenly, she was the wife of an abducted soldier held by the enemy, if not worse. She asked, for example, what she was supposed to do about the media, which was already swarming her mother's house. From an anonymous young woman—a student at the Technion who led a quiet life in Nahariya—she was destined to become one of the most exposed women in the country. She wouldn't even be able to sneeze in the street without the local media reporting about it.

I told Karnit that she would have to take into account that every word she said to journalists would immediately be spread around the world, that every little twitch of the muscles in her face would be caught on camera, and that they could end up being used by anyone—for better or worse. As someone who'd only had her pictures taken for her high school graduation ceremony and her Bat Mitzvah party, she would now find her face smeared across newspaper pages and TV screens, and we would have be prepared for it.

The simplest piece of advice I could give to Karnit was to avoid contact with the press at this initial stage, at least until she had more details. I also told her that she would have to decide who she wanted to involve in her life from now on. "Everyone will want to help you," I said, "and it could prove to be a drawback. You will have to learn to distance yourself, politely and with courtesy, from those whose help you have no interest in receiving."

Over the years, I've gotten rid of the clichés most people like to use. I have never used them in my meetings with any of the families. Never did I use phrases like "Be strong" or "Take care of yourselves," and I'd certainly never say, "It's going to be fine." I learned to speak without clichés.

In these kinds of meetings, I was asked a thousand questions and knew how to answer about three, as I made sure never to answer a question that I didn't know the full answer to. I had to face families that were anxious and frightened but also full of hope, and there was one thing I had to say to everyone, including Karnit: "Nothing happens fast in these matters." The son/husband/brother/grandson is not coming back tomorrow. Someone's going to want something in return for them. And it's going to take time. A lot of time.

And I also knew that the first meeting with me, even if it didn't include answers to all the questions that were posed, provided some comfort and relief for the family because they were meeting with someone who understood the predicament they were in, if nothing else.

* * *

Shortly after I arrived at Daniella's house, Mickey and Shlomo arrived. Karnit captured these touching moments, too, in her book *The Way to You*, in a way that is truly wonderful. I couldn't hope to do a better job than she did, so I allow myself to borrow her own words again:

> Shlomo and Mickey came into the house, looking gray and quiet, two people who had just been on a ten-hour flight while on tranquilizers, after two days without any sleep, having received the most tragic news anyone could hear. The only people in the house were us, Oded, and the Slonim couple. Shlomo recognized Slonim immediately. He didn't even put his suitcase down, didn't sit in the chair, no hugs, no water, nothing, he just said, perhaps to us and perhaps to Ory: "I want to know what tools we have. Who're the public figures involved? I know that when a carpenter has a problem, he needs a hammer, he needs nails. When a ship captain has a problem, he needs a map, a compass. When we have

a problem here, I want to know what tools we have at our disposal to bring Udi home." Only after saying these things, did he allow himself to hug, to drink some water, to crash into his armchair.

Ory accepted the challenge and explained how it was going to go. He said it would take time, that there was going to be a negotiation through mediators. The heads of the state themselves decide on what course of action needs to be taken, but there will probably be a representative from our side, in addition to an international mediator, and a mediator working on behalf of the Hezbollah. Negotiations will basically take place between these three figures. He explained that patience is of key importance, because it will take time, that there's nothing to do now but decide whether to go to the media, and most importantly—we have to survive. We've got to hold on, keep eating, keep sleeping, continue to function, even if partially. He also said that over time we would have to go back to some routine and later even think about going back to work. He didn't say anything that was new to me, seeing that we'd already heard similar things from Oded, but for Mickey and Shlomo, this was the first conversation they had with anyone, and beyond the content, the encouragement, embrace, moral support, and knowledge gained with experience were no less of value.

I felt a pinch in my heart as I read in Karnit's book about the less desirable people who entered their lives:

We learned some things we didn't know about the human condition and character in times of distress. For the first time we encountered the "hitchhikers." When such a catastrophe befalls a family, all sorts of people suddenly appear on the scene and offer to help—some of them known to the public, others anonymous. Initially, we expressed our gratitude to every one of them, but over time we came to see that our struggle was being exploited by people who wanted to take advantage of the situation to bring themselves to the forefront, and we realized that it was improper and unjust for them to be at center stage. We suddenly realized that these people spotted a chance to enter the captive and MIA niche, and comfortably hitch a ride on it—and on us too. Suddenly, some people came along and wanted to be like Ory Slonim, but without having to spend twenty years on the matter, like he did. And what a difference between him and them.

When we met Ory on that Friday in the beginning of the war, he told us one thing: "I'm with you for anything you want, whenever you want. But there's just one thing I don't want to do: I don't want to be your leader in the media. I'm not here to do public relations for myself." Much later, when I asked him to speak at rallies, it took quite a while for him to agree to do it. When all three families met together in order to decide on our course of action, he didn't show up. He told us, gently as always, that he's not here to lead us and doesn't make decisions for us. There was a real, strong feeling that he comes from a modest and pure place, from behind the scenes. That he wants to be a silent partner in this. Doesn't want to be heard of and doesn't want to be seen, but does want to take action. That was in stark contrast to others, who operated with distinct extravagance and showiness.

If Karnit hadn't been the one to write about it, I wouldn't have been so bold as to address the issue, certainly not to testify about myself. Over the years, I've also had a hard time dealing with the "hitchhiking" phenomenon. The issue of captives and MIAs is of interest to everyone in society and ignites the imagination of some people, who have the notion—and perhaps rightly, in some cases—that they have the capacity to help. In this good crowd, there are also people who have no abilities, experience, or knowledge to deal with the subject, which doesn't stop them from contacting the families with various requests and advice. When the families choose not to enlist their help, they try to get in the way. I had to learn to shoo them off over the years.

* * *

Since our first meeting in Nahariya, Karnit's life has been intertwined in mine, and I have accompanied her and the whole family until the bodies of Udi and Eldad were returned. We had a meeting every week in my office at Achad Ha'am Street in Tel Aviv or at the "Noir Café" across the street from the office. I preferred to meet with Karnit in my office and not in the coffee shop, since she had, as we fully expected, become an easily recognized public figure. People constantly approached her, voiced their support, gave her advice, told her everything they thought, and there were those who even asked for her autograph. This sudden exposure is very difficult for people who have been used to anonymity all their lives. Karnit, as the flag bearer—at least as far as the media was concerned— in the fight for the return of Udi and Eldad, was very well-liked. The intentions of the people who approached her were obviously good, but I wanted to use our meetings for talking and the exchange of opinions and to counsel each other and avoid anything unrelated.

Karnit spoke to me about everything. About Udi, her personal life, and the steps she was taking in her efforts to bring him home. She shared everything with me, like I was a big brother, and I tried to help as much as I could and make my experience available for her. As in other cases, I used my connections to arrange meetings for the family with any guests who arrived in Israel that might be able to help or with dignitaries abroad— the German prime minister, the Dutch foreign minister, an American senator. It's hard sometimes to slip a meeting with the family into their schedules, as tight as they are on official visits to Israel, but I insisted on it and wouldn't give up. You never know where you might find some help, and you have to be ready to utilize every single session with officials to keep the subject high on the agenda.

I told Karnit about the things I knew or was involved in whenever I could, and I heard from her about her independent activities. When she acted correctly, I didn't interfere, and if she did something that seemed to me useless or a waste of time, I didn't hesitate to tell her my opinion. In most cases, she did things the right way. I can't remember even one single day that Karnit lost hope. This statement is also true in regard to members of all the other families I have been in contact with: the dreams, the hope, and even the fantasies never stop coming.

In this case, the Regev and Goldwasser families were in terrible distress—in part, due to the high level of preoccupation among the public with the abduction—in an attempt to assess the situation and determine Udi and Eldad's status: Was there a chance that they survived under the circumstances, or did the findings on the ground and the evidence regarding their injuries in the initial incident unequivocally indicate that they were killed?

I will never forget the wording in the opinion of the doctors and researchers examining the bloodstains and injuries suffered from the blood on the road from which Udi and Eldad were abducted. The findings strongly indicated, according to the experts, that there was a 99 percent chance that Udi and Eldad were no longer among the living. The prime minister at the time, Ehud Olmert, commented thus on these assessments: "Never before did we attend the funeral of a person who had a 99 percent chance of being dead."

In parallel to the connection with the Goldwasser family, I was also in contact with the highly special Regev family—the father, Zvi, and the brothers Benny, Ofer, and Eyal. Theirs was a humble family that conducted itself with a lot of restraint, and my encounter with them was very moving. I did everything I could to make them feel better in those difficult times. I maintained an almost daily telephone connection with the family. In many of the conversations, we didn't even discuss the issue itself. I've always believed that even a conversation in which the missing person is not once mentioned is an important conversation. It's enough for the family to know that there's someone who is thinking about them and that they haven't been forgotten even for one moment.

* * *

At that point, I was less involved in the efforts to recover the kidnapped soldiers and the negotiations that were underway. Ofer Dekel, a senior Shin Bet officer, was appointed to be in charge of the captives and MIAs, and he performed his tasks faithfully and in a highly professional and sensitive manner. Ofer and I used to meet often. He updated me on the progress of the negotiations, and I updated him on my contacts with the families. We had a great working relationship with a lot of mutual trust and respect.

On June 29, 2008, the Israeli government approved the prisoner exchange deal, which was reached thanks to Dekel's efforts. The deal included the return of Udi and Eldad—who until the last moment had not been confirmed to be either alive or dead—and the provision of additional information about Ron Arad, in exchange for the release of five terrorists and the return of the bodies of 199 terrorists who had been temporarily buried on Israeli soil.

Among those released in the deal was Samir Kuntar. The Lebanese terrorist was only sixteen and a half years old when he led a terrorist squad on April 22, 1979, arriving in a rubber boat to the beach in Nahariya. The terrorists opened fire on a police vehicle, killed Israeli police officer Eliyahu Shahar, and then entered the Haran family's home in the city. The terrorists kidnapped Danny Haran and his four-year-old daughter, Einat. The mother, Smadar, managed to hide out with their two-year-old daughter, Yael, and a neighbor in the attic. The terrorists took Danny and Einat to the beach in an attempt to escape back to Lebanon, but a gunfight with Israeli security forces developed. Samir Kuntar shot Danny in front of his daughter and then murdered her too. Back in the home's attic, Yael suffocated to death as Smadar attempted to keep her silent so they would not be discovered by the terrorists.

Samir Kuntar was sentenced to five life sentences and forty-seven years in prison. Media reports about the intention to release him sparked harsh criticism by the Israeli public, even before the deal was approved and signed. Although I was not involved in the contacts or the decision-making process, I was called on for an urgent meeting with the team dealing with the issue. I was asked if I would be willing to meet with Smadar Haran and talk to her about the possibility that Kuntar, the despicable murderer who killed her family members in cold blood, might be released in exchange for the return of Udi and

Eldad. I wasn't personally acquainted with Smadar Haran and had never met her before. Despite that, I did not hesitate for one moment. I accepted this task. I called Smadar and asked to see her. I didn't tell her on the phone what the purpose of the meeting was. I can only speculate that, in her wisdom, she knew why I wanted to meet. Smadar invited me to her home in Nahariya, the same northern city where Udi and Karnit lived.

I went to see Smadar and found myself in a state of emotional turmoil. The evening before our meeting, I ran through almost every possible scenario. wondered if Smadar would be angry, ask me why I even bothered to come at all, claim that we should never release Kuntar, and perhaps even threaten to appeal to the Supreme Court in an attempt to stop the deal. Things like this have happened before. I would accept with complete understanding and respect any answer she gave me. If Smadar told me to go to the defense minister and tell him she was opposed to the deal, I would honor her request. I had no intention of convincing Smadar to agree to anything; I just wanted to hear her opinion. It didn't occur to me to say one word of persuasion or advocacy as to why the killer of her loved ones should be released, not even implicitly or with so much as a hint in my body language.

In none of the many scenarios that went through my mind did I manage to foresee what actually happened. In all the years I have dealt with the issue of captives and missing persons, my meeting with Smadar Haran has been one of the most touching and extraordinary events I have ever experienced. I will not reveal here the highly personal things said at that meeting. Suffice it to say that I witnessed rare moments of true human nobleness, the likes of which I did not think possible.

What little I can say about that meeting is that Smadar shared with me the feeling that family members of the victims of terrorist attacks are actually hostages in the continuous process, which is repeated each time the subject of terrorists being released is discussed. The public debate on the matter tormented her each and every single time, as she felt that everyone—both the victims of terrorism and the families of the MIAs—were on the same side of the barricade, that of pain and suffering.

Smadar expressed her feelings and state of mind in a letter she wrote in those days to Prime Minister Ehud Olmert and the ministers of the Israeli government. Her message was as follows:

In the coming days, you, the policymakers in the country, will be required to face ideological, moral, and human dilemmas, which contain a great deal of pain and internal contradictions. Your decisions will affect us all—the families of the abducted soldiers and the victims of the terrorist attacks.

Abductions are a strategic attack that has a rolling snowball effect: they impact the immediate and closest circle which includes the abducted persons and their families and the families of the victims of the terrorist attacks, those who were hurt and left without any power to defend themselves.

But those aren't the only people included in the circle of the affected population. Just like when a stone is thrown into the water, so too here, the waves spreading from the center outward touch each of us as individuals and as a state. Our lives here, in the state of Israel, are often characterized by uncertainty, as well as difficult and painful historical events. Often, in the rush of developing incidents, one must make a choice between conflicting values and priorities.

True, we're all right, and our wishes are all perfectly valid and legitimate. However, when making a decision, I recognize that in each case and in every decision, there will be a painful price to pay—the price for who and what we are. We are a people called time and time again to fight for their lives, a society that must fight terrorism, a sovereign state that holds fair trials and sentences terrorists to serve time in prisons, and not least: a society that sanctifies life, the redeeming of captives and the commitment to its soldiers—who are its emissaries.

All of these are up to you today to discuss and decide upon.

The abominable murderer Samir Kuntar is not and never was my private personal prisoner; Kuntar is a prisoner of the state of Israel, which sentenced him for his murderous crimes to five life sentences. His fate should be determined at this time according to the best interests of the state in terms of security, morality, and the values that constitute the good of the state and its citizens in the present and in the future.

Members of the government,

Beyond the fact of being a victim of terrorism, and maybe even before I turned into one, someone who has paid the price in blood, I am a loving and deeply devoted citizen of my country. From this standpoint, I ask that my personal pain should not be a consideration when discussing what lies ahead, but rather the substance of the issue in depth, with all its different aspects and its implications.

The burden of pain and longing for my beloved—Danny, Einat, and Yael—taken so cruelly from me, I shall bear for the rest of my life. Together with this, I do not forget the suffering of the Regev, Goldwasser, Arad, and Shalit families and the moral debt I feel I have incurred towards all those who have labored for the sake of my ability to live a peaceful life in safety, as well as for all the rest of us.

I have considered things for a very long time, and even if it is difficult for me, I will not challenge any decision that will be made here today.

Even if my soul is torn, my heart is whole.

Smadar Haran

Samir Kuntar was eventually released as part of the deal and returned to Lebanon. He also returned to his terrorist activities. On December 19, 2015, he was killed in Syria. According to the Hezbollah reports, the building he was staying in was hit by a missile launched by the Israeli Air Force. According to media reports, Kuntar and several Hezbollah commanders were eliminated while planning to carry out an attack against Israeli civilians.

* * *

On the morning of Wednesday, July 16, 2008, after 735 days in which the Regev and Goldwasser families moved between hope and despair, the boys were brought back to Israel.

And then, at nine o'clock in the morning, the prisoner exchange deal was aired on television.

Karnit wrote in her book:

The deal began to materialize, and Nasrallah invited the media to cover the return of Udi and Eldad. We were unable to speak as we sat in front of the screen, in the living room of my mother's house in Nahariya, and, like all the rest of the state of Israel, watched the horror show hosted by Wafiq Safa, the head of Hezbollah's coordination unit. He was bragging to the world media: "You still don't know what state they're in; we're going to open the door in just one second and find out," as if he were a magician at the circus about to reveal what was hidden behind curtain number two.

And then, he opened the door of the van, and we saw the two coffins.

23

Gilad Shalit—The Captive Who Returned

The news of Gilad Shalit's expected release made its way to me even in faraway Tibet. Tamy and I spent a long time preparing for this trip, which we went on with our travel partners of twenty-five years. We read Haim Be'er's book, *Wherever the Spirit Goes*, about a rabbi from Bnei Brak who travels to Tibet in pursuit of his dreams to meet a yak who is the reincarnation of one of his ancestors. By the time we reached Tibet, we felt like the sights and scents were already familiar to us.

I made an agreement in advance with David Meidan, who headed the negotiating team, that if there were any developments that would lead to Gilad's release, he would find a way to report it to me. One night, at a very luxurious hotel in Lhasa, the Tibetan capital, the long-awaited call suddenly came. As soon as I heard Meidan's voice, he didn't have to say anything further to me. Considering the long period we'd collaborated together in order to secure the release of Gilad Shalit, he obviously hadn't called to ask me what the weather was like out there.

After Tibet, we were supposed to continue with the tour group into China, but Tamy and I didn't spend even one minute thinking about it. We were going back to Israel. After a twenty-four-hour journey and three layovers, we landed in Israel at 3:00 a.m. Just a few hours later, we were already at Mitzpe Hila, sitting in the house of Shalit family, which we'd gotten to know so well.

Noam, the family's foreign minister, wasn't home. He was involved in a series of meetings in anticipation of his son's return from captivity. We sat down with Aviva—who was naturally in a state of incredible tension expecting her son's release—and with her best friend, Naomi Betser, the wife of my old friend Israeli Sayeret Matkal, veteran commando Muki Betser. I will never forget this exciting meeting at the magical small village community overlooking the hills of the western Galilee region, sitting on the balcony in the home of the parents who'd waited more than five years for their son's return. They were quiet and humble people, who had to give up their anonymity overnight and embark on a relentless campaign for the rescue of their son who'd been taken captive by Hamas. Noam was the more active of the two, but over time, we learned to appreciate Aviva's quiet and sensible demeanor and marvel at her tremendous strength.

Surprisingly, we didn't talk that morning about the long-awaited release, nor about Gilad, who was going to be home in just over twenty-four hours. Perhaps it was a defense mechanism of some kind, but Aviva didn't want to allow herself to rejoice quite yet. We had a very moving conversation about life and its purpose and essence. Naomi told us about the book she was reading at the time, which she held in her hand right that moment, *A New Earth—Awakening to Your Life's Purpose*, by the author and spiritual teacher Eckhart Tolle. The book's message, "There's a way out of your suffering and a path to peace," couldn't have been more appropriate for those moments when we sat with the mother of the IDF soldier who had lived for such a long time in the shadow of worry and nerve-racking uncertainty about her son's fate.

* * *

At another point—five years and four months prior to that exciting morning at Mitzpe Hila, on June 25, 2006—a squad of terrorists from Gaza infiltrated Israel early in the morning via an underground tunnel near the Kerem Shalom crossing. The terrorists attacked an Israeli Merkava tank stationed at the border near the perimeter fence, killed the tank commander, Lieutenant Hanan Barak, and the loader, Sergeant Pavel Slutsker, and abducted Corporal Gilad Shalit.

On the day of the abduction, I was contacted by Gilad's relative, and she asked if I would be willing to help and contact his parents, Aviva and Noam. I was no longer acting as a consultant for the defense minister at that time, but there was no doubt in my mind that I would come to their aid. I found myself engaged in that same ritual I have known for many years—traveling to the home of a stunned and terribly agitated family whose life had just been turned on its head. I couldn't possibly guess that two weeks later, I would make the trip down that same route again, but I'd be making that trip in the midst of a barrage of exploding rockets on my way to the home of a young woman whose husband had just been abducted.

I hadn't been to Mitzpe Hila before—I don't think I'd even heard of this beautiful place in the western Galilee until then. The posh and manicured look of the house, with colorful flowers blooming at its front path and the breathtaking vista from its windows unfolded, as if the scenery were a surrealistic theatrical backdrop, the decor for the storm that was raging inside the house and all around it. At the entrance, as always, media teams were waiting, on the prowl for every piece of information or photo angle of the family and anyone else who came to their home.

Immediately upon my arrival, and without me having any knowledge of it beforehand, a television crew came to the house to interview the family. For the first time in his life, Noam Shalit had to give an interview on television. I immediately called him aside and explained to him that there was a very good chance that the interview he was about to give would be shown to his son by the kidnappers and that he must take this into account. Therefore, I explained, it was very important that Aviva also stand by him during the interview. If she was missing, I warned, the kidnappers could take advantage of this to exert psychological pressure on Gilad by telling him false horror stories about his mother's condition and to try to break his spirits right at the first stages of his interrogation.

Between that day and the day when Tamy and I were sitting with Aviva and Naomi on the balcony talking about the meaning of life, more than five years had passed, during which I'd been involved in the negotiations for Gilad's release and the handling of the affair by the local intelligence community, and had stayed in contact with the family.

I had a special connection with Gilad's grandfather, Zvi Shalit, whose son Yoel was killed in action during the Yom Kippur War in 1973. Gilad's brother was named after his fallen uncle. Zvi, an impressive man who commanded respect, served for many years as an officer in the Israeli police. During our acquaintance, he invited me to the graduation ceremony at the police training base, the highlight of the ceremony being the issue of redemption of captives in general and Gilad Shalit in particular. At the exciting ceremony the cadets personally paid tribute to Zvi.

Zvi was an active and determined partner in the struggle to recover his grandson. You could learn about the character of this honest and special man, who always spoke his mind, from the letter he wrote to Prime Minister Benjamin Netanyahu on August 1, 2010:

I asked Hadas quite a few months ago to take action facing the Hamas in Gaza to acquire real signs of life from my grandson Gilad, the soldier, seeing that it's now been over eleven months since we received the videotape. Hamas announced back then that they wanted something in return for anything related to the soldier Gilad Shalit, and I believe what they're saying. The answers I received from Hagai Hadas were evasive/vague. You, the prime minister, who went so far as to raise (according to your own statements) the subject of the soldier Gilad in a meeting with the US president, have no desire to learn what became of Gilad since September of 2009?!

The terrible injustice you have been inflicting on an IDF soldier trapped in a dark pit at the hands of Hamas for a fifth year will not simply vanish into nothingness over time. This is far too grave to ignore. It is an incomprehensible cruelty, which I have already iterated in my previous letters to you. I ask again: give the necessary orders to bring Gilad back to his family, bereaved ever since Yom Kippur of 1973, with the hopes that he can still come back walking on his own feet. The media says that the prime minister is sensitive to the subject of bereavement...please, do not continue to use the subject of the soldier Gilad into this abyss whose depths are truly unfathomable.

The letter was signed: "Zvi Shalit, Gilad's grandfather, with increasing rage."

* * *

Public opinion in Israel focused on this subject throughout Gilad's captivity. Many joined the different activities initiated by the family and promoted the cause to recover Gilad Shalit—from the march from Mitzpe Hila to Jerusalem in a call to return Gilad, to the construction of the protest tent in front of the prime minister's residence, where Aviva and Noam lived for more than a year. Furious public debate ensued around the prisoner exchange deal to secure Gilad's return, which ultimately included the release of 1,027 terrorists imprisoned in Israeli jails. Against those who claimed that there was no price to human life—not least the life of an IDF soldier who was sent to war on behalf of the state—there were also those who voiced their alarm that the released terrorists would return to their former ways and murder others. Thus—facing Gilad, whose face we had already come to know—there were still anonymous victims whose faces we may well recognize in the future.

I sealed my ears to all those voices. All that mattered to me was the mission to bring Gilad back, because my position was, and always will be, that it is the supreme duty of the state which sends its troops into battle. I leave the public debate and controversy on these matters to others.

The negotiations were handled by a special team headed by Mossad officer Hagai Hadas, who was later replaced by David Meidan, also a Mossad man; he was there when the negotiations for Gilad's release were finally concluded. I had the honor of being a part of their team. Together we went through many days and nights, terribly hard and exasperating. It was a fascinating experience to work with these two and to be a close witness to a small part of the operational capabilities and performance—those visible to the eye and mainly the covert ones—that brought them to the top of Israel's intelligence apparatus.

The team that was run by Hadas and Meidan consisted of dozens of people from all the security agencies, intelligence personnel, and psychologists, who analyzed every last bit of information that could be gleaned. In Gilad's case, he was positively known to be still alive, and logic dictated that at some point an exchange deal would be formed. We had lots of ups and downs during this period. The other party was a terrorist organization, without a government, a parliament, or a cabinet. This group of terrorists' every move and word had to be analyzed.

As someone who maintained close contact with the Shalit family all through this period, I did my best to update them with every piece of new information before they'd read about it in the newspaper. They mainly wanted to know how this information should be interpreted.

During this time, we witnessed a beautiful and innocent romance begin to bloom between Yoel, Gilad's brother, and Ya'ara Winkler, a dominant activist in the fight for Gilad's return. How strange are the ways of destiny: at their wedding, which was held after Gilad got back home, we were sitting at the same table with Mickey and Shlomo Goldwasser.

* * *

When Hagai Hadas retired in May 2011, he wrote me a touching farewell letter. An equally moving letter was written to me by his successor, David Meidan, in January 2012, just a few months after Gilad's return to Israel. These letters truly reveal the warm, beating heart of the outwardly tough and rugged security personnel who worked behind the scenes to bring Gilad back to the plush little house in the Galilee village.

This is what Hagai Hadas wrote to me:

On the day I first got involved in the release of kidnapped soldier Gilad Shalit from captivity at the hands of the Hamas, many friends and professionals turned my attention to the fact that I must meet with you as soon as possible. To tell you the truth, no one could tell me exactly what you were doing in the field, except that everyone had the same insight: that without you something of the whole would be missing.

In our first meeting and in the course of our joint activities later, both of us often found ourselves in tears, due to the same physiological phenomena that allow the heart, otherwise safely hidden while it beats in the hollow of our bodies, to reveal its existence to the outside world. Later I plunged into the complex and sometimes gruesome activities, into periods of great hope and at times disappointment during the negotiations with a hard and pitiless opponent. Your presence gave me endless energies to keep pushing, to carry on and strive to achieve our common purpose, with another dimension that I couldn't quite explain to myself.

For many years I have been involved in state security, outlining strategies, as well as dealing with the details of one task or another. For many years I guided and commanded people out of responsibility for the fate of their lives, as well as the integrity of their families. Ory, working with you has added another element to me as a commander and as a person—that of passion and fervor. So, just as the heart expresses itself through the tears that cloud the eyes, you know how to translate the concept of passion, whose very existence is so elusive, into a sensitive, embracing, and supportive human art, a skill that provides human energies to those people who are working to save a captive's life in the face of a fierce, ruthless enemy. Just as a violinist has the skill to connect soul-ear-finger, the painter has the skill to connect soul-eye-hand, you have the skill to connect soul-heart-man. It is evident that you have attributes that are actually a kind of gift from the heavens.

I can appreciate today how difficult and demanding the task you've taken upon yourself over the years. Your capabilities and many years of work in this field are unique and rare and their contribution invaluable. I am honored that you agreed to share all this with me.

And David Meidan wrote to me:

Gilad returned home after five years and four months in captivity. Neither prayers brought him back nor miracles. The actions of individuals, their wisdom, their resourcefulness, the kindness of their hearts, their unrelenting faith—these and only these have been of service to him. You, Ory, were one of those unique people who, acting quietly, soundlessly, and without fanfare or fireworks from behind the scenes, provided support and encouragement, gave us advice, and were a shoulder to lean on in moments of stress, frustration, and deliberation, and you allowed us to finally perform this great undertaking. Your honors are many. They did not begin with Gilad's affair; they span decades and continue on and on. An anonymous hero, wise and warm, attentive to the weak and helpless, first to help, last to despair.

I was invited to the welcoming ceremony held for Gilad Shalit upon his return from captivity at the hands of the Hamas. I preferred to stay home in shorts and flip flops in front of the television and to be alone with myself, my thoughts, and my feelings after five difficult and exhausting years, but also full of activities.

Gilad Shalit was the only captive IDF soldier that I ever got to see come back to Israel alive.

24

Instead of Retirement

G en. (res.) Amos Gilad, in his capacity as the head of the Intelligence
Research Division in IDF Military Intelligence (AMAN) and later
as the head of the State-Security Division in the Israeli Ministry of
Defense, was one of my key allies in my endeavors on the issue of captives and MIAs. He was a confidant, someone I could always turn to
for advice. I am naturally an optimistic person, and Amos was always
pessimistic in nature, but we always managed to meet somewhere in the
middle. In June 1990, he wrote to me the following message:

> To my friend Ory! Today you are ending a long and very im-
> portant period of difficult and continuous struggle for a holy
> cause. As far as I'm concerned, my acquaintance with you was
> close to being the only point of light during this span of time. I
> do not shy away from admitting that I was happy that I chanced
> to have had the pleasure to work with you. First and foremost, I
> was impressed deeply by the spirit of volunteering, a rarity these
> days, that shrouds you, and by your uniquely humane and warm
> approach to those poor souls who found themselves in such a ter-
> rible predicament. Moreover, I have benefited from your wisdom
> and intellect, which have been such a crucial source of help in
> the difficult moments that, sadly, were far from being rare. Very

few people would ever learn about the extent and depth of your critical contribution to bolstering the spirit and perseverance of the families and breaking down the walls that separated us from them, which has contributed and changed the priorities in handling this top national mission, the fulfilment of which you've been entrusted with.

In fact, my retirement from the handling of captives and MIAs was gradual. Whenever a new defense minister was appointed, I wrote an official letter stating that I was ready to continue in my position. The defense ministers of those years—Yitzhak Rabin, Shimon Peres, Itzik Mordechai, Moshe Arens, Binyamin Ben-Eliezer, Shaul Mofaz, and Ehud Barak—requested that I continue my work, and so I did. I resigned from my position twice: once when I felt that I didn't have enough time to devote to the task and once when I wanted to express my dissatisfaction with how some negotiations were being handled.

Throughout the years, I wrote letters in which I argued that the subject of MIAs and POWs was not prominent enough on the agenda. To this day, there are still those who think the effort to bring these soldiers home is not the most important issue in this country's day-to-day affairs and that our preoccupation with it only weakens us. But I remained firm in my conviction that it is the responsibility of the state to bring back every soldier sent to serve in the army. Despite that, I have also always tried to promote the following understanding: don't wait for the next abduction, instead educate yourself on prevention. Because this issue, as in other areas of life, is also about risk management.

* * *

Even when I no longer carried the title of "Consultant to the Minister of Defense for Captives and MIAs," I continued to enlist and help whenever it was necessary. That's what I did after the abduction of Ehud Goldwasser and Eldad Regev, and during the years that Gilad Shalit spent in captivity. I minimized my involvement after the return of Gilad Shalit because I wanted to focus on my activities at the Variety charity, which drew all my mental strength and time. I visited the families of the soldiers Hadar Goldin and Oron Shaul immediately after they were kidnapped and told them I would always be available if they wanted to consult me.

But I never really broke with the world of captives and MIAs. I continue to lecture about the subject in various public forums, including to students, cadets at the IDF and Naval Academy, and to department heads at the Shin Bet. The subject is very engaging for young students, especially those graduating from high school and about to be recruited to the IDF. It remains a loaded subject and a highly problematic one, controversial to this day, even when discussing the prospect of a permanent ceasefire arrangement with Hamas.

When I started dealing with the captives and MIAs issue, I was asked to change the reserve unit at the Parachute Jump School, where I had been on IDF reserve duty for twenty-four years, and transfer to the EITAN unit, the IDF unit that deals with tracking down missing persons. I've served in the unit as a reservist to this day. EITAN holds courses every year that are open to senior-level officers and those who served in field units and became officers for locating missing persons. The subject to which I have devoted nearly thirty years of my life has become the domain of numerous IDF officers. I'm the one to give them the welcoming lecture at the start of the course, upon their arrival at the unit.

And the families of our missing people? I have never parted with them, and I never will.

Acknowledgments

I offer a huge bundle of thanks to the many people who were there during the process of writing this book. Its birth was sometimes all but unbearable due to the sensitivity of most of the subjects included in it and sometimes because of security and clearance issues.

First and foremost, I give endless thanks to my wife, Tamy, who was and continues to be a companion to most of the events mentioned herein. She was there at the book's birth and those of my three children, Erez, Anat, and Yonatan, without whose blessing, assistance, and faithful support and accompaniment, this book would never have seen the light of day.

Many thanks for being with me at all stages of the book publishing process in the US go to my dear and very special friend Steven Emerson and to my agent, Lynne Rabinoff, who have walked with me hand in hand on this special adventure to bring our messages of Israel's POWs and MIAs to English readers.

Thanks to the Post Hill Press family and especially those working with the Wicked Son imprint, Adam Bellow, Heather King, and all the wonderful crew who are walking with me through the book process in the US. Thank you all, my friends!

Lots of thanks to the book's translator, Tomer Zeev, who did a great job.

Many thanks to Efraim Halevi and Shabtai Shavit for their warm words, advice, and encouragement.

I'd also like to thank those who were with me on the journey as I wrote the book in its original Hebrew.

Thanks to my dear friend Dov Eichenwald and his team in Israel. And to my editor, Anat Sheinkman Ben-Ze'ev, who accompanied me during the difficult process of writing the book. She deserves every bit of appreciation and thanks I can possibly give her.

Thank you to the dozens of Israeli security personnel, IDF soldiers, and all those in the service who were involved in this mission: in the Israeli Ministry of Defense, the Mossad, the Shin Bet, and dozens of agents and foreign "collaborators" in Israel and other places in the world, some of whom could not be identified for security reasons.

A big hug of love and friendship to all the families of POWs and MIAs in Israel and the many human beings who are not allowed to be mentioned by name.

To the Variety organization's team in Israel and the rest of the world and especially to Udi Angel, my partner, soulmate, and an amazing brother in arms in our common venture. To all of Variety's staff and management to the many volunteers, who do their utmost to help every day and every hour, and to the thousands of children with special needs, a small group of whom participated in the writing of this book. For that, a special thank you. What you do is absolutely sacred and indispensable work.

A huge thank you to all my dear friends who have been there for me throughout my life, including the writing of this book.

And last but not least, much love to those who contributed their own chapters to this book with great love and without intervention from me or the editors.